Modern Arabic literature

Modern Arabic literature

PAUL STARKEY

GEORGETOWN UNIVERSITY PRESS
WASHINGTON, D.C.

As of January 1, 2007, 13-digit ISBN numbers will replace the current 10-digit system.
Paperback: 978-1-58901-135-9
Cloth: 978-1-58901-134-2

Georgetown University Press, Washington, D.C.

First published in the U.K. by Edinburgh University Press, 2006.

Library of Congress Cataloging-in-Publication Data

Starkey, Paul, 1947–
Modern Arabic literature / Paul Starkey.
p. cm.
Includes bibliographical references and index.
ISBN 1-58901-134-1 (cloth : alk. paper)—ISBN 1-58901-135-X (pbk. : alk. paper)
1. Arabic literature—1801—History and criticism. I. Title.
PJ7538.S73 2006
892'.709005—dc22

2006007879

This book is printed on acid-free paper meeting the requirements of the American National Standard for Permanence in Paper for Printed Library Materials.

13 12 11 10 09 08 07 06 9 8 7 6 5 4 3 2
First printing

Printed in the United Kingdom

Contents

Note on abbreviations

The following abbreviations have been used occasionally in the notes to refer to sources of additional information:

EAL = *Encyclopedia of Arabic Literature*, ed. J. S. Meisami and Paul Starkey, London and New York, 1998

EI^2 = *Encyclopedia of Islam*, new edn, Leiden, 1960 [also available in electronic version]

JAL = *Journal of Arabic Literature*

Preface and acknowledgements

This book is intended as a general introduction to the literature in Arabic that has been written during the course of the last two hundred years or so. Although the particular readership that I have had in mind has been that of the university undergraduate coming to the subject for the first time, I hope that it may also prove of interest to readers interested in comparative literature, as well as to those whose prime interests may not be literary, but who are in one way or another concerned with different aspects of the Middle East – a region of obvious and growing importance in the world today.

In accordance with the title of the series, the book aims to be a survey rather than an exhaustive account. Indeed, it may be questioned whether an 'exhaustive account' of the subject is any longer possible, since, as will be apparent from Chapter 8 in particular, there has been something of an explosion in literary writing in Arabic over the last few years, so that today, in addition to the traditional centres of literary activity such as Egypt and the Levant, vigorous and creative literary production can be found in every area of the Arab world, from Morocco and Mauritania in the west to the Gulf and Iraq in the east. Recent political events have also given a boost to the development of important new centres of publishing in Arabic outside the Middle East itself, in particular, London and Paris.

There have, of course, been a number of introductory surveys of this kind, both in English and in other European languages, since my Durham predecessor John Haywood published his now rather outdated *Modern Arabic Literature, 1800–1970* in 1971. Among works in English (details of which can be found in the bibliography), mention may be made of Pierre Cachia's *An Overview of Modern Arabic Literature*, published in the same series as the current volume in 1990, but which consists largely of reprints of previous articles by the author; the same author's *Arabic Literature: An Overview*, published in 2002, which covers both the classical and modern periods; M. M. Badawi's *A Short History of Modern Arabic Literature*, published in 1993; and Roger Allen's *An Introduction to Arabic Literature* (2000), based on his earlier *The Arabic Literary Heritage* (1998), which attempts to cover the classical and modern periods, probably for the first time, as a single tradition. I should be the first to acknowledge my debt to all these works (including even the much maligned Haywood), as well as to the numerous more specialised volumes on modern literature that have appeared in recent years — for the field is now so vast that no one scholar can hope to be an expert in anything but a fraction of it. All I can plead in adding to the volumes already existing is that, as Badawi noted in his own book, works of this sort inevitably need updating from time to time; and each writer will bring his or her own perspective to the task.

It would be invidious to single out particular colleagues for thanks, but I am pleased to acknowledge financial help in the form of travel grants from the British Academy and the University of Durham during the writing of this work, which for reasons beyond my control has extended over a rather longer period than I would have liked. I am also grateful to Janet Starkey, for her help in compiling the index; to Professor Carole Hillenbrand, the Islamic Surveys series editor, for her constant support and encouragement; and to the staff of Edinburgh University Press, in particular Nicola Ramsey, for their seemingly almost inexhaustible patience.

Paul Starkey
University of Durham
February 2006

Introduction: what is Modern Arabic literature?

The expression 'Modern Arabic Literature', which forms the subject of this survey, is a slightly problematic one, none of the three words that go to make up the phrase being quite as self-explanatory as they might at first appear. Before commencing our account of the topic, a brief word on definitions will therefore be in order, in order to define the scope of the work.

First, 'modern'. By 'modern', I refer, generally speaking, to literature written after the Middle East and North Africa had begun to be exposed to large-scale Western and European influence towards the end of the eighteenth and beginning of the nineteenth century AD. This process, which has been extensively discussed both in Arabic and in Western languages, was both a cumulative and a complex one. For practical purposes, 1798 (the date of Napoleon's invasion of Egypt) has often been taken as a starting point for this chain of developments, but though the date has merit as a convenient anchor-point (and I shall use it as such), it has less relevance for other parts of the Arab world, some of which remained remote from European influence, both from a social and a literary point of view, until way into the twentieth century, while a few (Lebanon is the obvious case in point) had enjoyed extensive, if selected, contacts with Europe for centuries before the emperor's French army set foot on Egyptian soil. As we shall see in the pages that follow, the pace of literary development (like social and political development) in the Middle East has been far from uniform, and rigid cut-off dates, though convenient, can be frequently misleading. In any event, as the following pages will again show, though much 'modern' Arabic literature does indeed show signs of influence by, or borrowing from, the Western tradition, any attempt to understand the development of modern literature without some appreciation of the classical Arabic heritage is unlikely to be productive.

Let us turn, then, from 'modern' to 'Arabic'. At first, this term appears less problematic: 'Arabic' literature must surely be 'literature written in Arabic', and this definition will indeed serve well for the vast majority of the material we are dealing with. But the political history of the Middle East over the last two centuries having been marked by an at times aggressive

Western colonialism, the interplay of cultures has sometimes been a less than straightforward one. In the countries of North Africa, in particular (though in different degrees), literature in Arabic was eclipsed by literature in French for part of the period under discussion. Although the present survey does not deal with literature written in French (though it will occasionally be mentioned), the phenomenon of Francophone literature cannot be entirely ignored: many of the authors in question wrote both in Arabic and in French, or consciously switched from one language to the other, a choice that often had political as well as literary significance. Such dilemmas have formed part of the general cultural context in which much North African Arabic literature was produced during the greater part of the twentieth century, and inevitably impinge on an account of modern 'Arabic' literature. Another phenomenon (albeit a less significant one, at least until recently) has been that of Arab authors, sometimes themselves resident in the West, writing in English, often with a view to a wider market than that provided by their Arabic-speaking fellow countrymen.

The third term, 'literature', also calls for a little explanation. For most Western readers, the term will almost certainly suggest 'imaginative literature' – novels, short stories, folktales, drama, poetry or their close equivalents in other cultures. For most of the discussion, we shall indeed be using the term in this sense. It will be as well, however, to bear in mind that the nearest Arabic equivalent for literature (*adab*) is a considerably more complex term that embraces, in addition to literature, 'culture', 'good manners', 'decency' and 'humanity', and whose parameters, even in the literary context, are by no means coterminous with those of the English term 'literature'.[1] Moreover, pre-modern readers and writers did not make the same distinctions between various types of 'literature' as do modern ones, so that 'literature', for the medieval Arabic period, has often been taken to include also other types of writing: history, geography, biography, philosophy and so on. Although 'literature' in the present work will usually mean imaginative literature, therefore, other *genres* will occasionally make an appearance, particularly in the initial background chapter and in the account of the early stages of the nineteenth-century literary revival (*nahḍa*) in chapter 2.

Note

1 Some further observations on the connections between these various meanings will be given below, see pp. 8–10.

1

The background

The medieval heritage: its origins and eclipse

It is impossible, in the space at our disposal, to do more than give a very brief sketch of some of the main features of classical, or medieval,[1] Arabic literature; for a fuller account, the reader is referred to the works listed in the Bibliography to the present volume.[2] However, no survey of 'modern' Arabic literature that fails to take account of the Middle Eastern literary background could be regarded as anything but incomplete. In the following section, therefore, I shall outline some of the main features of what is variously called 'classical' or 'medieval' Arabic literature, drawing attention to some of its main features by way of background to the account of the modern period that follows.

We should again begin with a few definitions. Like the literature of classical Greece, the origins of Arabic literature are literally lost in time; and because (again, as in Greece) the first specimens of literature derive from an oral rather than a written culture, the history of the first beginnings is inevitably somewhat speculative. For practical purposes, however, we may say that 'classical' Arabic literature makes its first appearance around the middle of the sixth century AD, when we find a corpus of tribal Bedouin poetry emerging in and around the Arabian Peninsula, with well-developed metrical and rhyme schemes indicating a considerable period (several centuries, presumably) of prior development. This corpus of poetry is usually described as 'pre-Islamic poetry' (though in fact it straddles the transition to the Islamic period) and forms one of the two primary starting-points for the subsequent development of most 'classical' Arabic literature; the other starting-point is provided by the revelation of the Qur'ān, the sacred book of Islam revealed to the Prophet Muḥammad over a period of approximately twenty years between AD 610 and AD 632. The subsequent evolution of the classical Arabic literary tradition, and indeed of the Arabic language itself, took place in the shadow of these two seminal literary events: for while Arabic poetry developed in a variety of ways over the succeeding centuries, the metrical and rhyme schemes developed by the pre-Islamic poets remained, with a few exceptions, essentially unchanged in the hands of most poets until the twentieth century, and the seven pre-Islamic *Mu'allaqāt*[3] have continued to be upheld as supreme examples of the poet's art. For its part, despite its unique status as the word of God (and by definition, therefore, 'inimitable'), the language and rhythms of the Qur'ān have continued to haunt and underpin much of the subsequent literary tradition, not only that written in Arabic, but also that of other languages widely spoken by Muslims, such as Persian, Turkish and Urdu.

As we shall see, the subsequent flowering of this rich tradition in its numerous branches owes much also to influences and importations from other civilisations, not least from those of India and pre-Islamic Iran. Nonetheless, the two indigenous foundations of pre-Islamic poetry and the Qur'ān never lost their pivotal position as the mainsprings of the Arabic literary tradition, and it is indeed the interplay between the two strands – one religious, the other supremely secular – that partly accounts for the distinctive pattern of development of Arabic literature in the classical, or medieval, period. Also relevant, however, is a third strand: for in parallel with the tradition of literature deriving from the Qur'ān and pre-Islamic poetry (sometimes described as 'high' or 'elite' literature), the medieval Arab world was also home to a tradition of 'popular' literature, almost entirely oral in nature, that (at least until recently) was not regarded as worthy of the name *adab*,[4] or included in the 'canon' of Arabic literary production. Ironically, perhaps, it is a work of this type, the *Thousand and One Nights*,[5] that, until recently at least, was arguably the best known work of Arabic literature to most Western readers.

If defining the origins and earliest manifestations of the Arabic literary tradition raises problems because of the lack of written evidence, defining an end point for classical, or medieval, Arabic literature involves difficulties of a different nature. There appears to be general agreement, however, that by the time of the fall of Baghdad to the Mongols in 1258, the best of 'classical' Arabic literature had already been written, and that though the succeeding centuries included a number of distinguished individual authors,[6] the tradition that had provided a link from generation to generation during the preceding centuries had been irrevocably broken. For some years already before 1258, the unified Islamic empire that had reached its peak under the 'Abbasids had begun to split apart, and from 1517, or thereabouts, Egypt and Syria came under Ottoman domination. Although Arabic retained its dominance as the language of the revelation of Islam, from the sixteenth century it was increasingly replaced by Turkish in the central Arab world as the language of administration and of educated discourse, and literature in Arabic appears to have become progressively more stylised and unoriginal. As a consequence, the years between the fall of Baghdad in 1258 and Napoleon's invasion of Egypt in 1798 have sometimes been described as the 'Dark Ages' of Arabic literature. In truth, this period remains seriously under-researched – a storehouse of potential lost treasures – partly because it lacks the obvious focal points of both classical Arabic literature and that of the modern period, but partly also, perhaps, because the socio-linguistic situation of the Arab countries during this period implies that any serious researcher should be proficient not only in Arabic but also in Ottoman Turkish. However significant or insignificant the productions of this period may be, however, it is clear that the term 'Dark Ages' is an unworthy one, and I shall therefore refer to it in this volume by the neutral term 'Transitional Period', implying no more than that it divides the better defined 'classical' period from the 'modern' literature that forms the main subject of this volume.

The Qur'ān and the religious tradition in Arabic literature

The Qur'ān (Arabic: 'reading', 'recitation', 'lesson' etc.), the Sacred Book of Islam that may be regarded as the first of the two main pillars on which the subsequent development of Arabic literature was based, is believed by Muslims to be the speech of God (Allāh) himself, revealed to His Prophet Muḥammad through the Angel Gabriel. Muḥammad himself had been born into the Quraysh, an aristocratic clan based in the religious and trading centre of Mecca, around AD 570. Little is known with certainty of his early life, but as his father had died before his birth, and his mother died when he was in his sixth year, he was brought up first by his grandfather, then by his uncle, Abū Ṭālib. For some time, he lived among the Bedouin, and probably visited Syria as a trader; later, he appears to have developed a taste for solitary meditation, and at the age of around forty began proclaiming a religious message in Mecca, the essence of which was that Allāh would subject the world to judgement, punishing the wicked and rewarding the virtuous. Although this message would already have been familiar to Jewish and Christian communities (of which there were several in the Arabian Peninsula at that period), Muḥammad encountered much opposition to his preaching in Mecca, and in AD 622 he migrated with a small band of followers to Medina, where he already had supporters; this migration, known in Arabic as the *hijra*, effectively divides Muḥammad's career into two, and provides the starting-date for the Islamic calendar.[7] After the *hijra*, as head of the fledgling Islamic community, Muḥammad's role evolved from that of preacher to that of politician and lawgiver; he died in AD 632, having subdued Mecca and consolidated his rule in most of the surrounding area.

No serious doubt has been cast on the authenticity of the revelations that were assembled into the Qur'ān after Muḥammad's death, though the process by which they were collected and organised into the Qur'ān in its present form is by no means clear. It consists of 114 chapters (Arabic: *sūras*), each *sūra* being divided into verses (Arabic: *āya*; plural *āyāt*), but instead of a chronological or thematic arrangement, we find an arrangement in approximate order of length, with the longer *sūras* being placed first; an exception to this general principle is provided by the first *sūra* – the *Fātiḥa*, or 'Opening' *sūra* – commonly used by Muslims as a short prayer. With one exception, each *sūra* begins with the formula *Bismi llāh al-raḥmān al-raḥīm* ('In the name of God, the Merciful, the Compassionate'), a formula commonly used by Muslims to preface actions of various sorts, from eating or drinking to embarking on a journey.

The language of the Qur'ān shows an evolution from the short *sūras* revealed in Mecca to the longer Medinan chapters. The earlier passages of the work are characterised by short verses, using rhyming oaths in the traditional style of the pre-Islamic *kāhin* ('soothsayer') to convey a message of the imminence of the Day of Judgement, which will bring paradise for the believers, and eternal torment for the wicked. The work's stress on the unity of God, and Muḥammad as His messenger, is reinforced by stories of previous prophets, both biblical and from pre-Islamic Arabia, and of peoples who were punished for their wickedness and disobedience. As Muḥammad's role evolved, however, he began to adopt a less dramatic and less lyrical style, using longer clauses – a style that more resembles prose as we understand it today, though retaining the loose monorhyme characteristic of the distinctive Arabic style called *saj'* ('rhymed prose').[8] This change of style reflects both a growing confidence in the use of language, and the development of the Prophet's own role: as the leader of the nascent Islamic community, he was now turning his attention to matters of social organisation and legal prescriptions, and we now find, in addition to the theological and revelatory material of the earlier *sūras*, passages containing regulations for marriage and inheritance, ordinances on fasting, almsgiving, pilgrimage and the like. Muḥammad the Prophet, to borrow Montgomery Watt's phrase, has by this time been replaced by Muḥammad the Statesman.[9]

Like that of much subsequent Arabic literature, the language of the Qur'ān is best heard rather than read to be fully appreciated. The imagery employed is at times startling, and the language capable of reaching great heights, which are seldom effectively conveyed in translation. Indeed, 'translating' the Qur'ān is to many Muslim commentators an almost blasphemous concept,[10] and later Islamic doctrine stressed its 'inimitability' (*i'jāz*) – a concept originating in the Qur'anic verses challenging the Prophet's opponents to produce anything like it. For this reason, direct imitation of the Qur'ān by subsequent writers has been only rarely attempted, and almost always with unfortunate results.[11] Despite this effective ban on imitation, the ideas, language and rhythms of the Qur'ān have been all-pervasive, reverberating through most subsequent Arabic literature until the present day. As the first Arabic book (*al-Kitāb*), both in a chronological sense and in terms of its status, memorisation of the Qur'ān was until recently the lynchpin of an Islamic education, and quotations and allusions to the text can be found in almost every type of literature. Nor is its importance confined to the literary sphere, for it was through the Qur'ān that Arabic established itself as a world language, serving as a common vehicle of thought for all Muslim scholars; the institutionalisation of Islam in the centuries following the death of the Prophet helped to reinforce the linguistic norms enshrined in the Qur'ān, which quickly became the standard for elevated, 'literary' Arabic.

At the time of the Prophet's death, the Qur'ān did not yet exist as a book. Parts had undoubtedly been written down during Muḥammad's lifetime, but, by common account, it was not until Zayd ibn Thābit, the Prophet's scribe, was commissioned to gather together the text 'from smooth stones, leather bits, camels' shoulder-blades, palm leaves and the breasts of men',[12] that any attempt was made to construct a complete version. Later, in about 650/1, the third caliph, 'Uthmān, set up a committee (including Zayd ibn Thābit himself) to compare all extant readings and establish a definitive text; and though some divergent readings continued to be preserved, the text of the Qur'ān as we know it today had effectively been established by around AD 660.

In the meantime, the second main source of religious authority in Islam – the body of narratives about the Prophet and his Companions known as *ḥadīth*[13] literature – had begun to take shape. For Muslims, God's will was not only revealed directly through God's words to Muḥammad but was also mediated through the words and actions of the Prophet, and this body of 'Traditions', as they are often called in English, soon came to be regarded as a second source of revelation that served as a supplement to the Qur'ān. The process of assembling these individual narratives into a reliable corpus of material was, however, considerably more complex than in the case of the Qur'ān itself, for the individual 'traditions', or *ḥadīths*, varied greatly in their provenance and reliability, and, being orally transmitted for at least the first three generations, were frequently used by rival political and theological factions to justify their own actions or point of view. The need critically to sift the *ḥadīth* material led to the formulation of scholarly criteria to establish the authenticity of each, in which the main weight was given to the reliability of the narrators involved, and the 'chains' of transmitters[14] that precede the narrative section of each *ḥadīth* form one of the most characteristic features of this body of literature. At first, the works that emerged from this process of sifting usually arranged individual *ḥadīths* by the name of their early transmitters, but later, classification by subject matter became more popular,[15] and as time went on they acquired an increasingly important status as sources of Islamic law; the best known and widely used collections in the Sunni tradition are those by Muslim (817?–875) and al-Bukhārī (810–70) – which in turn have given rise to numerous commentaries.

The scholarly discipline involved in the compilation of the early *ḥadīth* collections formed the basis for the emergence of the tradition of Arabic historiography, which reached perhaps its highest peak from the second century of the 'Abbasid period. The first serious historical work in Arabic was arguably the biography of the Prophet compiled by Ibn Isḥāq (d. 767) and subsequently revised by Ibn Hishām (d. 834); and much early historical writing was also intimately connected with religious questions. The earliest histories were essentially chronicles, one of whose main purposes was to enable the accurate dating of individuals involved in the transmission of *ḥadīths*. Similar concerns underlay the development of one of the most distinctive of medieval Arabic literary genres, the biographical dictionary,[16] the origins of which remain somewhat obscure but which probably go back to the pre-Islamic tradition of 'Battle Days' (*ayyām al-ʿArab*) – accounts of intertribal conflicts that constitute an at least partly factual history of pre-Islamic Arabia. The chronicle tradition found perhaps its finest expression in the *Ta'rīkh al-rusul wa-al-mulūk* ('History of the Prophets and Kings') by Muḥammad ibn Jarīr al-Ṭabarī (c. 839–923), which remains an indispensable source of historical data for the early Islamic period. Later writers extended the scope of these early works through attempts at historical analysis, and expanding geographical and cultural perspectives, in works which in some cases are as noteworthy for their literary qualities as for their historical acumen: the outstanding example of this tendency is perhaps al-Masʿūdī's (c. 896–956) *Murūj al-dhahab* ('Fields of Gold'), a universal history that reveals not only a deep and wide-ranging erudition but also an extraordinary curiosity about the affairs of civilisations beyond the boundaries of the Islamic world. However, it was not until the fourteenth century, with the work of Ibn Khaldūn (1332–1406), that Arab historiography can really be said to have moved beyond the compilation of data to an attempt to formulate a philosophy of history itself; unfortunately, though Ibn Khaldūn's *Muqaddima* is almost certainly the best known work of Arab historical writing in the West, it remained almost unread in the Arab world until the nineteenth century – an indication, perhaps, both of how far ahead of its time it was, and of the decline in intellectual activity during the period between the fifteenth century and the beginning of the literary revival (*nahḍa*) to be discussed in the next chapter.

In addition to, and closely connected with, *ḥadīth* literature, a number of other genres of religious literature began to emerge in the centuries following the revelation of the Qur'ān. Of these, the most directly related to the source text itself was the science of Qur'anic exegesis (Arabic: *tafsīr*), a body of writing that embraced all aspects of commentary on the Qur'ān, including the so-called *āyāt asbāb al-nuzūl* (the events associated with the revelation of particular verses), grammatical problems, the historical connections of the text, and comments on points of theological or juridical significance. The writing of such commentaries came to maturity with the same al-Ṭabarī already discussed as a historian,[17] whose massive *Tafsīr* in thirty volumes contains all the information, verse by verse, that he could glean from earlier commentaries. It in turn formed the basis for several subsequent commentaries by later writers. It should be noted that the use of earlier writers' work as a basis for more elaborate compositions forms one of the most characteristic patterns of medieval Islamic intellectual activity (extending far beyond the realm of religious literature) and that echoes of these patterns can still occasionally be found in modern writing.

In parallel with the science of *tafsīr*, though less immediately connected with the Qur'anic text, a more general literature of 'scholastic theology' (Arabic: *kalām*) began to emerge, which aimed at the more philosophical formulation of religious dogma. Motivated, in part at least, by the need to reconcile Islamic orthodoxy with the Greek philosophical tradition, this literature found its leading exponent in the person of al-Ash'arī (d. 935), whose *Kitāb al-ibāna 'an uṣūl al-diyāna* ('Book of Explanation of the Roots of the Creed') had a lasting influence on subsequent generations of theologians. The growth of this type of literature was aided by the establishment of religious academies in several cities, named 'Niẓāmiyyas' after their founder Niẓām al-Mulk. Not all religious literature was to follow such conventional philosophical or theological lines, however, for, like Christianity, Islam soon developed a 'mystical' tradition whose origins lay in ascetic practices developed by early believers meeting to recite the Qur'ān until its 'inner meaning' should be revealed. The pioneer of Islamic mystical literature is usually regarded as al-Ḥasan of Basra (d. 728). By a century or so later, the name 'Sufi'[18] had begun to be applied to devotees of such practices, and the movement had begun to show foreign influences such as Gnosticism which alarmed more orthodox Islamic theologians. This pantheistic tendency in the movement and the literature associated with it came to a head in AD 922 with the trial of al-Ḥallāj, charged with heresy for having identified himself with God and cruelly executed; his famous utterance *anā al-ḥaqq* ('I am the truth') succinctly encapsulates the spirit of these more extreme Sufi attitudes.

Islamic mysticism spawned a huge volume of writing, in both prose and poetry, which includes some of the best known names of classical Arabic literature, whose works have continued to be read and appreciated to this day. It also had a conspicuous influence on Persian and (to a lesser extent) other non-Arabic Islamic literatures. Particularly notable are the works of Ibn al-Fāriḍ (1181–1235), often thought of as the greatest mystical poet in Arabic, and his near-contemporary, Ibn al-'Arabī (1165–1240), a prolific writer in both prose and verse, whose *al-Futūḥāt al-Makkiyya* ('Meccan Revelations') provide a source text for the contemporary Egyptian writer Jamāl al-Ghīṭānī's *Tajalliyāt al-Ghīṭānī* (1983–6).[19] Some half a century later, al-Buṣīrī (d. 1294/5) composed his famous poem *Qaṣīdat al-Burda* ('Mantle Poem'), which has been used ever since on amulets and by devout Muslims to express devotion at gatherings. The writer who best succeeded in reconciling Sufism with the more orthodox formulations of Islam, however, was undoubtedly al-Ghazālī (1059–1111),[20] who is often reckoned the single greatest figure in Islamic religious thought, and whose story has a decidedly 'modern' flavour to it. Having received a fairly conventional religious education and embarked on a career as a teacher, he suffered what in modern terminology would probably be described as a nervous breakdown; withdrawing from the world, he set out to regain his lost faith, but could find no satisfaction until he rediscovered Islam through Sufism. His spiritual quest was described in his work *al-Munqidh min al-Ḍalāl*,[21] a work that perhaps comes closer than any other in the classical tradition to the modern concept of an 'autobiography', and which exemplifies the best traditions of mature classical Arabic prose – subtle but appealing at the same time. His full views on religion were set out in his *magnum opus*, *Iḥyā' 'ulūm al-dīn*, a massive work conspicuous for its emphasis on religion as a spiritual experience founded on love of God, rather than purely a system of ideas.

'Literary' prose in classical Arabic literature

As will be clear from the previous discussion, the boundaries between 'religious' and 'non-religious' in classical Arabic literature are at times difficult to distinguish, and are not identical to those of the Western tradition. Despite the strong influence of Islam on the development of the various genres noted above, however, the development of classical Arabic prose literature did not have an exclusively religious motivation, and from an early stage was subject to influences from outside the Islamic world that both enriched it and led to the establishment of new literary forms. In this process (as was also the case both with Islamic philosophy noted above, and with the modern cultural revival to be discussed in the next chapter), translation into Arabic played a significant part.

The first examples of 'literary prose', as we would normally understand the term today, are usually held to be three epistles composed by 'Abd al-Ḥamīd ibn Yaḥyā, secretary to the last Umayyad caliph Marwān II (r. 744–50).[22] These, however, appear to have been a comparatively isolated phenomenon. The first work to have had a substantial influence on succeeding developments was almost certainly Ibn al-Muqaffa''s *Kalīla wa-Dimna*, a translation from Persian of a series of maxims and anecdotes put into the mouths of animals that is regarded by most commentators as a model of elegant style and is still widely read to this day; the source of these stories may ultimately be traced back to the work known in Sanskrit as the *Panchatantra*, or 'Fables of Bidpai'. Ibn al-Muqaffa''s work had many imitators, whose productions are unfortunately now lost, and he is generally regarded as the founder of what is sometimes called the 'secretarial school' of Arabic literature – an essentially didactic genre,[23] also referred to as 'Mirrors for Princes', that purports to give advice on conduct to rulers and administrators. This genre, which draws on the Persian imperial tradition of government (Ibn al-Muqaffaʿ himself was a Persian), was subsequently adopted and developed by a number of major medieval Arabic writers, not least the theologian al-Ghazālī already mentioned, whose *Naṣīḥat al-Mulūk* (originally written in Persian) combines the traditional concerns of the 'secretarial school' with a strongly Islamic orientation.

Many works of the 'Mirrors for Princes' type combine their function as vehicles for advice with a complementary aim of entertaining the reader, and this tendency to change tone in order to hold the reader's attention may indeed be regarded as one of the main characteristics of medieval imaginative prose literature (*adab*) generally.[24] There is general agreement that this type of literature found its most eloquent expression in the works of al-Jāḥiẓ (c. 776/7–868/9),[25] whose enormous output included not only works of *adab* ('artistic prose') proper, but also theological tracts, works on rhetoric, philological works, and a number of books that today might be described as 'social criticism': among his best known works are the seven-volume *Kitāb al-ḥayawān* ('Book of Animals'), a description of the animal kingdom that aims to demonstrate the unity of creation; the *Kitāb al-bukhalā'* ('Book of Misers'), a witty compilation of anecdotes illustrating the decline in the traditional Arab virtues of hospitality and generosity; and the *Risālat al-qiyān* ('Epistle on Singing-Girls'), a document containing much valuable material on the relations between the sexes, not only in 'Abbasid but also in earlier periods.

Little purpose would be served by attempting to trace in detail the way in which al-Jāḥiẓ's style and approach to *adab* were developed by subsequent medieval writers such as Ibn Qutayba (828–89), al-Masʿūdī (c. 896–956) or al-Thaʿālibī (961–1038).[26] A few general characteristics of this literature may, however, be stressed. The most obvious is perhaps that, in addition to the frequent changes of tone previously noted, this style of writing is both non-specialist and all-embracing: rather than binding itself by the rules and traditions of particular genres (*ḥadīth*, *kalām*, *tārīkh* etc.), it takes from any discipline whatever is necessary for the general education and amusement of the reader. Few works exhibit much sense of artistic 'unity', as it is generally understood in the West, and digressions of various kinds are frequent. In addition, many works of *adab* rely heavily on previous writings to illustrate their themes, and quotations from a variety of sources –whether in poetry or prose – are frequently interspersed in the main narrative. As noted earlier,[27] the use of previous writers' works as a basis for developing one's own composition was a frequent characteristic of religious literature, and this tendency can be found in works of *adab* also.

The traditional styles of *adab* literature continued to be cultivated over the succeeding centuries – not least by court officials, whose duties included the drafting of correspondence and other official documents, and for whom some degree of literary skill was a *sine qua non* of their appointment. In the meantime, a new genre had come to maturity that both represents one of the most distinctive of medieval Arabic literary forms, and has also been regarded by some as the nearest approach in this tradition to the 'short story'; employed by certain authors even into the twentieth century, it therefore forms an important link between medieval and modern Arabic literature. This form, known as the *maqāma* ('standing'),[28] is usually thought to have been originated by Badīʿ al-Zamān al-Hamadhānī (969–1008),[29] and makes use of the rhymed prose (*sajʿ*) format previously noted as a feature of the pre-Islamic soothsayers.[30] Typically, the *maqāma* consists of a short vignette related by a narrator (*rāwī*), who encounters a vagabond wandering from place to place, using his eloquence to secure his livelihood or escape from a tricky situation; in al-Hamadhānī's *maqāmāt*, the narrator goes by the name of ʿĪsā ibn Hishām, while the 'hero' is usually called Abū al-Fatḥ al-Iskandarānī.[31] At the end of the *maqāma* the 'hero' is exposed, often through a surprise twist of events, and the whole sketch is usually interspersed with verses designed to show off the writer's poetic talents.

This new genre reached its highest achievement in the works of al-Ḥarīrī of Basra (1054–1122), who preserved the basic format of al-Hamadhānī's creation, while changing the hero's name to Abū Zayd al-Sarūjī and that of the narrator to Ḥārith ibn Hammām. Although they are unashamed imitations of al-Hamadhānī's work, they are almost universally held to be superior, and have frequently been held up as a model of literary and linguistic genius. The secret of their attraction is probably that, despite the obscurity of much of their language, and the endless verbal tricks that make the form inaccessible to many Western readers, their author never lost sight of the fact that their principal purpose was to entertain.

Unfortunately, the linguistic virtuosity that, used in the right way, could add sparkle and polish to a composition of this sort, appears almost to have contained within itself the seeds of its own destruction. Al-Ḥarīrī himself, despite the brilliance of his *maqāmāt*, was also responsible for producing a number of works in which verbal jugglery clearly has the upper hand over wit and imagination: among these may be mentioned *al-Risāla al-sīniyya* and *al-Risāla al-shīniyya* (works in which the letter *s* or *sh* respectively occurred in every word), poems using only undotted letters, and so on. With the passage of time, such features appear to have become the principal hallmark of the *maqāma* form; the achievements of al-Ḥarīrī and al-Hamadhānī were never equalled in subsequent centuries, and the proliferation of linguistic 'trick-compositions' of this sort has been held to be a measure of the decline of Arabic *adab* literature to a state from which it only began to recover in the nineteenth century.[32]

Poetry

As has already been suggested, poetry in the medieval Arabic tradition held a place that may perhaps be regarded as second only to the Qur'anic revelation itself. As an oral art form, the origins of Arabic poetry are essentially unfathomable; what can hardly be doubted, however, is that the Arabic poetry that first emerged into the light of history in the century or so preceding the Prophet Muḥammad's revelation was the outcome of several centuries of development. In its emergence, apparently from nothing, as a fully-developed art-form, the phenomenon of pre-Islamic poetry presents a parallel to the emergence of Greek literature in Homer and the Homeric hymns; in most other respects, however, both structurally and thematically, there is almost nothing to link the two traditions.

Pre-Islamic poetry may be subdivided into two main types: the *qiṭʿa*[33] (a short poem, usually on a single theme) and the longer, structurally more complex *qaṣīda* (sometimes translated into English as 'ode').[34] The themes of the *qiṭʿa* include elegy (*marthiya, rithā'*), praise (*madīḥ*), boasting (*fakhr*) and invective (*hijā'*); all these themes are also found in the longer *qaṣīda*, though the precise relationship between the two genres remains a matter of some controversy.[35]

Although the *qaṣīda* shares with the *qiṭʿa* the characteristics of monorhyme, and the use of a fixed set of metres based on syllable length,[36] their overall structure is considerably more complex. Most *qaṣīdas* range between about 30 and 100 lines, of up to thirty syllables each, divided more or less equally over two hemistichs. Within this structure, the range and arrangement of themes varies considerably. The Arab writer Ibn Qutayba (828–89), however, quickly identified a pattern that seemed to him to encapsulate the essence of the pre-Islamic *qaṣīda*, and his account has been widely quoted:

> I have heard ... that the composer of Odes began by mentioning the deserted dwelling-places and the relics and traces of habitation. Then he wept and complained and addressed the desolate encampment, and begged his companion to make a halt ... Then to this he linked the erotic prelude (*nasīb*), and bewailed the violence of his love and the anguish of separation from his mistress ... Now, when the poet had assured himself of an attentive hearing, he ... went on to complain of fatigue and want of sleep ... and how his camel had been reduced to leanness ... And when, after representing all the discomfort and danger of his journey, he knew that he had fully justified his hope and expectation of receiving his due meed from the person to whom the poem was addressed, he entered upon the panegyric (*madīḥ*), and incited him to reward.[37]

Although Ibn Qutayba's description can be literally applied in all its detail to only a proportion of extant *qaṣīdas* from the pre-Islamic period (and to an even smaller proportion of later productions), it nonetheless provides a useful benchmark against which to analyse the development of the *qaṣīda* from its earliest appearance into the Umayyad and ʿAbbasid periods. Most of the best-known pre-Islamic *qaṣīda* are analysable, at least in outline, into three main sections, of which the first, the *nasīb*, is undoubtedly the most characteristic: the predominant mood of this section is almost invariably nostalgia, as the poet recalls an encounter with his beloved at a now deserted encampment (a situation deriving from practice in pre-Islamic Bedouin society, where neighbouring tribes would camp together during the fertile spring season). In the second section, the poet breaks free from his attachment to the past through a 'release' (*takhalluṣ*) to a journey episode (*raḥīl*), usually involving a camel-ride, and often accompanied by vividly drawn vignettes of desert animals such as the antelope, ostrich or wild ass. The final section of the poem is the most varied, and may include one or more of the themes already noted as subjects of the *qiṭʿa*: satirical verses against a rival tribe; boasts of his own, or his own tribe's, prowess; or a panegyric addressed to the poet's patron. The greater freedom allowed to the poet in this final section probably argues for the combination of *nasīb* and camel theme having existed as a convention before the development of the fully fledged *qaṣīda* as usually understood.[38]

As will probably be apparent from the above, the average modern Western reader is unlikely to find the pre-Islamic Arabic poem an 'easy read', even in translation, and there are a number of serious obstacles to an easy appreciation of the genre. The linguistic problems posed for the translator by a hundred-line monorhymed poem replete with archaic vocabulary will be obvious enough;[39] but for many readers the alien desert environment and the unfamiliar social structure of pre-Islamic Bedouin tribal society are at times equal, if not greater, barriers to comprehension. Although in the best of the poetry artistic qualities that transcend cultural constraints are apparent in abundance, the role of the poet as the spokesman of his tribe is quite foreign to the modern West – and indeed, even within the Middle East, it had before long become an anachronism, as the centre of gravity of Islamic society moved from the desert environment of its conception to the courts of Damascus, Baghdad and elsewhere.

Despite these problems of appreciation, pre-Islamic poetry has continued to be admired and upheld as perhaps the supreme example of the Arabic poet's art until modern times, and echoes of its main themes may be found even in some modern compositions.[40] Although attempts were made in the early twentieth century by the Egyptian critic Ṭāhā Ḥusayn[41] and others to cast doubts on the authenticity of this poetry, arguing that it was in fact the product of a later age, this view – always a controversial one – no longer commands serious credence, and it is now generally accepted that the majority at least of the corpus of poetry ascribed to the Arab poets of the sixth century is authentic. Passed down from generation to generation by a chain of *rāwīs* ('reciters'), the best of these poems had by the tenth century AD been assembled into an anthology known as the *Muʿallaqāt*, a term the meaning of which remains elusive – the traditional explanation that the poems had been 'suspended' (*muʿallaqa*) in the Kaʿba in pre-Islamic times being almost certainly false. Though the precise contents of the anthology varied somewhat from collection to collection, most compilers centred on a core of seven varied poems (the so-called 'Seven Odes'), including works by ʿAntara,[42] Labīd and Imruʾ al-Qays, whose *Muʿallaqa*, with its famous opening line 'Stay, let us weep ...' has some claim to be considered the best-known Arabic poem of all time.

Although the Prophet Muḥammad had a so-called 'court poet', Ḥassān ibn Thābit, his attitude to poets and poetry remained ambiguous, when not openly hostile. Indeed, the association of poetry with the pagan values rejected by the Prophet meant that poetry continued to be viewed by suspicion by many influential members of the early Muslim community for some time. Perhaps for this reason, the great waves of Arab expansion out of the Arabian Peninsula that followed the death of the Prophet (the perfect subject, one might have thought, for a war poet like ʿAntara) went almost entirely unrecorded in poetic form.

By the time that Arabic poetry resurfaced in the Peninsula itself, changes both in structure and in theme had become apparent, and the full-length *qaṣīda* had begun to give ground to the shorter *ghazal* ('love lyric'), characterised by a more straightforward and less contrived style. The first exponent of this new trend was probably the Meccan ʿUmar ibn Abī Rabīʿa (d. c. 720), whose *dīwān* contains some 440 poems and fragments, characterised by passion, tenderness and a generally light-hearted tone. Not a few of these poems were composed during the pilgrimage season, which the poet welcomed as an occasion for the pursuit of amorous adventures, and the style of this poetry was favoured in the Umayyad capital, Damascus, where it may well have blended with a native tradition of wine song.

By contrast, the poetry of the other sacred city of the Peninsula, Medina, was notable for its depiction of hopeless love. Originally the creation of the poet Jamīl ibn Maʿmar of the Banū ʿUdhra tribe, this style quickly became known as *ʿUdhrī* poetry, spawning a series of poets whose fate was to remain devoted and faithful, but separated from their loved ones until death. Some of these pairs of lovers – Jamīl and Buthayna, Qays and Lubnā, Majnūn[43] and Laylā – in time acquired a legendary quality,[44] forming the subject of romantic stories in which the original historical figures were effectively forgotten. The story of Majnūn and Laylā in particular had many imitators, and the tearful introspection of this style of poetry spread beyond the boundaries of the Arabic-speaking world, to be copied by Persian, Turkish and, later, even Urdu poets over a period of several hundred years. It also subsequently influenced the Sufi tradition of mystical poetry, and arguably played a part in the development of the European concept of 'courtly love' – though the precise relationship between these two traditions is by no means clear.[45]

For all the fascination of the Umayyad period, however, it was not until the ʿAbbasids brought a shift in the centre of gravity of the Islamic empire from Damascus to Baghdad in AD 750 that the way was cleared for the second great flowering of classical Arabic poetry. This shift reflected a change in balance between Arab and non-Arab Muslims, opening the door for the spread of Persian and other influences from the East. Like much prose literature, the poetry of the early ʿAbbasid period is characterised by a tension between, on the one hand, the traditional values of Arabian desert culture that had produced the pre-Islamic *qaṣīda*, and, on the other, the more sophisticated urban lifestyle of Baghdad, influenced by the Iranian tradition. Conservative tendencies were reinforced by the philologists' view that the imitation of pre-Islamic styles of poetry was the only worthy poetic objective, and we continue to find poets starting their poems with reflections on deserted camp sites. Other poets, however, presented a more faithful reflection of contemporary society, both in their subject matter and in their attitudes, which were often surprisingly unorthodox; for all that, Arabic poetry remained both metrically and linguistically conservative during the ʿAbbasid period – as indeed, it did until the nineteenth century AD.

The new attitudes of the early ʿAbbasid years are well exemplified by two of the best known poets of this period, Bashshār ibn Burd (d. 794) and Abū Nuwās (c. 756–810/1), both of whom were of part-Persian extraction, and both of whom were notable for their irreverent attitude towards the norms of conventional morality. The poetry of Bashshār ibn Burd, the first of a line of blind poets and writers culminating in the twentieth-century Egyptian man of letters Ṭāhā Ḥusayn is of particular interest for the contrast that he draws between the ancient civilisation of Persia and the uncouth habits of the Bedouin Arabs; many critics also considered him both as the first of the 'modern' (*muḥdath*) poets and as an early exponent of a style of poetry known as *badīʿ*,[46] characterised by the heavy use of rhetorical devices and figures of speech. Of the two, however, it is Abū Nuwās who has acquired the greater reputation for his irreverent and iconoclastic attitude, not only towards Islam, but also towards the conventions of the traditional *qaṣīda*, explicitly ridiculing the custom of starting a poem with a reference to a deserted encampment.[47] Of all the classical Arab poets, Abū Nuwās has perhaps the most modern 'feel' to him for a Western reader;[48] for all the slightly exaggerated reputation that he has acquired, there can be little doubt that pleasure was the main business of his life and he is known, *inter alia*, as the most important exponent of the Arabic *khamriyya* (wine song).

Space forbids any detailed account of the development of Arabic poetry through the ʿAbbasid period.[49] A few general points are, however, worth making for their relevance to subsequent developments. The first is that, although – as in any age – many poets were renowned for their profligate and unconventional lives, the formal structure of Arabic poetry remained surprisingly resistant to change, and almost all productions continued to adhere to the pattern of metres codified by al-Khalīl ibn Aḥmad in the eight century AD.[50] The main exception to this generalisation is the strophic poems known as *muwashshaḥāt*, which originated in Islamic Spain in the late ninth century AD, and whose linguistic and metrical features have generated both scholarly interest and heated debate, not only because they seem in some respects to bridge the gap between 'high' and popular culture, but also for the role they may have played in the development of vernacular poetry in Europe.[51] The second general point to note is the increasing importance of patronage in the development of poetry during this period. For this, there were precedents: as previously noted,[52] the Prophet had employed a 'court poet' (Ḥassān ibn Thābit), and Abū Nuwās had later enjoyed the patronage of Hārūn al-Rashīd and his son al-Amīn in Baghdad. Already from the tenth century AD, however, a political trend towards the decentralisation of power was leading to the establishment of effectively independent dynasties in the more remote provinces of the Islamic Empire, several of which are important for the support they offered to literature and other cultural activities.

The rewards, as well as the perils, offered by employment at the courts of these new patrons are well illustrated by the career of al-Mutanabbī[53] (d. 965), who spent some nine years (948–57) at the court of Sayf al-Dawla, a member of the short-lived Ḥamdānid dynasty in north-east Syria. For a time, he was richly rewarded by his patron; but his immodest and overbearing nature made him many enemies, and in 957 he fled to Egypt, where he enjoyed the patronage of the Ikhshīdid ruler Kāfūr for some five years, before again fleeing, this time to Iraq and Persia. A few years later, he was killed when his caravan was set upon by brigands near Baghdad.

Al-Mutanabbī's poetry, though admired by many later Arab writers, was not without its detractors, who criticised it even during his lifetime for plagiarism and errors of language, as well as for the poet's supposedly heretical beliefs. Based on the principle that poems should be constructed as organic unities, at its best it successfully combines the heroic ideals of the pre-Islamic tradition with the technical ingenuity developed by later poets; yet ironically, it has often been appreciated most by Arab critics as a source of short quotations. Many Western critics have also failed to be impressed by his poetry, perhaps because of his over-fondness for figures of speech such as antithesis and *jinās* (the use of words having the same root letters but different meanings).[54] Nicholson went so far as to comment that 'lovers of poetry, as the term is understood in Europe, cannot derive much aesthetic pleasure from his writings, but, on the contrary, will be disgusted by the beauties hardly less than the faults which Arabian critics attribute to him',[55] and though this judgement is obviously an extreme one, it is by no means unique.

Be that as it may, al-Mutanabbī's reputation quickly spread to other parts of the Islamic world, from al-Andalus to Iran, and the style of his poetry was imitated by a number of important later poets, not least the blind Abū al-'Alā' al-Ma'arrī (973–1058), whose distinctive combination of a humanistic, pessimistic, rationalist spirit with an extraordinary knowledge of the Arabic language and its literature made him one of the most important figures in Arabic literary history.[56] More importantly perhaps, from the point of view of the development of modern literature, his work quickly became established as one of the yardsticks of the literary canon to which the pioneers of the neo-classical movement turned for inspiration – the poetry of al-Bārūdī, among others, offering many examples of intertextual references to al-Mutanabbī's work.[57]

The 'transitional' period

Traditional accounts of the development of Arabic literature have tended to categorise the early 'Abbasid period as a sort of 'Golden Age', to be followed by a long descent – slow or rapid, depending on the perspective of the writer – into mediocrity or worse. In this process, the main demons have usually been the Mongols, whose sacking of Baghdad in AD 1258 put an end to the independent caliphate; and the Ottoman Turks, whose occupation of Egypt and Syria at the beginning of the sixteenth century AD ushered in a long period of foreign dominance in which Arabic had to compete with Turkish as a means of expression throughout much of the central Islamic world. The language in which some commentators have described these processes has in some cases bordered on the melodramatic: Gibb, for example, speaks of 'a profound intellectual lethargy' that seemed to settle on the Arab lands after the Ottoman conquests;[58] while Nicholson, having noted that the Mongols 'did their work of destruction so thoroughly that no seeds were left from which a flourishing civilisation could arise', goes on to observe that '[North] Africa was dominated by the Berbers, a rude, unlettered race, Egypt and Syria by the blighting military despotism of the Turks'.[59]

It would be absurd to pretend that these disparaging comments about the state of Arabic literature and learning in the period following the Mongol invasion are entirely without foundation. A contemporary observer, the traveller and geographer Ibn Baṭṭūṭā,[60] visiting Basra in 1327, observed that 'when the preacher [at Friday prayers] rose to deliver his sermon, he committed many serious errors. I was astonished at this and spoke of it to the qādī, who answered "In this town there is not one left who knows anything about grammar"'.[61] On another level, the statement repeated almost ad nauseam both by Western and by Arab commentators in one form or another to the effect that the literature of this period is 'characterized by the virtual absence of originality and loss of vigour'[62] can be backed up by a host of examples. Like many phenomena in the development of Arabic literature, this 'loss of vigour' can probably be attributed to the interplay between general cultural factors (in this case, foreign domination) and other developments having a more specific literary orientation – in poetry, the appeal of the *badīʿ* style itself, whose reliance on verbal artifice contained the seeds of its own destruction, while in prose, the *maqāma*, with its intricate *sajʿ*, while retaining its appeal for writers with a philological bent, in the longer term similarly lost its creative potential.[63] At the same time, it is clear that to such broad generalisations about the 'loss of creativity' there are at least a fair number of conspicuous exceptions, including, for example, the historian Ibn Khaldūn (1332–1406),[64] the traveller Ibn Baṭṭūṭā himself, already mentioned, and the poet 'Abd al-Ghanī al-Nābulsī (d. 1731). Two general points may, however, be made. The first is that there appears to have been a shift in the focus of many of the most creative writers of the period away from 'literature' in the modern sense and towards related fields of history, geography and the religious sciences. The second is that this period has hitherto suffered from a serious lack of research, both in the West and in the Middle East itself – with the result that, in the absence of systematic analysis, commentators have been forced back on broad generalisations unlikely to stand the test of time.[65] Fortunately, this gap is gradually being filled, not least by the imminent publication in the 'Cambridge History of Arabic Literature' series of a volume exclusively devoted to the years between the classical and the modern periods, which promises to illuminate several areas that have so far remained comparatively unresearched.[66]

The popular heritage and the literary 'canon'

Little has been said so far about 'popular' or 'folk' literature in the Arabic tradition. As previously noted, however, it is somewhat ironic that, at least until recently, the work of Arabic literature best known to Western readers was almost certainly the collection of stories entitled in Arabic the *Alf Layla wa-Layla*, or in English the *Thousand and One Nights* or *Arabian Nights* – a work with no fixed text, and no single author, but rather a fluctuating collection of tales originating over a period of centuries in a succession of cultural environments, most obviously including India, Persia, Baghdad and Cairo.[67] The text incorporates a number of story cycles that appear to have had an independent origin; some of the best known tales reflect the environment of 'Abbasid Baghdad, most obviously the court of Hārūn al-Rashīd, but the collection continued to grow until the late eighteenth or early nineteenth centuries, and no single 'authentic' text exists. In these respects, the collection exhibits the typical features of 'oral' literature, passed down through a succession of storytellers and reciters – as also seen, for example, in other traditions such as that of the ancient Greek epics discussed by A. Lord in his study entitled *The Singer of Tales*, 1960. Moreover, although the

Alf Layla wa-Layla is by far the best known of such 'popular' works in the West, the Arab tradition in fact contains a considerable corpus of 'popular' works in both prose and verse, some but not all of which might be described as 'folk literature': they include romances such as the Romance of ʿAntar, originally based on the pre-Islamic poet ʿAntara ibn Shaddād (6th century AD),[68] and the Romance of the Banū Hilāl, which describes the wanderings and migrations of the Bedouin tribe of that name; popular religious stories; fables of various sorts, and humorous literature, including, most famously, collections of stories based on the pseudo-historical character Juḥā.

This is not the place to embark on a detailed discussion of what might almost be termed a 'parallel literature' – a rich corpus of material that for a variety of reasons remains seriously under-researched by comparison with what is today generally termed the 'high literature' of the Arab-Islamic tradition.[69] Suffice it to say that, for what were originally largely religious reasons, both linguistic and literary development in the Arab world has been heavily influenced (some might even say 'hampered') by traditional views of linguistic excellence based, in a religious context, on the Qur'ān, and in a secular context, on the language of pre-Islamic poetry. This attachment to the ideal of the *fuṣḥā* (literary Arabic) is at least in part responsible for the wide gap that exists between the standard written language (usually termed 'Modern Standard Arabic') used today in all Arab countries, and the spoken or colloquial language (*ʿāmmiyya*), which differs widely from region to region. Traditionally, works written (or, in many cases, recited) in the colloquial language have seldom if ever been admitted to the literary 'canon', and this attitude has persisted until modern times, reinforced by the pronouncements of distinguished *literati*. Ṭāhā Ḥusayn,[70] for example, famously declared that 'I am, and shall remain, unalterably opposed to those who regard the colloquial as a suitable instrument for mutual understanding and a method for realising the various goals of our intellectual life because I simply cannot tolerate any squandering of the heritage, however slight, that classical Arabic has preserved for us. The colloquial lacks the qualities to make it worthy of the name of a language.'[71] Najīb Mahfūz, the Arab world's only literature Nobel Prize winner to date, used even stronger terms, declaring that 'The colloquial is one of the diseases from which the people are suffering and of which they are bound to rid themselves as they progress. I consider the colloquial one of the failings of our society, exactly like ignorance, poverty and disease'.[72]

These views have tended to be reinforced in modern times by nationalist and political considerations – the use of the shared *fuṣḥā* being seen as a unifying factor in the Arab world. As we shall see in the discussion that follows, however, practice has not always kept pace with theory, and the evolution of a middle-class readership in many Arab countries, combined with the introduction of Western literary forms, has prompted some increased flexibility, particularly in fictional dialogue and in the theatre, where spoken *fuṣḥā* usually sounds unnatural. The growth and spread of various forms of mass media, including radio, television and the cinema, during the twentieth century has also increased the pressure for the acceptance of colloquial Arabic in situations that share at least some of the characteristics of 'literature'. For a more detailed discussion of the linguistic aspects of diglossia, as it is termed, the reader is referred to more specialist studies such as those by Clive Holes.[73] The chapters that follow will, however, contain several references to the dilemmas and debates that these questions have prompted among modern and contemporary Arab authors – questions that even now, at the beginning of the twenty-first century, remain in many respects unresolved.

Notes

1 The two terms are effectively used synonymously by different scholars.
2 See below, pp. 199–209.
3 Ten poems are sometimes included in the collection. For an explanation of the term and discussion of these poems, see below, pp. 11–13.
4 For an explanation of this term, see below, pp. 8–10.
5 Or *Arabian Nights*; in Arabic *Alf Layla wa-Layla*. See further below, pp. 17–18.
6 Among whom we may mention (taking *adab*/literature, for the moment, in a more extended sense), Ibn Khaldūn (1332–1406), Ibn Baṭṭūṭa (d. 1368-9/1377?), etc. See also below, pp. 16–17.
7 Usually abbreviated in Latin to AH (Anno Hegirae). It should be noted that the most widely used form of the Islamic calendar is based on lunar rather than solar months, and that the Islamic year accordingly advances on the solar one by approximately ten days per annum.
8 The question of whether the language of the Qur'ān could be described as *saj'* was to cause controversy, largely because of the doctrine of *i'jāz* ('inimitability'), for which see below, p. 4.
9 On this, see, for example, W. Montgomery Watt, *Muhammad at Mecca*, Oxford, 1953, and *Muhammad at Medina*, Oxford, 1956.
10 Hence, for example, Arberry's decision to call his translation *The Koran Interpreted*, and other titles referring, for example, to the translation of the *Meanings of the Qur'ān*, etc.
11 The best known example in 'classical' times is perhaps that of Abū al-'Alā' al-Ma'arrī (973–1058); for a modern example, cf. the Tunisian writer 'Izz al-Dīn al-Madanī (1938–), discussed below, p. 156.
12 Quoted in R. A. Nicholson, *A Literary History of the Arabs*, p. 142.
13 Strictly speaking, the term *ḥadīth* (plural: *aḥādīth*) refers to a single narrative unit; but the term is also used generically to refer to the body of literature made up of the individual narratives.
14 Arabic *silsila* ('chain'); also *sanad*, or *isnād*, denoting the 'support' for the *ḥadīth*'s credibility.
15 *Musnad* and *muṣannaf* respectively in Arabic.
16 Arabic *tarjama* (plural: *tarājim*), or *sīra* (plural: *siyar*).

17 Although al-Ṭabarī is probably better known in the West as a historian (not least because of the massive project, sponsored by UNESCO, to translate his masterwork *Ta'rīkh al-rusul wa-al-mulūk* into English), most Muslims probably think of him primarily as a theologian.
18 The origins and significance of this term are somewhat obscure. For a discussion, see *EI²*, s.v.
19 See below, pp. 144–5.
20 Also spelled al-Ghazzālī.
21 Translated into English by W. M. Watt as 'Deliverance from Error ...' in *The Faith and Practice of al-Ghazali*, London, 1953.
22 On these, see Beeston *et al.* (eds), *Arabic Literature to the End of the Umayyad Period* (Cambridge History of Arabic Literature), Cambridge, 1983, pp. 154–80.
23 The genre roughly corresponds to that often known in the Western literary tradition by its German name, *Fürstenspiegel*.
24 The term *adab* is a problematic one, being used in modern Arabic for 'literature' in a more general sense than its medieval usage, while retaining its original sense of 'manners'. On this, see Bonebakker, S. A., '*Adab* and the concept of *belles-lettres*' in *'Abbasid Belles-Lettres*, ed. Julia Ashtiany *et al.* (Cambridge History of Arabic Literature), Cambridge, 1990, pp. 16–30.
25 A nickname meaning 'goggle-eyed', and implying something approaching physical deformity. There were many stories of al-Jāḥiẓ's ugliness.
26 For a guide to this fascinating and extensive literature, the reader is referred to Leder, Stefan and Kilpatrick, Hilary, 'Classical Arabic prose literature: a researchers' sketch map', *JAL* 23 (1992), pp. 2–26.
27 See above, pp. 6–7.
28 This name is somewhat enigmatic, but may be intended as a contrast to the *majlis* ('sitting, session') of the 'proper' Islamic scholar.
29 For whom, see J. T. Monroe, *The Art of Badī' al-Zamān al-Hamadhānī as Picaresque Narrative*, Beirut, 1983. The nickname 'Badī' al-Zamān' ('Wonder of the Age') was given to him at an early age in recognition of his verbal dexterity.
30 See above, p. 4.
31 This character appears in most, but not all, of al-Hamadhānī's *maqāmāt*.
32 On this, see below, Chapter 2.
33 Literally, 'piece', or 'fragment'.
34 The derivation of this term has been the source of much debate. Related to the root *qaṣada* ('aim for'), it has been held to refer to the fact that the poet does not approach his subject directly but rather reaches it in a roundabout way. Other explanations have, however, also been proposed.
35 On this, see M. M. Badawi, 'From primary to secondary *qaṣīda* ...' *JAL* 11 (1980), pp. 1–31.
36 For a succinct account, see *EAL*, s.v. 'prosody'.
37 *Kitāb al-Shi'r wa-al-Shu'arā'*, quoted in Nicholson, *A Literary History of the Arabs*, pp. 77–8.
38 On this, see *EAL*, s.v. *qaṣīda*.
39 For details of some English versions, see *EAL*, s.v. '*mu'allaqāt*'. The most successful modern translations are probably those by Michael Sells, for example in *Desert Tracings: Six Classic Arabian Odes*, Middletown, 1989.

40 See, for example, the poem *al-'Awda* ('The Return') by the Egyptian Romantic poet Ibrāhīm Nājī, discussed below, p. 71. An English translation of the poem is available in Arberry, A. J., *Modern Arabic Poetry: An Anthology of English Verse Translations*, Cambridge, 1980 [1950], pp. 49–51.
41 For whom, see below, pp. 103–4.
42 For whom, see also below, p. 18.
43 An epithet given to the poet Qays ibn al-Mulawwaḥ, whose frustrated love for his beloved Laylā drove him mad (from the root *j-n-n*, 'mad' or 'obsessed').
44 On this, see, for example, A. E. Khairallah, *Love, Madness and Poetry: An Interpretation of the Mağnūn Legend*, Beirut, 1980.
45 See, for example, J. S. Meisami, 'Courtly love', in *EAL*, I, pp. 176–7.
46 Literally, 'novel' or 'original'. For a discussion of the term, see *EAL*, I, pp. 122–3.
47 See, for example, Nicholson, *Translations of Eastern Poetry and Prose*, pp. 33–4.
48 Desmond O'Grady's collection of translations of modern Arabic poetry entitled *Ten Modern Arab Poets* (Dublin, c. 1992) actually includes a translation of a poem by Abū Nuwās.
49 For such an account, see, for example, *'Abbasid Belles-Lettres* (Cambridge History of Arabic Literature), ed. by Julia Ashtiany, Cambridge, 1990.
50 For a convenient summary of the Khalilian system, see *EAL* under 'prosody'.
51 For a selection of essays on various aspects of these poems, see *Studies on the Muwaššah and the Kharja: Proceedings of the Exeter International Colloquium*, eds Alan Jones and Richard Hitchcock, Reading: Ithaca Press for the Board of the Faculty of Oriental Studies, Oxford University, 1991.
52 Above, p. 13.
53 The name, meaning 'one who claims, or aspires, to be a prophet', is probably an allusion to his leadership of a political/religious revolt in early life.
54 For a convenient summary of some of the most common of these figures of speech, see A. J. Arberry, *Arabic Poetry: A Primer for Students*, Cambridge, 1965, pp. 21 ff.
55 Nicholson, *A Litterary History of the Arabs*, p. 308.
56 On Abū al-'Alā' al-Ma'arrī, see 'Ā'isha 'Abd al-Raḥmān, 'Abū 'l-'Alā' al-Ma'arrī', in *'Abbasid Belles-Lettres* (Cambridge History of Arabic Literature), ed. Julia Ashtiany, Cambridge, 1990, pp. 328–38.
57 On this, see below, pp. 42–59, and especially pp. 44–5.
58 Gibb, *Arabic Literature*, London, 1926, p. 106.
59 Nicholson, *A Literary History of the Arabs*, pp. 442–3.
60 On whom, see Ross Dunn, *The Adventures of Ibn Battuta*, London, 1986; English translation by H. A. R. Gibb, *The Travels of Ibn Battuta*, Cambridge, 1958–71.
61 Quoted by Gibb, *Arabic Literature*, pp. 141–2.
62 Badawi, *A Short History*, p. 2.
63 See R. Drory, *EAL*, II, 508. *s.v.* 'maqāma'. See also, Haywood, *Modern Arabic Literature*, London, 1971.
64 For whom, see A. Al-Azmeh, *Ibn Khaldun: an Essay in Reinterpretation*, London, 1982; repr. 1990.
65 To be fair, this point was already made, almost a century ago, for example by Nicholson, *A Literary History of the Arabs*, p. 448: 'The poets of this period are almost unknown in Europe, and until they have been studied with due attention it would be premature to assert that none of them rises above mediocrity …'

66 *Arabic Literature: the Post-Classical Period*, ed. Roger Allen and Donald Richards (Cambridge History of Arabic Literature), Cambridge, 2006.
67 There is an enormous body of secondary literature on the *Alf Layla wa-Layla*, mainly (for reasons touched on below) in Western languages rather than in Arabic. For some initial suggestions, see the bibliography following the article '*Alf Layla wa-Layla*' by D. Pinault, *Encyclopedia of Arabic Literature*, pp. 69–77.
68 English translation as *'Antar and 'Abla: A Bedouin Romance*, by Diana Richmond, London, 1978.
69 A useful starting point for those interested in pursuing this topic further is U. Marzolph, 'popular literature (*al-adab al-sha'bī*)' in *Encyclopedia of Arabic Literature*, pp. 610–11, together with the references given therein to other relevant entries.
70 For whom, see below, pp. 144–5.
71 *Mustaqbal al-Thaqāfa fī Miṣr*, Cairo, 1954, p. 86.
72 Cachia, Pierre, *Arabic Literature: An Overview*, London, 2002, p. 37.
73 Clive Holes, *Modern Arabic: Structures, Functions and Varieties*, London and New York, 1995.

2

The revival

The conventions of classical Arabic literature outlined in the first chapter were fundamentally and irrevocably altered by the growing interrelationship between the Arab world and the West during the nineteenth and early twentieth century. In literary terms, the main effect of this process was the progressive substitution of Western literary forms (drama, novel, short story) for the traditional Arabic ones as the main (though not the only) means of literary expression in prose, with a corresponding (though rather later) loosening of the classical forms in poetry. Though it is impossible to give firm dates for the process, the resulting *nahḍa* (a term probably first used by Jirjī Zaydān,[1] and usually translated as 'revival' or 'renewal' in English) may be said to have extended roughly from the middle of the nineteenth century to the end of the First World War. In describing this process, however, it is important to bear in mind that literary development did not proceed at the same pace in every part of the Arab world, and that many areas failed to feel the influence of developments in Egypt or Syria[2] (the leaders in the *nahḍa*'s early stages) for a considerable time. Moreover, as with most literary developments, stages of development overlapped – to the extent, indeed, that it is still possible to find poets, in particular, in some parts of the Arab world, still using forms of verse that would be regarded as 'classical' even today.

The conventional starting date usually given for the start of this process – 1798, the date of Napoleon's invasion of Egypt – prompts a number of questions, literary, political and economic. If some commentators are open to the charge of being over-eager to characterise the years following 1258 (or 1516–17) as a period of unremitting gloom (the 'Age of Depression', to use Haywood's term),[3] others (or, more frequently, the same ones) may with some justification be accused of attaching undue significance to 1798. Broad generalisations abound, often accompanied by a touch of hyperbole, as a substitute for rigorous analysis. Badawi, for example, observes simply that 'Out of this complacency [i.e., the complacency induced by Ottoman rule] Arabic culture was rudely awakened when Bonaparte invaded Egypt in 1798',[4] while Haywood takes it for granted that, left to its own devices, Arabic literature – and, by implication, the Arab world more generally – had reached a point of no return and that, 'In this situation, only contact with another culture could arouse Arabic literature from its torpor'.[5]

Whatever the significance of Napoleon's invasion for the socio-economic development of the country, however,[6] its status as a turning-point in Egyptian culture is difficult to ignore; as Muhammad Siddiq has noted, 'the postulation of the French occupation ... as the original event that stirs modern Arabic literature to life ... is heavily documented and cannot easily be gainsaid.'[7] But we should beware of supposing that political events of immediate significance to the development of culture in one Arab country were necessarily of equal significance elsewhere. As already noted, literary developments did not occur at the same pace throughout the Arab world. At least in its early stages, the *nahḍa* was largely confined to Egypt and Greater Syria; but the cultural background and consequent contribution even of these two areas to the development of the movement were quite different; Napoleon's invasion of 1798 was of little or no immediate significance for literary development in nineteenth-century Syria, whose links both with the West and with the Ottoman Empire during this period differed radically from those of Egypt.

These considerations imply, first, that any discussion of the *nahḍa* must have a geographical dimension, and second (and more radically), that the concept of the *nahḍa* as a unified movement is almost certainly illusory. Against this background, the remainder of this chapter will therefore be divided largely on a geographical basis – even though, as we shall see, cross-fertilisation between the various areas is a decisive factor at certain crucial junctures.

Egypt

As already suggested, the picture presented by Haywood[8] and others of an 'Age of Depression' devoid of culture extending for a period of some three hundred years from the Ottoman conquest is almost certainly an exaggerated one. As Nelly Hanna has shown,[9] the forms of literary expression in Egypt underwent significant changes during the Ottoman period, reflecting both a change in the political status of Egypt, and a redefinition of the different social groups in the processes of cultural expression. One result was that popular art forms, often including use of colloquial and dialectal Arabic (*'āmmiyya*), assumed a greater importance than hitherto. From this perspective, Arabic literature of the Ottoman period may well be judged inferior to the productions of the early 'Abbasid period. It is also arguable, however, that the popularisation of culture in the eighteenth century and earlier had already (albeit to a limited extent) laid the foundations for the growth of a modern, 'middle-class' reading public in the nineteenth century under new Western influences. One possible theoretical model for the development of modern Arabic literature would indeed see its development as the product of an underlying tension between three distinct strands of cultural activity: an Arabic-Islamic 'elite' tradition, primarily associated with literature in *fuṣḥā* (classical, or formal Arabic); a parallel, though less well documented, tradition of 'popular' literature, frequently involving the use of *'āmmiyya* (colloquial Arabic); and new influences and literary forms derived from the West. These tensions are of relevance not only to nineteenth-century Egypt, but will reappear at various points in the narrative that follows – the interplay between the 'popular' and Western traditions being of particular interest for the development of modern Arabic drama.[10]

Be that as it may, the brief French occupation of Egypt that followed Napoleon's invasion saw developments that were radically to alter the cultural and educational development of the country. Although primarily a military adventure, heavily grounded in Anglo-French imperialist rivalry,[11] the invasion was also in part an intellectual adventure: teams of scholars and scientists accompanied the French military, and a comprehensive survey of the country was undertaken, subsequently published as *Description de l'Egypte*.[12] The French also founded a scientific institute in Cairo, and set up a series of provincial councils, thus introducing the Egyptians to Western representative institutions for the first time; most significantly, perhaps, for a history of literary development, they also introduced a printing press, used not only for printing proclamations for the local public but also for the production of a newspaper, *Le courier de l'Egypte*, and a scientific and educational journal, *La décade égyptienne*, both of which publications contained occasional literary material.[13]

As one recent commentator has observed, the three years of the French occupation of Egypt 1798–1801 have received more scholarly and popular attention than any comparable period in the country's history.[14] This attention has not been confined to Western commentators: unsurprisingly, the invasion quickly evinced reaction not only from Egyptian observers but also from others in the Middle East – including, among others, the Lebanese historian and poet Niqūlā al-Turk, who was sent by the Druze Amir Bashīr to report on the French occupation.[15] The reaction of the Egyptian scholar and historian al-Jabartī, however, is of particular interest, as it exemplifies the ambivalent reaction of educated Egyptians to this first encounter with Western culture – an ambivalence that pervades much of the subsequent development of modern Arabic literature, and indeed, of modern Arab culture more generally. Writing of the year of the invasion, he first describes it in almost apocalyptic terms as 'the beginning of a reversal of the natural order and the corruption and destruction of all things', and accuses the French of being materialists 'who deny all God's attributes, the Hereafter and Resurrection and who reject Prophethood'.[16] Later, however, his attitude appears to have changed, as he makes clear his admiration for the scientific and cultural achievements of the French, contrasting their sense of justice with that of the Ottomans and commenting that 'all the transactions of the Muslims are fraud while all of the transactions of the Europeans are honest'. In the judgement of Shmuel Moreh, 'This awareness of the shortcomings of Islam heralds the demands of the later generations of Muslim reformers for moral, social, religious and scientific revival in the Arab world. It confirms the French occupation of Egypt as the true starting-point of the *nahḍa*.'[17] One may add that, in its explicit and implicit comparisons between Arab and Western civilisation, it also heralds one of the most enduring motifs of modern Arabic literature, as Arab writers have striven to define themselves, and their culture, in relation to European values.

Although technically still a part of the Ottoman Empire, from the departure of the French in 1801 until the British occupation beginning in 1882, Egypt was effectively an independent country. If Napoleon's invasion had given the Egyptians a first glimpse of an alternative civilisation, credit for much of the country's development during the nineteenth century (and, in consequence, for much of the development of modern Arab culture) must belong to an ambitious soldier of Albanian descent, Muḥammad ʿAlī, who had come to Egypt with the Ottoman troops sent to expel the French. Taking advantage of the chaos following the departure of Napoleon's men, he was able to establish himself as ruler of Egypt in 1805 and put into place a range of policies which, while primarily designed to further his political and military ambitions, had important cultural side-effects.[18] The principal cultural innovations of his reign were in the sphere of education. This was a two-way process. Foreign teachers, at first Italian but later mainly French, were imported to train the officers, administrators and other skilled professionals needed to run the new Egypt. About fifty primary schools were set up, together with some higher educational institutions. At the same time, Egyptians were dispatched to study in Italy and France. On return from abroad, these students were required to translate the books from which they had studied, and Western Orientalists and Syrian Christians were also co-opted to assist in the task of providing texts for the new schools. In 1822, the Būlāqiyya printing press was founded, and in 1828 the first issue of the official Egyptian gazette, *al-Waqāʾiʿ al-Miṣriyya*, appeared, at first in both Turkish and Arabic, then (from c. 1847) in Arabic only.[19]

These developments had a number of important implications for the development of modern Arabic literature in Egypt, and indeed in the Arab world generally. The opening of the Būlāq press marks the first stage in the shift from a manuscript-based readership (largely confined to the *ʿulamāʾ*, or traditional Islamic scholars) to one based on the printed word – a readership that was, moreover, constantly expanding in number as a result of Muḥammad ʿAlī's educational reforms.[20] The increased scope for the easy dissemination of texts that printing allowed undoubtedly played a major part in promoting the cultural and national awareness that was later to find fruition not only in the cultural *nahḍa* of the later nineteenth century but also in the subsequent rise of Arab political nationalism.[21] This process was also closely connected with the growth of journalism, which soon began to play a crucial role, not only helping to forge a new sense of national consciousness, but also providing a vital training ground for young writers – a role it has continued to play until today. Associated with these developments were a gradual replacement of Turkish by Arabic as the main language of education and administration, as well as changes in the Arabic language itself, involving the evolution of a more modern, less convoluted prose style and a vocabulary capable of dealing with modern concepts in a manner accessible to the expanding reading public.[22]

From the point of view of literary development, however, the most crucial role was undoubtedly that played by translation. As already noted, Egyptian students returning from abroad had from an early date been required to translate the textbooks they had studied and in 1835, a new impetus was given to the translation movement with the founding of a School of Languages in Cairo for the teaching of Italian, French and English, under the directorship of Rifā'a Rāfi' al-Ṭahṭāwī (1801–71). Al-Ṭahṭāwī, who had been sent to Paris by Muḥammad 'Alī as *imām* to the first Egyptian educational mission to France, may be reckoned one of the most distinguished Egyptian *'ulamā'* of the nineteenth century, with a public service career that included, for a time, the editorship of the official newspaper *al-Waqā'i' al-Miṣriyya*, the Directorship of the Translation Bureau set up in 1841, and several other official positions under Muḥammad 'Alī's successor Ismā'īl (1863–79). The first translations, often into Turkish rather than Arabic, were largely limited to military and technological works, but in time, works of literary and historical value also began to attract the attention of the Egyptian students, and al-Ṭahṭāwī's own translation of Fénelon's didactic novel *Les Aventures de Télémaque*, published in Arabic in Beirut in 1867, set a precedent that was enthusiastically followed during the remaining years of the century.[23]

In addition to his role as a translator and educator, al-Ṭahṭāwī made a more direct contribution to the development of Egyptian literature through his authorship of some four literary works that provide a fascinating insight into how traditional Egyptian culture was evolving under Western influence.[24] The best known of these, *Takhlīṣ al-ibrīz ilā talkhīṣ Bārīz*, written soon after his return to Egypt from Paris,[25] provides a fascinating account of his impressions of France and reveals a surprisingly sympathetic attitude towards Western culture, comparing Western education, in particular, favourably with that of al-Azhar and other Egyptian institutions, with their emphasis on traditional learning. The work is also important on another level, for it set a pattern for a series of works, both by Egyptian writers and those from other parts of the Arab world, in which they recorded their impressions of the West on their return, and reflected on the differences between Western and Arab civilisation. Among the most interesting of these accounts is that by the Egyptian educator and official ʿAlī Mubārak (1823–93), whose four-volume semi-fictional *ʿAlam al-Dīn* describes the adventures of an Azhar *shaykh* (himself possibly modelled on al-Ṭahṭāwī), who travels to the West with an English orientalist[26] to educate himself in the ways of Western civilisation.[27] This motif found further expression in Muḥammad al-Muwayliḥī's seminal work *Ḥadīth ʿĪsā ibn Hishām* (1898–), later editions of which contained an additional section entitled *al-Riḥla al-thāniya* ('the second journey'), in which the author, following a path already mapped out by several writers at the end of the nineteenth century, describes the visit made by himself to the Great Paris Exhibition of 1900.[28] As we shall see later,[29] with the rise of a genuine fictional tradition in the twentieth century, the student who goes to the West to pursue his studies, and whose life is thereby both challenged and changed, is a recurrent figure in the works of both Egyptian and other Arab writers, among them the Egyptian Tawfīq al-Ḥakīm, the Lebanese Suhayl Idrīs, and the Sudanese al-Ṭayyib Ṣāliḥ.

Although it was Muḥammad ʿAlī's reign that arguably saw the beginning of a genuine Egyptian middle class, the educational and other cultural development of his reign rested on a precarious basis, which was heavily dependent on the personality and military fortunes of the ruler himself. As these declined, the translation movement lost much of its momentum. Few, if any, cultural innovations of significance were made during the reigns of Ibrāhīm (1848), ʿAbbās I (1849–54) or Saʿīd (1854–63). With the accession of the French-educated Ismāʿīl (1863–82), however, the pace of innovation once again began to pick up. More interested than Muḥammad ʿAlī in education for its own sake, the new Khedive dispensed his patronage, for whatever motives, with a seeming lack of religious prejudice: the number of European-run schools increased; Catholic missions set up orders in Egypt; and the state school system was revitalised, incorporating for the first time a clear distinction between 'civil' and 'military' establishments. Al-Ṭahṭāwī's School of Languages, originally founded in 1835, was reopened in 1868; the Khedival (now the National) Library (Dār al-Kutub) was established in 1870; the following few years saw the establishment of the first higher training college (Dār al-ʿUlūm) in 1872 and the first Egyptian state girls' school (1873).[30] The number of Europeans living in Egypt increased dramatically during Ismāʿīl's reign, and a radical development programme transformed the topography of Cairo with new buildings, roads and European-style suburbs in imitation of Hausmann's Paris. Many of these developments were implemented under the supervision of the indefatigable ʿAlī Mubārak, already mentioned above for his work *ʿAlam al-Dīn*,[31] and paved the way for the city's seemingly inexorable growth, both in area and population, during the twentieth century.

Particularly significant in a cultural context was that in 1869, as part of the celebrations to mark the opening of the Suez Canal, the Cairo Opera House was founded, opening with a performance of Verdi's *Rigoletto*. Although an institution known as the 'Comédie' had been established during the French occupation in 1800, and occasional performances had been given by amateur European companies in the first half of the nineteenth century, the Opera House gave the Egyptian public their first opportunity to develop a regular acquaintance with Western works and techniques. Many European companies visited Cairo over the succeeding years,[32] and the Opera House, situated in the Ezbekiyya Gardens, remained a focal point in Egyptian cultural life until it was destroyed by fire in 1971.[33]

It is somewhat ironic that Ismāʿīl's policies, designed to make Egypt 'part of Europe', should have indirectly led, in 1881–2, to the British occupation of Egypt that lasted, in one form or another, until 1956. At all events, the succeeding period saw a rapid growth in political awareness, which manifested itself both in an increase in the number of newspapers and magazines, and in a re-examination by a number of Egyptian intellectuals of the relationship between Islam and the West, and of the need for religious and social reform. Among the most significant of this group of intellectuals was the pioneer of Islamic modernism, Muḥammad ʿAbduh (1849–1905), and the social reformer Qāsim Amīn (1863–1908), whose writings on the position of women in Islam signalled the first stirrings of Egyptian feminism.[34] A further indication of a growing self-awareness on the part of Egyptian women was the appearance of the first Egyptian women's magazine, Hind Nawfal's *al-Fatāh*, in 1892.

Although Egypt had had an official newspaper since 1828, it was not until 1866 that the first non-governmental journal, *Wādī al-Nīl*, had appeared, and it was not until the 1870s that independent journalistic activity in Egypt truly began to flourish. In 1877, an Egyptian Jew, James Sanua (1839–1912),[35] published a satirical magazine, *Abū Naḍḍāra Zarqā'*, but the publication incurred the wrath of the Khedive and Sanua was exiled to Paris. A leading role in the development of the Egyptian press, however, had already begun to be played by Syrian émigrés, many of whom, fleeing the periodic inter-communal strife in Lebanon, had found sanctuary in Egypt, where they helped to stimulate the search for new forms of literary expression. Among those involved in this process were a number of writers who also made major contributions to other fields of literary activity, including Salīm al-Naqqāsh and Adīb Isḥāq.[36] Although many of their publications were short-lived, others flourished and acquired prestige; indeed, the Taqlā brothers' *al-Ahrām*, originally founded in Alexandria in 1876, went on to become for many years the leading newspaper of the Arab world.[37]

Syria

To understand the contribution of these Syrian intellectuals to the literary and cultural developments discussed above, some general background will be necessary, for the existence in Syria and Lebanon of indigenous Christian communities with long-standing links to the West implied a starting point rather different from that in Egypt. Unlike in Egypt, where the Christian Coptic tradition had survived in comparative isolation from the West, the Catholic Church had begun to establish regular contact with the eastern Christian communities in the Levant as early as the sixteenth century; Jesuit and other missionaries were sent to the area, a network of Catholic schools was gradually established, and in 1736 the Maronites concluded a Concordat with Rome guaranteeing their local liturgical traditions in exchange for recognition of the Pope's supremacy. European editions of Arabic material, mainly biblical and liturgical texts, began to circulate among these communities, and through this route Arabic typography was introduced into the Arab world, with the printing of a Melkite Arabic Psalter at Aleppo in 1706.[38]

As a result of these and other developments, an educated priesthood had emerged, knowledgeable not only in the history and languages of the Near East, but also in Italian and Latin, and through the development of the educational system, a class of educated laymen also grew up, who not only began to occupy key positions in trade, finance and administration, but also to develop a taste for scholarship, including an interest in Arabic language and literature, and in the history of their own region.[39] Starting with the Patriarch Iṣṭifānūs al-Duwayhī (1603–1704), who wrote a 'History of the Times' (*Ta'rīkh al-azmina*), a number of historians published works centred on the changing fortunes of the Maronites; the Amir Ḥaydar Shihāb (1761–1835) himself produced what was in effect a political history of Lebanon, and Tannūs al-Shidyāq,[40] the brother of the renowned [Aḥmad] Fāris al-Shidyāq,[41] wrote a history of the noble families of Lebanon, embracing not only the Maronites but also Muslim and Druze families.

Among the most notable characteristics of intellectual life in Greater Syria during this period was the emergence of a number of exceptionally well-educated families, with scholars often spanning more than one generation – among the best known being the Yāzijī, Bustānī and Shidyāq families. Many of these scholars had been educated at the Maronite seminary of 'Ayn Waraqa, and many subsequently found employment, for part at least of their careers, in foreign consulates or with foreign missions. As Christians in a predominantly Muslim environment within the Ottoman empire, this group of intellectuals developed a distinctive outlook quite different from that of the mainly Muslim pioneers of the *nahḍa* in Egypt: not only was their relationship to the West radically different, but their attitude to the Arabic language (whose development had been intimately linked to the Qur'ān and Islam) was also more complex. Less bound by tradition than their Muslim counterparts elsewhere, they developed a particular concern with fashioning Arabic as a means of expressing the life and ideas of the contemporary world – a concern that manifested itself not only through literary expression as such, but also through the compilation of dictionaries and encyclopaedias, and a range of journalistic and associated activities.

The 'father' – for want of a better term – of this group of writers was the Maronite poet and teacher Nāṣīf al-Yāzijī (1800–71), whose work stands at the crossroads between classical and modern literature. Although his most important publication, *Majma' al-baḥrayn* (1856), has been described as a 'pioneering work',[42] there is little original in the author's use of the traditional *maqāma* form,[43] and indeed it is clear that its purpose was primarily didactic.[44] Al-Yāzijī's importance, however, lies less in his originality than in his passionate concern for the language and literature of the Arabs, and with the impetus that this concern gave to the pioneers of the *nahḍa* in Syria and Lebanon, many of whom had indeed been his students. At least four of his children – Ḥabīb, Ibrāhīm, Warda and Khalīl – were active in literary circles, and the family as a whole may be accounted one of the leading contributors to the nineteenth-century literary revival.[45]

Although the origins of the literary revival in Syria were to some extent independent of those in Egypt, developments in the two areas during the nineteenth century quickly became interwoven. In 1831, anxious to secure a stable regime on his eastern frontier, Muḥammad 'Alī invaded Syria, and for the next decade or so, Syria was effectively under Egyptian occupation, ruled by the Khedive's son, Ibrāhīm Pasha. One immediate result was a rapid increase in Western educational and missionary activity in the country. Not only were a number of new missionary schools opened during this period but the seeds were also sown for the subsequent development of higher education in the region: in 1847, the Americans founded a College that subsequently (1866) became the American College, later evolving into the prestigious American University of Beirut; a few years later, in 1874, the Jesuits opened a College in Beirut that later became the University of St Joseph. Important as the cultural effects of the brief Egyptian occupation were, however, the political and social side-effects of Muḥammad 'Alī's brief foray into the Levant were far from universally positive. Ibrāhīm's attempts to promote religious equality and social reform provoked widespread opposition, and when the regime further aroused Western opposition by marching into Asia Minor, a revolt broke out leading to the evacuation of the Egyptians from the country in 1840.[46] A period of political confusion followed, characterised by an increase in Western interference, a hardening of Ottoman rule, and a growing tension between the various religious communities. In 1860, war broke out between the Druze and Maronite communities, and many

Syrians (including many intellectuals) left the country – a pattern that was to be repeated on several occasions over the succeeding years. Some of these émigrés went to Egypt, where they helped to stimulate the search for new forms of literary expression – their contribution being particularly important in the fields of the theatre[47] and the press. Other émigrés sought sanctuary in the Mahjar[48] communities of North and South America, where a number of literary groups and societies were soon established, bringing together writers such as Mīkhā'īl Nu'ayma and Jibrān Khalīl Jibrān, who were later to play a major role in transmitting the experience of contemporary Western literature to the Arab East.

In Syria, as in Egypt, a major role in the development of the literary renaissance had been played by the press. In 1851, an Arabic journal, *Majmū' fawā'id li-nukhbat afāḍil*, had been founded by the American Protestant missionaries in Beirut, and the succeeding years saw a major expansion of commercial printing and publishing activity, which established Beirut as one of the major publishing centres of the Arab world – a status that, together with Cairo, it still enjoys. A number of influential publications were founded during this period, including the fortnightly *al-Jinān* (1870–86), particularly associated with the Bustānī family, and the monthly review *al-Muqtaṭaf* (1876–1952), initially edited by Ya'qūb Ṣarrūf and Fāris Nimr, which moved from Beirut to Cairo in 1885. Arabic publications of this type also made an appearance in Istanbul, the seat of the Ottoman Empire, where *al-Jawā'ib* (1861–84), edited by the Lebanese [Aḥmad] Fāris al-Shidyāq,[49] played an important part in the literary revival, stimulating debate on linguistic and literary development and achieving a circulation that stretched as far afield as India, Zanzibar and North Africa. As in Egypt, these and other publications of a similar type served a variety of functions, conveying much information to the general reader about Western thought, civilisation and science, while at the same time serving as a vehicle for the publication of literary texts –whether translations, adaptations, or original works. An additional function – in some cases, at least – was to propagate political ideas, and they thus played an important part in the development of ideas of Arab nationalism within the context of the Ottoman Empire.[50]

A particularly important part in the Syrian *nahḍa* was played by Buṭrus al-Bustānī (1819–83) who, in addition to founding the magazine *al-Jinān*, published a number of translations of Western literary works, including John Bunyan's *Pilgrim's Progress* and Daniel Defoe's *Robinson Crusoe*. His most distinctive contribution, however, was probably in the field of lexicography: his *Muḥīṭ al-Muḥīṭ* (1867–70) is usually reckoned the first dictionary by a modern Arab lexicographer, and he also compiled the first volumes of the first Arabic encyclopaedia, *Dā'irat al-Ma'ārif* (1876–82). Buṭrus's activities were continued by other members of his family, including 'Abd Allāh al-Bustānī (1854–1930), who, in addition to work as a journalist and translator, compiled a massive dictionary entitled *al-Bustān*; by Salīm al-Bustānī (1846–84), an important pioneer in the development of Arabic fiction;[51] and Sulaymān al-Bustānī (1856–1925), who not only assisted his cousin Buṭrus with work on his encyclopaedia, but also produced a verse translation of Homer's *Iliad*, the first modern attempt to translate a major classical literary work into Arabic.

Major contributions to lexicography and related linguistic sciences were also made by Fāris al-Shidyāq, undoubtedly the most fascinating of this group of writers, whose career also best exemplifies the complex relationships both between East and West, and within the Middle East itself, at this time. Shidyāq's literary output stands at a number of crossroads, drawing as it does on both the Arabic and Western literary traditions, and occupying a pivotal position at the transitional point between 'classical' and 'modern' Arabic literature; in addition, the man himself, both through his travels and through his acquaintance with, and adherence to, different religious and social communities, epitomises the tensions and choices that fell to be faced by many nineteenth-century Middle Eastern intellectuals, confronted as they were with the growing influence of the West.

Born in 1804 into a Maronite family in 'Ashqūt (Lebanon),[52] Fāris al-Shidyāq worked for a time as a copyist for the Amīr Ḥaydar Shihāb, before being recruited by the American Protestant missionaries, for whom he worked as a translator in Malta. He subsequently travelled to England to work (mainly in and around Cambridge) on the translation of the New Testament into Arabic. Over the next few years, he travelled frequently between London and Paris, and also visited Tunis, where he converted to Islam, adding the name Aḥmad to his original name. The final phase of his life was spent in Constantinople, where he had been invited by the Sultan Abdülmecid ('Abd al-Majīd); in 1861 he launched the periodical *al-Jawā'ib*, to which he devoted much of the rest of his life, and which enjoyed an astonishingly wide circulation throughout the Arab world and beyond. After his death in 1887, his body was returned to the family plot at al-Ḥadath, Lebanon, for burial, though the story repeated by Hourani (among others)[53] that he reconverted to Catholicism on his death-bed is almost certainly false, for his tombstone bears a Muslim symbol.

Al-Shidyāq left three substantial works in which his experience of, and views on, the West play an important part: *al-Wāsiṭa fī ma'rifat aḥwāl Māliṭa* (Malta, 1836), which provides a description of the history, geography and customs of the island where al-Shidyāq spent much of his early working life; *Kashf al-mukhabba' 'an funūn ūrubbā* (Tunis, 1866), an account of contemporary Europe that clearly stands in a direct line of descent from Rifā'a Rāfi' al-Ṭahṭāwī's work *Takhlīṣ al-ibrīz ilā talkhīṣ Bārīz*; and a part-fictional, part-autobiographical work entitled *al-Sāq 'alā al-Sāq fī mā huwa al-Fāriyāq* (Paris, 1855).

Of these three works, it is *al-Sāq 'alā al-Sāq* that is by far the most significant from a literary point of view. Indeed, it has been described, not without exaggeration, as 'the first real approach to fiction in modern Arabic literature'.[54] Clearly indebted to Lawrence Sterne's *Tristram Shandy*, al-Shidyāq's narrative technique was, by comparison with his Arab contemporaries, equally clearly ahead of its time: he adopts, for example, the 'distancing device' of referring to himself in the third person;[55] his humour, by turns mocking, sarcastic, or sometimes merely flippant, is invariably based on a close observation of his fellow human beings; and his narrative tone varies so much that at times the reader is uncertain of the precise relationship between fact and fiction.

Al-Shidyāq's work was perhaps too idiosyncratic to have had any direct successors, but his career provides a useful reminder that the channels by which the Arabs 'rediscovered' Europe in the nineteenth century (and arguably, through the process of defining their relationship to the West, attempted to redefine themselves), were considerably more complex than some conventional accounts of the process would suggest; marginalised as he was for much of his career, Shidyāq may be regarded as a striking example of the power of an individual personality both to transcend and to reflect the circumstances of his time. In fact, he presents us with one of the most fascinating life stories of the nineteenth-century Middle East – and one that is certainly overdue for further study.

In the meantime, the theatre had also begun to make an appearance in Syria. The first significant step towards the establishment of a modern Arabic drama was taken in 1847, when the Lebanese Mārūn al-Naqqāsh staged an adaptation of Molière's *L'Avare* in his Beirut home; this was followed in 1849 by an original Arabic play, *Abū al-Ḥasan al-Mughaffal aw Hārūn al-Rashīd*, based on a story from the *Thousand and One Nights*. Mārūn's early death was a blow to the development of Arab theatre, but his enthusiasm for the genre, originally acquired on business trips to Europe, was passed on to other members of his family: his plays were published by his brother, Niqūlā al-Naqqāsh (who also wrote plays of his own), and his nephew, Salīm Khalīl al-Naqqāsh, later formed his own troupe. In 1876, at the invitation of the Khedive Ismāʿīl, Salīm established himself in Alexandria, and the exodus of theatrical talent from Lebanon to Egypt continued in the 1880s and 1890s.[56]

Although, as will be clear from the above account, most cultural developments in the Levant during this period were centred in Lebanon, the cities of Aleppo and Damascus were not without their share of intellectual activity. In Damascus, Aḥmad Abū Khalīl al-Qabbānī (1841–1902) had begun staging plays after the fashion of Mārūn al-Naqqāsh, some deriving their plots from the *Thousand and One Nights*, until in 1884 his theatre was closed down, and he joined the exodus of theatrical talent from Syria to Egypt. In the embryonic field of fiction, his contemporary, Nuʿmān ʿAbduh al-Qasātilī (1848–1920), contributed three romances to al-Bustānī's periodical *al-Jinān*.[57] In Aleppo, mention should be made of Fransīs Marrāsh (1836–73), a Melchite writer and poet, whose allegorical work *Ghābat al-ḥaqq* (1865), mainly in dialogue, revolves around the issue of how to achieve 'the kingdom of civilisation and freedom'. Marrāsh's writing career was cut short by his premature death, but his original style (bordering on prose poetry) was later to influence Jubrān Khalīl Jubrān,[58] and, although little read today, he has been described as having some claim to being regarded as 'the first truly universal Arab intellectual of modern times'.[59]

Other areas

Although the most significant developments in the early phases of the *nahḍa* largely centred on Egypt and Greater Syria, it would be an exaggeration to suggest that literary activity was entirely absent elsewhere. Following the founding of the Būlāq Press in Egypt in 1822, Arabic printing presses had begun to appear in most large centres of the Arab Middle East from the mid-nineteenth century onwards, including (among others) Jerusalem (1847), Damascus (1855), Mosul (1856), Tunis (1860), Baghdad (1863), Sana'a (1877), Khartoum (1881), Mecca (1883) and Medina (1885).[60] In most cases, these presses produced not only books but also newspapers and periodicals of various kinds. Although the main intellectual driving forces for cultural and national revival continued to emanate from Cairo, Beirut and Damascus, changes in the pattern of dissemination of texts had therefore become evident in most areas of the Arab world by the last quarter of the nineteenth century (though the practical effect of these changes varied widely from country to country according to the literacy rate and general level of education).[61] Almost everywhere, original works in Arabic were continuing to be written. Often, however, these continued to follow traditional patterns of historical and religious literature, and held little interest for readers outside the immediate locality. Nontheless, although – like many aspects of the earlier 'transitional period' – this is an under-researched area, in Iraq and North Africa, if nowhere else, it is possible to identify a number of individual writers and families whose work echoes, at the very least, the more radical development in the central Arab world.

Iraq

The historical background to literary development in Iraq is a complex one, for the country's geographical position on the eastern extremity of the Arab world had periodically exposed it to Persian influence, be it political, literary or linguistic. By 1800, however, Iraq had been firmly reincorporated into the Ottoman Empire for some 150 years, while its literature for the most part followed a similar pattern to other parts of the Arab world, with the *maqāma* form continuing to enjoy considerable favour.

Although, by comparison with Egypt and the Levant, Iraq in the nineteenth century remained comparatively unaffected by contact with the West, we can nonetheless detect in Iraq some of the same trends and tensions apparent in Egypt and Greater Syria during the same period. As in Syria, for example, a number of families had emerged with a leading role in the development of literary activity. ʿAbd Allāh al-Suwaydī (1692–1761) produced poems, commentaries, and a set of *maqāmāt*, and his talents were continued by his three sons, Muḥammad Saʿīd al-Fatḥ Ibrāhīm, ʿAbd al-Raḥmān, and Abū al-Maḥāmīd (1740–95),[62] the last-mentioned of whom produced a *maqāma* full of rich imagery revolving around an enchanted garden. The most influential family of the nineteenth century, however, was undoubtedly the Ālūsī family, who had already been active in the traditional religious and literary fields for some time. The most significant members of the family were Abū al-Thanāʾ Shihāb al-Dīn Maḥmūd (1802–54) and his grandson, Maḥmūd Shukrī Abū al-Ma ʿālī (1857–1924). Abū al-Thanāʾ, who had studied in Damascus, Beirut and Istanbul and worked as a teacher for a time, wrote three books describing his travels, as well as a collection of *maqāmāt* in which, while following the traditional format and linguistic conventions, he also demonstrated a concern with the present day through his criticism of the Sufi orders for attempting to influence contemporary youth. For his part, the prolific Maḥmūd Shukrī produced some fifty works on a variety of subjects, including history, biography, *fiqh*, lexicography and religion. There can be little doubt that these writers have been unjustly neglected in most discussions of the nineteenth-century *nahḍa* and are due for a reappraisal – as are, indeed, such poets as ʿAbd al-Ghanī Jamīl (1780–1863) and ʿAbd al-Ghaffār al-Akhraṣ (1805–75), in whose verse one may see the beginnings of an attempt in the Iraqi context to free poetry from its traditional conventions.[63] Other noteworthy Iraqi poets of this period include Ṣāliḥ al-Tamīmī (1762–1845); Ḥaydar al-Ḥillī (1831–86), best known for his elegies; and ʿAbd al-Bāqī al-ʿUmarī (also known as al-Fārūqī, 1790–1862), described as the *imām* of the poets of his time.

North Africa

The relevance of the concept of the *nahḍa* to the countries of the Maghrib (North Africa west of Egypt) is perhaps slightly less clear. Indeed, with the conspicuous exception of the Tunisian statesman and reformer Khayr al-Dīn al-Tūnisī (1832/3?–89), many accounts of the nineteenth-century revival appear to disregard the *nahḍa* in North Africa altogether.[64] The achievements of Khayr al-Dīn, however, suggest that, had it not been for the protracted French occupation of the region,[65] the evolution of Arabic literature and culture in North Africa might well have taken a different turn. Born in the Caucasus, Khayr al-Dīn had experience of life in Paris and other foreign capitals; he served as Prime Minister of Tunisia from 1873 to 1877, before being forced into exile, and subsequently served as grand vizier from 1878 to 1879. In 1867–8, he produced a monumental work, *Aqwam al-masālik fī ma'rifat al-mamālik*, in which he reviewed the history and political and economic structures of a number of European countries, as well as those of the Ottoman Empire itself; in the most interesting part of the work, the *Muqaddima* (a title borrowed from his illustrious fellow-countryman Ibn Khaldūn [1332–1406]), the author argued in favour of trying to emulate the progress of the West, which in his view sprang from a combination of representative government and the fruits of the industrial revolution. Khayr al-Dīn's works were certainly known to the Egyptian writer Rifā'a Rāfi' al-Ṭahṭāwī, and may indeed have influenced his views in this area.

In other respects also, we may also note parallels between the experience of Egypt following the Napoleonic invasion, and that of the countries of the Maghrib. In each of the countries of North Africa, a quest for national (or at least, indigenous) identity developed alongside a struggle against French (or in the case of Libya, Italian) colonialism, which exerted a powerful grip on the countries concerned, not only in political but also in linguistic terms. The phenomenon of bilingualism, and the propensity of Arab writers for writing in French rather than Arabic, has been a powerful influence on the development of modern Arabic literature in North Africa – particularly, though not only, in Algeria and Morocco.[66]

In Algeria, at all events, the first of the North African countries to be occupied, French-language newspapers had been published as early as 1832, and the first bilingual paper, *al-Mubashshir*, appeared in 1847. The discovery of what appears to be the first known Arabic-language play written under the influence of European models and published in Algiers in 1847,[67] has given additional weight to the argument that the *nahḍa* in North Africa has been seriously under-studied, at least by English-speaking researchers, and deserves more serious consideration.[68] In this regard, the contribution of the *amīr* 'Abd al-Qādir al-Jazā'irī (Abdel Kader) (1808–83) is also of some interest: better remembered as a staunch nationalist and opponent of the French, he was also a versatile writer who, in addition to technical and military works, composed poetry and philosophical works. Despite this, however, the literary *nahḍa* of Egypt and the Levant appears to have had little significant influence on the course of events in Algeria until some time after the First World War, when 'Abd al-Ḥamīd ibn Bādīs (Ben Badis), who was acquainted with the reformist ideas of Muhammad 'Abduh, founded the *Jam'iyyat al-'Ulamā' al-Muslimīn*, and a period of concentrated journalistic activity ensued, with several publications devoting considerable space to poetry, short stories and even novels:

among the writers who came to prominence during this period, Aḥmad Riḍā Ḥūḥū (1911–56) is the best known. In Tunisia, literary development followed a generally similar pattern – the founding of the official journal *al-Rā'id al-tūnisī* in 1869 being followed by that of the first privately-owned daily newspaper, *al-Zahra*, in 1889. Much writing remained traditional in both form and theme during the nineteenth century, though a few writers such as the poet Maḥmūd Qabādū (1815–71) were beginning to try to find ways of making their craft more relevant to the modern world. Muḥammad al-Sanūsī (1851–1900), author of the *Majma' al-dawāwīn al-tūnisiyya*, compared Christian and Muslim habits in a way that recalls that of Fāris al-Shidyāq,[69] but it was not until the 1930s – extremely late by comparison with Egypt – that we see the beginnings of a modern literary tradition. In Morocco, the process began a little later still, with the foundation of the first Arabic-language newspaper, *al-Maghrib*, in Tangiers in 1889; from then on, literary development followed a broadly similar path, though the linguistic structure of the country has been complicated by the existence of a substantial number of Berber speakers.

Conclusion

By its very nature, the *nahḍa* was a fluid process: it is difficult, if not impossible, to posit any rigid 'end date' for its completion. In the central parts of the Arab world, by the end of the 1920s, most of the initial problems involved in adapting Western literary forms for use in an Arab context had been tackled, and the groundwork laid for the future development of modern Arabic literature in the remainder of the twentieth century; the process, however, was an uneven one, and literary development in most genres took place at different paces in different countries. The countries most associated with the *nahḍa* in its early phases had been Egypt and Greater Syria; but the exodus, for political and other reasons, of a considerable number of intellectuals from the latter area left Egypt as the undisputed leader in most areas of literary activity at the beginning of the century – with exile communities in North and South America acting as an intellectual bridge between Western influences and indigenous development. In the following chapters, we shall see how these processes evolved over the following century or so in the three main genres of poetry, prose fiction, and the drama.

Notes

1 See below, pp. 99–100.
2 Which at this date included not only present-day Syria, but also the territories now known as Lebanon, Jordan, and Palestine/Israel. For reasons discussed below, the contribution made by inhabitants of Lebanon was particularly important at various

stages of the *nahḍa*.

3 Haywood, *Modern Arabic Literature*, London, 1971, pp. 26ff.
4 Badawi, *A Short History*, p. 2.
5 Haywood, *Modern Arabic Literature*, p. 29.
6 On this, see Daly, M. W., *The Cambridge History of Egypt: Vol. 2*, especially chapters 3, 4, 5 and 11.
7 Muhammad Siddiq, review of M. M. Badawi (ed.), *Modern Arabic Literature*, in *Journal of Arabic Literature*, 26 (1995), p. 270.
8 See above, pp. 23–4.
9 Nelly Hanna, 'Culture in Ottoman Egypt', in Daly (ed.), *The Cambridge History of Egypt: Vol. 2*, pp. 87–112.
10 See below, pp. 163–97.
11 For a succinct account, see Darrell Dykstra, 'The French occupation of Egypt, 1798–1801', in Daly (ed.), *The Cambridge History of Egypt: Vol. 2*, pp. 113–18.
12 Commission des Monuments de l'Egypte, *Description de l'Egypte*, 1st edn, Paris, 1810–29.
13 On these publications, see Wassef, Amin Sami, *L'Information et la presse officielle en Egypte jusqu'à la fin de l'occupation française*, pp. 49–108.
14 Dykstra in Daly (ed.), *The Cambridge History of Egypt: Vol. 2*, p. 113.
15 See al-Turk, Niqūlā, *Chronique d'Egypte*, 1798–1804, ed. G. Wiet, Cairo, 1950.
16 al-Jabartī, 'Abd al-Raḥmān, *Napoleon in Egypt*, Moreh, 1993, p. 47.
17 S. Moreh, s.v. 'al-Jabartī, 'Abd al-Raḥmān', *EAL*, I, p. 403.
18 For a detailed account of Muḥammad 'Alī's reign, see Khalid Fahmy, 'The era of Muhammad 'Ali Pasha, 1805–1848', in Daly (ed.), *The Cambridge History of Egypt: Vol. 2*, pp. 139–79.
19 On this, see 'Abduh, Ibrāhīm, *Ta'rīkh al-Waqā'i' al-Miṣriyya, 1828–1942*, Cairo, 1942.
20 On this, see Roper, G., 'Fāris al-Shidyāq and the Transition from Scribal to Print Culture in the Middle East', in *The Book in the Islamic World*, ed. G. N. Atiyeh, pp. 209–32.
21 On this, see Hourani, A., *Arabic Thought in the Liberal Age, 1798–1939*, London, 1962.
22 On this, see Stetkevych, J., *Modern Arabic Literary Language: Lexical and Stylistic Development*, Chicago, 1970.
23 On al-Ṭahṭāwī, see Hourani, *Arabic Thought in the Liberal Age, 1798–1939*, pp. 67–83; Crabbs, J. A., *The Writing of History in Nineteenth-century Egypt*, Detroit, 1984, pp. 67–86.
24 For details, see Crabbs, *The Writing of History*.
25 English translation by Daniel Newman as *An Imam in Paris*, London, 2004.
26 Possibly modelled on Edward Lane.
27 On 'Alī Mubārak, see Crabbs, *The Writing of History*, pp. 109–119, and S. Fliedner, *'Alī Mubārak und seine Ḥitat* (Islamkundliche Untersuchungen, 140), Berlin, 1990.
28 On al-Muwayliḥī, see below, pp. 97–9; a translation of al-Muwayliḥī's work, with a useful study may be found in R. Allen, *A Period of Time*, Reading, 1992.
29 See below, for example, p. 116.
30 On these developments, see J. Heyworth-Dunne, *An Introduction to the History of Education in Modern Egypt*, London, 1939, repr. 1968.
31 See above, p. 28.

32 On this, see P. C. Sadgrove, *The Theatre in Nineteenth-Century Egypt*, London, 1996.
33 It has since been replaced, on a different site, by a new construction donated by the Japanese.
34 On 'Abduh and Amīn, see Hourani, *Arabic Thought in the Liberal Age*, pp. 164–70.
35 Otherwise Ya'qūb Ṣanū', for whom, see below, pp. 167–8.
36 On the theatrical activities of al-Naqqāsh, Isḥāq, etc, see below, pp. 166–7.
37 For a general history of the Arab press, see Ayalon, Ami, *The Press in the Arab Middle East: A History*, New York, 1995.
38 See Roper, *EAL*, II, 614, s.v. 'Printing and publishing'.
39 See Hourani, *Arabic Thought in the Liberal Age*, pp. 54ff.
40 See A. Hourani, 'Historians of Lebanon', in B. Lewis and P. M. Holt (eds), *Historians of the Middle East*, London, 1962.
41 For whom, see below, pp. 33–4.
42 P. C. Sadgrove, *EAL*, II, 812, s.v. 'al-Yāzijī, Nāṣīf'.
43 See above, p. 10.
44 See Introduction to *Majma' al-baḥrayn*, p. 3.
45 On the Yāzijī family, see Kratschkowsky, I., 'Yāzijī' , *EI*[1], viii, p. 1171.
46 See Hourani, *Arabic Thought in the Liberal Age*, pp. 60–1; Khaled Fahmy, 'The era of Muhammad 'Ali Pasha', in Daly (ed.), *The Cambridge History of Egypt: Vol. 2*, pp. 165 ff.
47 See below, Chapter 9.
48 Literally, 'place of emigration'.
49 For whose literary activities, see below, pp. 33–4.
50 See Ayalon, *The Press in the Arab Middle East*.
51 See below, pp. 99, 107; also, S. Hafez, *The Genesis of Arabic Narrative Discourse*, London: Saqi, 1993, pp. 111–13; Matti Moosa, *The Origins of Modern Arabic Fiction*, 2nd edn, Boulder & London: Lynne Rienner, pp. 157–83.
52 The date and place of al-Shidyāq's birth have been disputed. See, for example, *EI*[2], s.v. 'Fāris al-Shidyāk'.
53 See Hourani, Albert, *Arabic Thought in the Liberal Age*, London, 1970, p. 98.
54 Boutros Hallaq, 'Love and the Birth of Modern Arabic Literature', in R. Allen, H. Kilpatrick and E. de Moor (eds), *Love and Sexuality in Modern Arabic Literature*, London, 1995, p. 17.
55 A technique that can also be seen in many later, more conventional autobiographies such as Ṭāhā Ḥusayn's *al-Ayyām* (for which, see below, p. 103).
56 See below, pp. 000; also Badawi, M. M., *Early Arabic Drama*, Cambridge, 1988, pp. 43–67.
57 See Moosa, *The Origins of Modern Arabic Fiction*, pp. 191–5.
58 For whom, see below, pp. 61–4, 88–90.
59 P. C. Sadgrove, *EAL*, II, pp. 510–11, s.v. See also, Moosa, *The Origins of Modern Arabic Fiction*, pp. 185–95.
60 Roper, *EAL*, II, p. 614, s.v. 'Printing and publishing'.
61 On this, see Findley, C.V., 'Knowledge and Education in the Modern Middle East', in G. Sabagh (ed.), *The Modern Economic and Social History of the Middle East in its World Context*, Cambridge: Cambridge University Press, 1989.
62 Haywood, *Modern Arabic Literature*, pp. 67–8.

63 On al-Akhraṣ, see Jayyusi, *Trends and Movements in Modern Arabic Poetry*, pp. 29ff.

64 See, for example, Badawi, *Modern Arabic Literature* (Cambridge History of Arabic Literature), in which even Khayr al-Dīn al-Tūnisī is apparently unmentioned, either in the index or the text.

65 The French occupation of Algeria lasted from 1830 to 1962; of Tunisia, from 1882 to 1956; and of Morocco, from 1912 to 1956. The Italian occupation of Libya lasted from 1911 to 1943.

66 On this, see Jacqueline Kaye and Abdelhamid Zoubir, *The Ambiguous Compromise: Language, Literature and National Identity*, London and New York, 1990.

67 On this, see S. Moreh and P. Sadgrove, *Jewish Contributions to Nineteenth-Century Arabic Theatre*, Oxford, 1996.

68 For historical reasons that should need no further explanation, the French contribution to scholarship on North African literature is considerably more comprehensive than that of the English-speaking world. Indeed, it is scarcely possible to conduct serious research on North Africa literature without a knowledge of French.

69 For Tunisian literature generally, see J. Fontaine, *Histoire de la littérature tunisienne par les textes*, Bardo, 2 vols, 1988, 1994; idem, *La littérature tunisienne contemporaine*, Paris, 1991; S. Pantuček, *Tunesische Literaturgeschichte*, Wiesbaden, 1974.

3

Neo-classical poetry

In the chapters that follow, we shall attempt to explore some of the main trends and manifestations of the movement of 'revival' through the three main areas of poetry, prose fiction, and the theatre, beginning with poetry. As already explained in Chapter 1, Arabic poetry not only had a longer tradition than any of the European poetic schools to which any early Arab nineteenth-century traveller to Europe might have become exposed; in addition, Arabic poetry itself, from the time of the pre-Islamic poets onwards, had acquired a status that was effectively second only to the Qur'ān itself. It is therefore little surprise that when the poets of the second half of the nineteenth century sought to 'renew' their craft, they turned not to new Western forms, as their counterparts in prose generally did, but rather to models from the classical, or medieval, Arabic tradition. As we shall see, this represented a literary reaction radically different from that of their prose-writing colleagues to the Western influences that had begun to spread through the Arab world since the end of the eighteenth century. It is for this reason that the first stirrings of 'renewal' in the context of modern Arabic poetry are usually given the name of 'neo-classical'.

The history of modern Arabic poetry from the middle of the nineteenth century has often been held to be divisible into three clearly distinguishable phases: neo-classical, Romantic, and modernist. In terms of poetic technique, this is indeed a useful division, since each of these categories has specific formal features that mark it off from the others, and there are few examples of modern Arabic poetry that could not, in broad terms at least, be almost immediately assigned to one category or the other.[1] In giving an account of the development of the main schools of modern poetry, a useful starting-point has been to state that the 'neo-classical period' extends from the second half of the nineteenth century to roughly the time of the First World War; that the Romantic period covers roughly the inter-war period, and that 'modernism' became a major feature of modern Arabic poetry from the time of the introduction of various forms of 'free verse' in the period following the Second World War. Although this periodicisation may be helpful in terms of the leading poetic practitioners, it should be noted that these labels refer to 'schools' or 'movements' rather than to periods, and that viewed in terms of formal technique, 'neo-classical' poetry continued to be produced well into the so-called 'Romantic' period – even, indeed, in the more conservative parts of the Middle East, until this day – and it is likewise still possible, even in Egypt, to find new poetry being produced using the formal conventions of what would usually be regarded as the 'Romantic' school of poetry. As we shall also see later when considering prose fiction, literary evolution can and has proceeded at widely varying paces in the different parts of the Arab world.

With that caveat, we can fairly say that the 'heyday' of neo-classical Arabic poetry extended from the second half of the nineteenth century, when a number of poets, mainly in Egypt, first began consciously to become aware of the need to adapt the classical Arabic conventions to modern needs, while attempting at the same time to reread the classical heritage in an effort to utilise the best literary achievements of the past as a source of inspiration. What is clear is that there is a fundamental difference here between 'renewal', as used in the case of poetry, and 'renewal', as used when speaking of prose – and even more of the theatre – which involved the almost immediate importation of Western-inspired forms. In the case of poetry, it was not until the second stage of modern evolution (the so-called 'Romantic' period) that Western-inspired forms began to dominate Arabic poetic literary production.

Since poetic renewal did not immediately involve any major formal structural change, a starting date for the process is slightly arbitrary. There nonetheless appears to be general agreement that the first poet of significance who could be described as 'neo-classical' was the Egyptian Maḥmūd Sāmī al-Bārūdī (1839–1904). That is not to imply, of course, that there had not been poets writing earlier in the nineteenth century whose poetry had adapted to the modern context, at least to the extent of using traditional Arabic verse to describe features of the modern world. Since some competence in composing verse was almost an essential feature of literacy at the time, a number of writers already mentioned in the context of the development of Arabic prose – not least, the maverick Aḥmad Fāris al-Shidyāq (1807–82) – had also composed verse of some interest, if not of great significance.[2] In any event, despite the general trend of Arabic poetry to lapse into frivolous 'word play' of various kinds during the so-called 'transitional period' from the fall of Baghdad in 1258 to the French occupation of Egypt in 1798, some positive traditions of the medieval poetic tradition had been preserved, and court patronage had continued, intermittently at least, on a local basis in Lebanon, Syria, Iraq and elsewhere. In Lebanon, for example, the *amir* Bashīr al-Shihābī had employed poets such as Niqūlā al-Turk (1763–1828) (who also wrote an account of the French occupation of Egypt)[3] and Buṭrus Karāma (1774–1851), who not only wrote poetry in praise of their patron but also produced verse reflecting contemporary developments. Nāṣīf al-Yāzijī (1800–71), possibly the greatest Arabic scholar of his time, was also employed by the same ruler; his output includes not only poetry, but also an important work, *Majma' al-baḥrayn* (1856), employing the traditional *maqāma* form, in which he attempted to use the style of al-Ḥarīrī to reflect the concerns of the contemporary world.

These literary activities in Lebanon also had their counterparts in Egypt, where poets such as 'Alī Abū al-Naṣr al-Manfalūṭī (1811–81), 'Alī al-Laythī (c. 1820–96), Maḥmūd Ṣafwat al-Sā'ātī (1825–81) and 'Abd Allāh Fikrī (1834–90) were active in and around the salons of the khedivial family, sometimes as court officials (*dīwāniyyūn*), sometimes as a more modern equivalent of the *nudamā'* (sing. *nadīm*) of medieval Arab court society – a role described by Salma Khadra Jayyusi as 'perhaps one of the most degrading roles to have been played by poets in the history of Arabic poetry'.[4] Two poets in particular illustrate the extent to which the literary life of this period had become (or remained) bound up either with court and political activity or with that of the opposition: the Egyptian official 'Abd Allāh Fikrī and the radical Egyptian propagandist 'Abd Allāh al-Nadīm (1843/4–96), both of whose fortunes became entwined with those of the 'Urābī rebellion of 1882. Despite their radically different careers and outlooks, both men essentially operated on the fringes of court life – even though in both cases their lasting contribution to the development of Egyptian literature seems likely to have lain in the development of a simpler Arabic prose style rather than in their poetic compositions.

Neo-classicism in Egypt

Despite the literary activity already alluded to in Lebanon and Syria, however, it was not these writers so much as the Egyptian poet Maḥmūd Sāmī al-Bārūdī (1839–1904) who gave the main initial impetus to the neo-classical poetic movement, seeking to find a 'new departure' through the revival of the style and spirit of the great practitioners of the medieval poetic tradition, such as al-Mutanabbī, Abū al-'Alā' al-Ma'arrī, and Abū Tammām. One impetus for this movement was almost certainly provided by the growth of new, rival forms of literary expression influenced by the West; another was the wider availability of editions of classical Arabic poetic *dīwāns* made possibility by the printing press.

Soldier and statesman as well as poet (a combination reflected in his sobriquet *shā'ir al-sayf wa-al-qalam* – 'poet of sword and pen'), al-Bārūdī took part in the 'Urābī uprising of 1881–2 and was exiled for his part in it by the British to Ceylon, where he spent seventeen years, returning to Egypt only in 1900. His poetry combines a new attempt at an expression of his own personality and experience with a traditional approach to the use of language and poetic technique, such as the use of metre, rhyme and *aghrāḍ* (thematic types), including satire, elegy and various types of *waṣf* ('description'). Such a conscious attempt to return to the poetic style of a previous age reflected the need to reassert an Arab cultural identity in a world of rapidly changing political realities.

Much of al-Barūdī's poetry prior to his exile was political in nature, attacking the harsh rule of the Khedives Ismā'īl and Tawfīq and calling for greater democracy, and in this, he laid the groundwork for subsequent neo-classical poets, not only in Egypt, but also elsewhere, particularly Iraq. His most distinctive poetry, however, was composed during his period of exile, during which his health deteriorated, his wife and daughter died, and he lost a number of close friends. His poetry of this period is characterised by an intense consciousness of exile and yearning for his native Egypt and includes several poems on the beauties of the Egyptian countryside.

Although much of al-Bārūdī's poetry is intensely personal, his status as a political activist – if one may use this term for a nineteenth-century poet – was not untypical of the leading figures of the neo-classical movement, most of whom showed a keen awareness of the political and social issues of the day, and used their poetry as a means of addressing both the literate public and the authorities, whether Arab or those imposed on them by the West. Many of these poems were composed for, and declaimed at, public gatherings of one sort or another, effectively a sort of 'platform poetry', and though in retrospect it is easy to pour scorn on some examples of this practice (Aḥmad Shawqī's collected poetry, for example, includes a poem to be declaimed at the opening of a new branch of the Egyptian Bank), their importance in the contemporary context can hardly be overestimated.

Although neo-classical poets of sorts could be found in almost every part of the Arab world, the main centres for its development were Egypt and Iraq. In the case of Egypt, the name of al-Bārūdī is often linked with that of Ismā'īl Ṣabrī (1854–1923) who, like most of the figures already mentioned, combined literary activity with an official career: after obtaining a law degree from Aix-en-Provence University, he embarked on a legal career, served as Governor of Alexandria (1896–9) and then held a position in the Ministry of Justice. Ṣabrī's poetry, hovering at times on the metaphysical, was perhaps the first to reflect a modern sensitivity to the conflict between the medieval heritage and modern progressive thought; but his poetry, like that of the Turko-Egyptian Walī al-Dīn Yakan (1873–1921), was soon eclipsed by more illustrious successors whose poetry, despite often retaining its official, 'public' flavour, was more successful in standing the tests of time.

In Egypt, the example of al-Bārūdī was taken up in particular by two poets, contemporaries of one another, whose names are often mentioned together, and contrasted with each other: Aḥmad Shawqī (1868–1932) and Ḥāfiẓ Ibrāhīm (1872–1932).

Of these two poets, it is Aḥmad Shawqī who is the more widely known throughout the Arab world: indeed, he has some claim to be the best known modern Arabic poet of all. Born of mixed Arab, Turkish and Circassian parentage, he was educated in the modern Egyptian secular system and studied law and translation at the Cairo Law School, where one of his teachers was Shaykh Muḥammad al-Basyūnī, himself a poet, who encouraged his poetic talent. In 1887, Shawqī was sent to France by Khedive Tawfīq to complete his legal education at the University of Montpellier. On his return to Egypt in 1891, he was appointed to a court position and became effectively the poet laureate at the court of Khedive ʿAbbās. The position involved the composition of a considerable number of poems of eulogy and panegyric, with which Shawqī does not always appear to have been entirely comfortable. In 1915, however, Shawqī's so far rather privileged career took a dramatic turn, as ʿAbbās was deposed by the British authorities, Ḥusayn Kāmil appointed in his place, and Egypt was declared a British protectorate. Shawqī, whose attachment to ʿAbbās and the Ottoman cause was well known to the British, was exiled to Spain, where he remained until 1919.

Like his predecessor Bārūdī, however, Shawqī was able to turn his period of exile to positive effect, and he wrote some of his effective poetry in Spain, expressing his deep sense of nostalgia for his home country. On returning to Egypt, he assumed a somewhat different role; freed of his court and public duties, he became, as it were, the poetic spokesman for the Egyptian people. His poetry became more obviously concerned with political and social topics and his poems echoed many contemporary events in the Arab world. He also developed an interest in the potential of Arabic drama,[5] which was attracting increasing interest as a literary form, and composed most of his verse dramas during this period. He was honoured in 1927 with the title 'Prince of Poets' (*Amīr al-Shuʿarā'*) at a ceremony in Cairo, attended by delegations from a number of other Arab countries.

The first volume of Shawqī's poetry, known collectively as *al-Shawqiyyāt*, was published in 1898, but his collected works only appeared much later: volumes 1 and 2 appeared in 1926 and 1930 respectively, and volumes 3 and 4 appeared posthumously, in 1936 and 1943. Many individual poems had originally appeared, after the custom of the time, in newspapers and magazines such as *al-Ahrām* and *al-Majalla al-Miṣriyya*. The contents of his collected works give an indication of the vast range of his poetic themes: the first volume contains poems on political, social and historical themes; the second volume largely consists of descriptive and amatory poems (*waṣf* and *nasīb*); the third elegies; and the fourth is a miscellaneous collection, including also some poems for children. A further volume, entitled *al-Shawqiyyāt al-majhūla*, was published in 1961, though the authenticity of some of the poems contained in this volume is doubtful. In addition to his poems in 'classical' verse, Shawqī also experimented with poetry involving 'popular' verse forms, or *zajal*, though these poems have tended to be ignored or relegated to a subordinate status in most discussions of his work.[6]

During his studies in France, Shawqī had gained a first-hand acquaintance with French literature, reading Hugo, de Musset and Lamartine; he is said to have translated Lamartine's *Le Lac* into Arabic (though this translation has been lost), and his reading of La Fontaine's fables inspired him to produce in Arabic some fables of his own. Unlike many later poets, however, he never allowed Western influences of this sort to displace the classical Arabic tradition as the dominant influence on his own work.

Despite the obvious excellence of his poetic technique, and the continuing popularity of his verse not only in Egypt but throughout the Arab world, Shawqī's poetry has never enjoyed universal praise. His detractors nicknamed him 'Poet of Princes' as opposed to 'Prince of Poets', in reference to his position as effectively the last court poet of the Arab world. Writers and critics of a younger, often Western-educated, generation such as Ṭāhā Ḥusayn, ʿAbbās Maḥmūd al-ʿAqqād and Ibrāhīm al-Māzinī, attacked him as an outmoded traditionalist whose poetry was irrelevant to the contemporary Arab world. Despite the obvious classical basis for Shawqī's poetic technique and, indeed, for many individual poems, however (he does not hesitate to use the classical device of *muʿāraḍa*[7] on a number of occasions), these attacks seem exaggerated, and indeed, in most cases, appear to have been motivated more by personal jealousy than by any genuine literary arguments. Like all poets of the neo-classical school, Shawqī modelled many of his poems on those by earlier Arab authors, including al-Mutanabbī, al-Maʿarrī and Abū Tammām; his period of exile in Spain also sharpened his interest in the poetry of Muslim Spain and he became an admirer in particular of the poetry of Ibn Zaydūn. His indebtedness to the classical tradition can be seen in his use of traditional Arabic similes and metaphors, the surging of the sea being compared to horses in the thick of battle, and women referred to as gazelles or wild cows etc. As an overall judgement on Shawqī's poetry, however, the accusations of his detractors seem decidedly unfair. Far from being irrelevant to the modern world, many of Shawqī's poems have an immediacy that must have struck a chord in the hearts of his compatriots from the very moment of their composition: welcoming the departure of the autocratic Lord Cromer from Egypt, for example, supporting the struggle of the Syrian nationalists against French imperialism, or celebrating the conference convened by the Egyptian nationalist leader Saʿd Zaghlūl in 1927.[8] Equally impressive are his powers of description: his interest in history was evident throughout his poetic career, and he seems to have been particularly fascinated by buildings (mosques, churches, or the remains of antiquity) and their power to invoke feelings in the visitor or beholder. A common theme that runs through much of Shawqī's poetry (as well as that of several of his contemporaries) is the contrast between the past glory of the civilisation of the ancient Egyptians and the present state of the country: a good example of this is his poem on the Sphinx (*Abū al-Hawl*, I, 158).

Ahmad Shawqī's name is frequently linked to that of Muḥammad Ḥāfiẓ Ibrāhīm (1872(?)–1932), his contemporary and rival, and the careers of the two men provide a study in contrasts and similarities. Their backgrounds and upbringings were very different, for Ḥāfiẓ Ibrāhīm was born into a poor family, and enjoyed few of the educational advantages of the aristocratic Shawqī; he never studied abroad, and his attempts to master a European language appear to have met with very limited success – his free translation of extracts from Victor Hugo's *Les Misérables* being presumably done with the aid of an assistant. After attending schools in Cairo and Tanta, Ḥāfiẓ Ibrāhīm entered the Military Academy in Cairo, and in 1896 was sent to the Sudan, where he was involved in an Egyptian mutiny against the British that ended his military career. For several years he was effectively unemployed; but he secured the patronage of the religious reformer Muḥammad ʿAbduh, who introduced him to the leading political and intellectual figures of the day, and in 1911 he succeeded in obtaining a position as director of the literary section of the Egyptian National Library (Dār al-Kutub), a position which he held until shortly before his death.

Despite their differences of background and experience, Ḥāfiẓ Ibrāhīm shared many characteristics with his contemporary Aḥmad Shawqī. As youths, both men had enjoyed reading Ḥusayn al-Marṣafī's influential publication *al-Wasīla al-Adabiyya*, which had introduced them not only to the finest specimens of classical Arabic verse but also to the poetry of the neo-classical pioneer al-Bārūdī, whom they both admired and whose work was a major formative influence on both men. An additional formative influence in the case of Ḥāfiẓ Ibrāhīm was the medieval writer Abū al-Faraj al-Iṣfahānī's *Kitāb al-Aghānī*, which he had apparently read several times.

Like that of his contemporary Shawqī, much of Ḥāfiẓ Ibrāhīm's verse can best be regarded as 'platform', or public, poetry of one sort or another, written for social or political occasions. His poetry, nonetheless, has a distinctive feel. Lacking both the 'grand sweep' and the aristocratic connections of either Shawqī or al-Bārūdī himself, Ḥāfiẓ Ibrāhīm's poetry is characterised by a simpler and more natural approach whose gentle humour seems almost to typify the Egyptian people. Dubbed *Shāʿir al-Nīl*, or *Shāʿir al-shaʿb*, early in his career, his verse seems to encapsulate what the 'average Egyptian' of the time might be thinking on contemporary issues. At times, the contradictions inherent in his situation produce results that can only be described as naïve: for example, in his treatment of modern inventions such as the train or aeroplane in terms recalling the camel of the pre-Islamic poet. However, his elegies on the death of public figures such as Muḥammad ʿAbduh, Muṣṭafā Kāmil and Saʿd Zaghlūl, combining personal emotion with the expression of a communal grief, were particularly admired. Also notable was his use of irony, not least in his political poems directed against the injustices of British rule: for example, his poems on the Dinshaway incident of 1906; on the Egyptian women's demonstration in support of Sa'd Zaghlūl; or his address to Lord Cromer.[9] Despite the power and vividness of many of these poems, however, and despite the obvious popular patriotism of poems such as that on the Dinshaway incident, his reputation as an Egyptian nationalist rests on a slightly shaky foundation, for despite his obvious Egyptian popular patriotism, he also composed poems in praise of the Ottoman Sultan; and while understandable in the context of the intellectual climate of the time, these poems drew criticism from later commentators. In addition to his poetry and his translations, Ḥāfiẓ Ibrāhīm also wrote a prose work, *Layālī Saṭīḥ*, in the *maqāma* form, somewhat in the style of Muḥammad al-Muwayliḥī's *Ḥadīth 'Īsā ibn Hishām*, discussed below.[10]

Neo-classicism in Iraq

The second main area associated with the blossoming of the neo-classical movement was Iraq. Unfortunately, although later Iraqi poets such as al-Zahāwī, al-Ruṣāfī and al-Jawāhirī have always been accorded a high position in this movement and continue to be extensively discussed for their own merits,[11] the background to the neo-classical movement, and indeed the *nahḍa* generally, in Iraq is very much less well documented or researched. What does seem clear, however, is that a thriving tradition of poetry had continued in Iraq, based partly at least on the religious *madrasas*, and that the complex social and political environment of nineteenth-century Iraq succeeded in producing a number of poets whose work not only remains of interest but whose verse may also perhaps be regarded as a forerunner of later attitudes, both personal and nationalist. In this respect, the two most important figures are probably 'Abd al-Ghanī al-Jamīl (1780–1863) and 'Abd al-Ghaffār al-Akhraṣ (1805–75).[12] The poetry of al-Akhraṣ, whose nickname ('the mute one') was derived from a speech impediment, is perhaps of particular interest as an early example of the sort of spontaneity and authenticity of feeling associated rather with the modern period than with the medieval tradition. Although al-Akhraṣ's career, like that of most of his Iraqi contemporaries, revolved around court life (in his case, the court of Dawud Pasha, governor of Baghdad), he was nicknamed the 'Abū Nuwās of his age' for his wine poetry and his work clearly betrays an unconscious attempt to free itself from the constraints of the classical mould.

The work of these and other poets, including Ḥaydar al-Ḥillī (1830–86), 'Abd al-Baqī al-'Umarī (1789–1860) and Muḥammad Sa'īd al-Ḥabbūbī (1849–1916), laid the groundwork for the subsequent development of the neo-classical school in Iraq during the early years of the twentieth century. This was not only a matter of a progressive change in sensibility; it was also connected with the fact that, because of Ottoman misrule, the poetic tradition in Iraq during the nineteenth century had been uniquely open to latent nationalist influences of a sort that came to fruition in the better known poets of the twentieth century.

In this context, two poets are worth mentioning who provide a sort of 'bridge' (in spirit, if not chronologically) between the nineteenth-century poets already mentioned and their more famous compatriots: ʿAbd al-Muḥsin al-Kāẓimī (1870–1935) and Muḥammad Riḍā al-Shabībī (1890?–1966). Although both may be regarded in many ways as poetic and social 'conservatives', both men's poetry deserves to be better known, and both illustrate a number of contemporary trends. Al-Kāẓimī's poetry, for example, is rich in references to Bedouin culture, and indeed it is Bedouin values that seem to underlie much of his nationalism, as he transports the old poetic ideal of *fakhr* into the modern world; forced to take refuge from the Ottomans outside Iraq, he has been described as 'the first self-exiled Iraqi poet in this [i.e. the twentieth] century'.[13] For his part, al-Shabībī may be regarded as a staunch conservative, both in his use of the established poetic conventions and in some of his social attitudes, but the charm of his language and style was nonetheless firmly rooted in a belief in the relevance of poetry to contemporary political and social events.

The two poets who have continued best to represent the political and social aspirations of the Iraqi people during the twentieth century, however, are undoubtedly Jamīl Ṣidqī al-Zahāwī (1863–1936) and Maʿrūf ʿAbd al-Ghanī Maḥmūd al-Ruṣāfī (1875–1945). Like those of their Egyptian 'counterparts', Aḥmad Shawqī and Muḥammad Ḥāfiẓ Ibrāhīm, the names of al-Zahāwī and al-Ruṣāfī are often linked, for in addition to their obvious features in common (they both combined poetic with political activities, for example), they were also at times bitter rivals. Among their principle achievements was the restoration of the tradition of Iraqi poetry to the mainstream of modern Arabic poetic development, after the isolation which it had suffered through the nineteenth century. At the same time, their careers are also an excellent illustration of how, in order to flourish in the intellectual climate of the final stages of the Ottoman Empire, it was necessary to embrace a number of different disciplines, in a style that almost recalls that of the medieval polymath.

Jamīl Ṣidqī al-Zahāwī was born in Baghdad to parents of Kurdish origin descended from the Baban royal family of Sulaymaniyya; his father was a learned scholar who held the post of Mufti of Baghdad. Al-Zahāwī received a traditional Islamic education, which did not include Western languages, but he quickly developed an interest in modern Western science, literature and ideas, through Turkish, Persian and Arabic translations. His career embraced posts in a number of fields, including journalism, education, publishing and law. For a time, he was the editor of the official Iraqi newspaper *al-Zawrā'*, and in the course of a somewhat stormy official career visited Egypt, Yemen and Istanbul; from 1908 he taught philosophy and jurisprudence in Istanbul, before returning to Baghdad, where he lectured in the Law School. He convened a committee during the British Occupation. charged with translating Ottoman laws into Arabic, and served for four years (1925–9) as a Senate member in independent Iraq.

Al-Zahāwī published five volumes of poetry during his lifetime, and a further two volumes appeared after his death. His best poetry is characterised by a simplicity and directness of approach, as well as a readiness to tackle controversial and unpopular themes; in addition to original works, for example, he also translated the Persian poet Omar al-Khayyam's *Quatrains* [*Rubay'iyyāt*] into Arabic. No less importantly, he also wrote extensively about his own philosophy and conception of the function of poetry.[14] His output, however, reflects a certain ambiguity in his attitudes, for while his theoretical writing appears progressive, even revolutionary, his calls to liberate Arabic poetry from the accepted conventions are seldom reflected in his own verse: most of his poetry, at least in formal terms, adheres strictly to the Khalilian metres, and his language remains essentially grounded in the classical tradition. Moreover, although al-Zahāwī has been widely hailed as the father of modern Iraqi poetry, some critics have in fact argued that it is not so much his poetry as his freethinking temperament that constituted his true importance: Jayyusi, for example, draws attention to '[H]is love of freedom; his radical call for the emancipation of women, and for the woman's right to divorce her partner ...; his love of experimentation; his call for secularism; his delightful ridicule of the sterile-minded clergymen ...' etc.[15]

One poem of al-Zahāwī is worth particular mention, as not only being possibly unique in terms of its scale and structure, but also as illustrating the poet's freethinking attitudes: his 'Thawra fī'l-jaḥīm', an extraordinary poem of over four hundred lines in monorhyme, in which the influence of the medieval poet Abū al-'Alā' al-Ma'arrī's *Risālat al-Ghufrān* (as well as, less certainly, the indirect influence of Dante) is apparent throughout.[16] Cast in the form of an extended dream, the poem relates how the poet is tested after his death by two angels, who give him a brief glimpse of paradise before sending him to hell, where he is not only reunited with his beloved Laylā but also meets the greatest thinkers, poets and philosophers of history, including Plato, Aristotle, Imru' al-Qays and his own favourite poet, Abū al-'Alā' al-Ma'arrī, who proceeds to lead a revolt of the inhabitants of hell against the angels. The ironic nature of the account is reinforced by the poem's conclusion, when we learn that the experience was no more than a bad dream caused by the poet's eating too much watercress.

Al-Zahāwī's contemporary and rival, Ma'rūf 'Abd al-Ghanī Maḥmūd al-Ruṣāfī (1875-1945), was, like al-Zahāwī himself, partly of Kurdish descent. Born into a modest family, he received a traditional *kuttāb* education before joining the al-Rushdiyya Military Academy, but he failed to complete the course and left to continue his education in Arabic and the Islamic sciences under the scholar Shukrī al-Ālūsī for a further twelve years. For some years, he worked as a schoolmaster, teaching Arabic, until 1908, when the Ottoman Constitution was declared, when he left for Istanbul to edit the newspaper *Sabīl al-Rashād.* He represented the al-Muthannā district of Iraq in the Ottoman Parliament from 1912. Following the end of the First World War, he spent brief periods in Damascus and Jerusalem, before returning to Iraq, where he held various posts in the fields of journalism, politics and education. He became a member of the Iraqi Parliament in 1930 and was a supporter of Rashīd ʿAlī al-Kīlānī, but after the failure of the al-Kīlānī rebellion he lived in virtual self-imposed isolation from 1937 until his death, supplementing his pension by working in a tobacconist's shop.

Al-Ruṣāfī's first poems and articles on social and political issues were published in journals such as *al-Mu'ayyad* and *al-Muqtaṭaf*. His first *Dīwān*, or collection of poems, was published in Beirut in 1910, and an enlarged collection was published there in 1932.[17] His background and career bear an obvious resemblance to those of al-Zahāwī, both in terms of the interplay of their literary and political activities – closely related to the situation of Iraq at the time of the dissolution of the Ottoman Empire – and because neither man knew any European languages. Despite this, both men, through their knowledge of Turkish, were able to become acquainted with a wide variety of Western literary works at second hand. Many of the themes of their poetry were also similar, covering, from a progressive standpoint, a range of philosophical, political and social issues such as the emancipation of women, the lot of the poor and the oppression of ordinary people, and lamenting the passing of the glories of Arab civilisation. Both men also, influenced by the medieval poet al-Maʿarrī, had a reputation for freethinking, even at times heretical, religious attitudes; despite this, however, and despite al-Ruṣāfī's occasional use of stanzaic forms based on the *muwashshaḥ*, both remained essentially conservative in their attitude to structural innovations in Arabic poetry. There are also, however, clear differences. Compared with that of al-Zahāwī, much of al-Ruṣāfī's poetry has a directness and passion that often stands in contrast to that of the more cerebral al-Zahāwī, and it is perhaps these qualities, together with the musicality of his verse, that helped to give his poetry added popularity. Perhaps the real reason for al-Ruṣāfī's enduring pre-eminent reputation, however, is that he was able in his poetry to capture the spirit of the Iraqi people at a certain moment in their history, embodying the role of the poet as a spokesman for his people in a way that few others had been able to do. His poetry has a simplicity of language that made it obviously comprehensible to the ordinary Iraqi and as the Iraqi 'poet of freedom' par excellence, he was honoured with a bronze statue in Baghdad's al-Amīn Square.

Al-Ruṣāfī and al-Zahāwī are widely regarded as having 'paved the way' for the poetry of Muḥammad Mahdī al-Jawāhirī (1900–97), whose poems represent perhaps the height of the tradition of neo-classical political poetry in twentieth-century Iraq. Born and educated in the predominantly Shi'a city of Najaf, his career included diplomatic as well as educational and journalistic appointments: in Baghdad, he edited the periodicals *al-Furāt*, *al-Inqilāb* and *al-Ra'y al-'āmm*, and for a time in the early 1960s he served as Iraqi ambassador in Prague, but his rebellious nature and outspoken poems and articles constantly brought him into conflict with the authorities, and for much of the time he led a life of self-imposed exile, spending periods in Egypt, Syria and Czechoslovakia.

Al-Jawāhirī's first collection of poems, *Bayna al-shu'ūr wa-al-'āṭifa*, was a rather conventional and unremarkable publication, consisting largely of eulogies, and it was not until after the Second World War that he began to acquire the reputation as a 'revolutionary' poet that he now enjoys, through collections such as *Barīd al-ghurba* (1965), *Barīd al-'awda* (1969), and *Ayyuhā al-'araq* (1971). Like his predecessors in the Iraqi neo-classical tradition, al-Jawāhirī was essentially a conservative in matters both of language and of poetic form, but it is precisely this formal conservatism that seems to gives his verse the strength to express his commitment to the struggle against foreign domination and feudalism so forcefully, in a way that evokes powerful responses in his audience. It is for this reason that, like that of al-Ruṣāfī, al-Jawāhirī's verse became almost a symbol of emancipation, not only for the Iraqis, but for the Arabs as a whole, during the latter half of the twentieth century.

One further Iraqi poet is worth considering in this context, less perhaps for his contribution to the tradition of political poetry in his own country than as an illustration of the sort of roving life led by many Arab poets and writers during the twentieth century as a result of political factors beyond their control. Aḥmad al-Ṣafī al-Najafī (1897–1977) was born in Najaf to an Iraqi father and a Lebanese mother, but was forced to leave his native country in 1920 after becoming caught up in the struggle against the British occupation of Iraq. He remained in Iran until 1927, during which time he learned Persian and, like al-Zahāwī before him, translated Omar al-Khayyām's *Rubay'iyyāt* into Arabic. After three years in Baghdad, he decided, for health reasons, to settle in Lebanon, where in 1941 he was briefly imprisoned because of his support for Rashīd al-Kīlānī. He only returned to Iraq in 1976, a year before his death, after having been wounded in the Lebanese Civil War.

Al-Najafī's poetry has had the misfortune to be somewhat overshadowed by that of his more famous compatriots, but it is nonetheless worthy of attention, and Arab critics in particular have recognised his considerable contribution to the modern Arabic poetic tradition.[18] He was a prolific writer, publishing more than twenty volumes of poetry in all, on a variety of topics and in a variety of styles ranging from the satirical to the pastoral; what distinguishes it from the poetry of the better known Iraqi neo-classicists is that the poet's simplicity of language appears in al-Ṣafī's case to reflect the simplicity of attitude of an essentially private man, who bore poverty, loneliness and exile without undue fuss, and whose first commitment, despite his obvious political sympathies and activities, was essentially to the honest depiction of life around him rather than to any particular ideology.

Neo-classicism elsewhere in the Arab world

Although Egypt and Iraq are usually, and rightly, regarded as the main centres of the Arabic neo-classical movement, a number of poets who have some claim to the label 'neo-classical' were, and indeed, arguably still are, active in other parts of the Arab world, laying the groundwork for the transition from traditional forms to the later Romantic and modernist trends. Indeed, the continuing prevalence of neo-classical styles and attitudes long after the school had lost its position of supremacy in Egypt and Iraq provides a striking example of a more general feature of modern Arabic literary development – the fact that different genres have evolved at different (often, radically different) paces in different parts of the region. In Syria, for example, the journalist and intellectual Muḥammad Farīd Kurd ʿAlī (1876–1953), though not a poet of major consequence himself, was responsible for fostering a revival of interest in Arabic literature and culture that included, among other things, the emergence of a group of poets influenced by what has been labelled by one critic 'the Kurd ʿAlī school of thought'.[19] Kurd ʿAlī himself, in addition to founding and editing an important review, *al-Muqtabas*, had been largely responsible for the establishment in 1919 of the Arab Language Academy of Damascus, inspired by the example of the Académie Française, and his outlook combined a strong sense of Arab nationalism with a return to the classical roots of Arabic culture and civilisation.

Of the poets who came under Kurd ʿAlī's influence, the most prominent were Khayr al-Dīn al-Ziriklī (1893–1976), Muḥammad al-Buẓm (1887–1955), Khalīl Mardam Bek (1895–1959) and Shafīq Jabrī (1898–1968?). Less well known than their Egyptian and Iraqi counterparts, their often strongly nationalistic poetry, though less original than that composed elsewhere, is almost certainly due for reappraisal. Of the four, Khayr al-Dīn al-Ziriklī is today best known for his ten-volume biographical dictionary, *al-Aʿlām*, a work steeped in the medieval Arabic literary tradition, while Muḥammad al-Buẓm's work appears to have been almost entirely forgotten. For his part, Shafīq Jabrī is today remembered less for his poetry itself than for his autobiographical lectures given in Cairo in 1959 and 1960,[20] in which he discusses the influence of the classical tradition, as well as that of Europe, on his own writing, and describes his own method of composing poems, which he constantly revised with the help of classical dictionaries. The most influential of the four was probably Mardam Bek, whose distinguished career included the posts of president of al-Rābiṭa al-Adabiyya, and who served as Syrian minister of education on three occasions, in 1942, 1949 and 1952. Like the other members of the 'Kurd 'Alī school', his poetry, published posthumously in 1960, combines a nationalistic orientation with a neo-classical concern for the Arabic literary and linguistic heritage, and his influence has extended, in his homeland at least, down to the present day.

More obviously appealing than the poetry of the 'Kurd 'Alī school', perhaps, is the work of the slightly later Muḥammad Badawī al-Aḥmad (1907–81), who wrote under the pen name of Badawī al-Jabal. Like Khalīl Mardam Bek, Badawī al-Jabal,[21] who came from an Alawite community, combined his literary interests with political activities, serving as a member of parliament six times and as a minister on four occasions; active in al-Ḥizb al-Waṭanī, he suffered both imprisonment and exile in the course of his career. Much of his early poetry, like that of other neo-classicists, may be classed as public 'poetry of occasion', but unlike some of his colleagues, he succeeds, particularly in his elegies, in transcending the limitations of the occasions to produce work that is both creative and personal. His style, which has frequently been compared to that of the classical poet al-Buḥturī, is clear and delicate; moreover, despite his innate conservatism in regard to stylistic matters, his later work shows a clear line of creative development, not least because of the strong influence of Sufi literature, particularly the poetry of Ibn al-Fāriḍ, with its at times almost pantheistic vision of beauty.

In Lebanon, which had produced some of the most important figures of the nineteenth-century *nahḍa*, a group of poets known as the *mukhaḍramūn*, because they united a neo-classical outlook with an acceptance of certain aspects of modernism,[22] were active in Beirut during the first decades of the twentieth century. This group included poets such as Salīm Iskandar 'Āzar (1855–1916), Amīn Taqī al-Dīn (1884–1937), Niqūlā Fayyāḍ (1873–1958), Shakīb Arslān (1870–1946) and at least one member of the eminent Bustānī family, Sulaymān al-Bustānī (1856–1925), the cousin of Buṭrus. Of these, the most eminent was perhaps the conservative Shakīb Arslān, though it is today for his essays and writing on Arab history and nationalism that he is remembered rather than for his poetry. For his part, Sulaymān al-Bustānī, who like many intellectuals of this period combined his literary enthusiasms with political activity, has the distinction of being the first to translate into Arabic verse a major work of classical Greek literature, Homer's *Iliad*. The most forward-looking of the group, however, was undoubtedly Niqūlā Fayyāḍ, a prolific translator as well as an author who was widely read in French literature and who advocated a form of free verse with an irregular number of feet and an irregular rhyme scheme, thus anticipating by some two decades the Arabic free verse movement that was later to dominate modern Arabic poetry in the period after the Second World War.[23]

More widely known than the poetry of the so-called *mukhaḍramūn* is the poetry of Bishāra 'Abd Allāh al-Khūrī (1884? [1890?]–1968), who wrote under the pen-name al-Akhṭal al-Ṣaghīr.[24] An enthusiast for French romantic poetry, his work forms a bridge between the neo-classical school and the Arabic Romantic poets who were to come to prominence in the years that followed. In 1908 he founded the newspaper *al-Barq*, which became a literary weekly after the First World War and which played an important part in disseminating French romantic poetry through translation, as well as publishing the works of other Lebanese and Mahjar poets. Al-Akhṭal's own poetry, some of which is in stanzaic form, is distinguished by a lyricism and simplicity of expression that has led some critics to suggest a link with Lebanese folk poetry.[25] Although his main themes are those of beauty and love, however, he was also, like most other poets of this period, an ardent nationalist, and like many other poets of the neo-classical school had a penchant for public 'platform poetry' little to the taste of later generations. The impression of a slightly anachronistic personality was reinforced by the fact that, although he had started composing poetry at an early age, his collected poems were not published until comparatively late in his career: *al-Hawā wa-al-shabāb* appeared in 1952, and *Shi'r al-Akhṭal al-Ṣaghīr* only in 1961, by which time the free verse movement and other experimental poetic developments were making some of his public verse at least look decidedly outdated. In 1961, he was hailed as the 'Prince of Poets' at a grand ceremony in Beirut, but the occasion seemed to many to belong to a previous era.

The link with the tradition of Lebanese folk poetry that we have noted in the discussion of al-Akhṭal al-Ṣaghīr may be seen also in the work of the poet and journalist Rashīd Nakhla (1873–1939), who composed poetry in both classical Arabic and in colloquial Lebanese. In 1933 he was elected the 'prince of *zajal* poetry',[26] and his popular verse had a considerable influence on later Lebanese Romantic and symbolist poets. His popular poetry was later collected by his son Amīn Nakhla (1901–76), who himself published three collections of poetry in the neo-classical tradition; as Jayyusi notes, Amīn's name is often linked with that of al-Akhṭal al-Ṣaghīr,[27] but his work is characterised by a narrowness of vision and experience, and his poetry never attained the popularity of his fellow countryman.

In Jordan and Palestine also, a number of poets were writing at this time who shared some at least of the characteristics of the neo-classical school, at least in terms of their formal adherence to the classical patterns of metre and rhyme, which was usually, as we have seen, combined with a nationalist orientation.

The Palestinian Ibrāhīm Ṭūqān (1905–41), for example, born in Nablus, and the brother of the poetess Fadwā Ṭūqān,[28] is commonly regarded as the foremost spokesman of the Palestinian cause in the 1920s and 1930s; much of his poetry was originally published in Arabic newspapers before being collected and published posthumously in his *Dīwān* (1988). Ṭūqān's verse, which combines the personal and the national, is characterised by the use of irony and sarcasm that recalls the tone of some more prominent neo-classical poets such as Ḥāfiẓ Ibrāhīm, but his early death from a recurrent stomach illness brought a tragic end to a promising career. Other Palestinian poets of this generation whose patriotic tone anticipated the later, better known flowering of Palestinian resistance poetry in the 1960s and 1970s include ʻAbd al-Raḥīm Maḥmūd (1913–48), who died in the 1948 Arab-Jewish war, Muḥammad al-ʻAdnānī, ʻAbd al-Karīm al-Karmī (1906–80), who wrote under the pen name Abū Salma, and Burhān al-Dīn al-ʻAbbūshī (1911–), who in addition to several volumes of poems, published four historical plays in verse, characterised by a strongly didactic tone. A Jordanian counterpart to these Palestinian poets may be found in Muṣṭafā Wahbī al-Tall (1899–1949), known as ʻArār, Jordan's foremost poet, whose restless, Bohemian lifestyle has been compared to that of the pre-Islamic *ṣuʻlūk* poets, and whose poetry, despite its frequent grammatical mistakes, continues to touch the Jordanian reader with its strong local flavour.

Despite the intrinsic interest of the work of poets such as Ibrāhīm Ṭūqān and Muṣṭafā Wahbī al-Tall, however, the influence of their work generally remained limited by comparison with that of the neo-classical poets of Egypt and Iraq. The same is at least as true of the neo-classical poets of North Africa who flourished in the 1930s and 1940s, including the Moroccan ʻAllāl al-Fāsī (1910–79), a champion of the *salafiyya*, or traditionalist movement, the Algerian Muḥammad al-Khalīfa al-ʻĪd (born 1904), and the Tunisian Aḥmad Khayr al-Dīn (1906–67). Much of these poets' work, like that of their neo-classical counterparts elsewhere, was closely linked to the struggle for national independence, and the strength of this link arguably delayed the introduction of free verse and other innovations during the period following the Second World War. In the Arabian Peninsula itself, as well as in the Gulf states, neo-classical poetry did not make any tangible impression until the 1940s and 1950s, but continued to be in vogue long after it had been overtaken by Romanticism and various forms of free verse in the main urban centres of the Arab world such as Cairo and Beirut. Indeed, the continuing popularity of poetry in the neo-classical style in these countries provides yet another striking illustration of the different pace of literary evolution in different parts of the Arab world.

It is only necessary to browse in a good Arabic-language library or bookshop, or indeed to surf the Internet, to convince oneself that, even at the beginning of the twenty-first century, much Arabic poetry continues to be written in the traditional forms of classical verse used by the neo-classical poets and that the Khalilian system of prosody is by no means yet extinct. Nevertheless, by the time of the First World War, a number of poets had already begun to show signs of rebellion against the constraints both of the thematic concerns and of the structural conventions of traditional poetic forms. The resulting movement, Romanticism, was fuelled, at least in part, by contacts between the Mahjar writers and their Western counterparts, and came to dominate the Arabic poetic scene in the period between the two world wars. It is to this movement that we shall turn in the following chapter.

Notes

1 'Popular' poetry clearly falls outside the scope of this generalisation.
2 For al-Shidyāq, see above, pp. 33–4, and for an example of his verse, conventional not only in its construction but also in its purpose, see his ode to Queen Victoria, in Arberry, *Arabic Poetry*, pp. 136–49.
3 Al-Turk, Niqūlā, *Chronique d'Egypte*, *1798–1804*, ed. G. Wiet, Cairo, 1950.
4 Jayyusi, *Trends and Movements*, p. 36.
5 For which, see below, Chapter 10.
6 See, for example, *al-Mawsū'a al-Shawqiyya*, ed. Ibrāhīm al-Abyārī, Beirut: Dār al-Kitāb al-'Arabī, 1994–5, I, p. 527.
7 *mu'āraḍa*: the imitation of a prior literary text, often with the purpose of honouring the model and/or trying to surpass it.
8 Respectively I, 206; II, 88; and II, 190 in his collected works
9 Respectively II, 20; II, 87; and II, 25 in his collected works. See also Vatikiotis, *The Modern History of Egypt*, pp. 194–5.
10 See below, Chapter 6.
11 See, for example, the extensive discussions in Badawi, *A Critical Introduction*, chapter 2.
12 For whom, see Jayyusi, *Trends and Movements*, pp. 29–32.
13 Ibid., p. 176.
14 See, for example, his *Dīwān* (1924), pp. 240–62.
15 Jayyusi, *Trends and Movements*, p. 185.
16 For al-Ma'arrī, see above, p. 16; for a study of the poem, see Jamīl Sa'īd, *al-Zahāwī wa-thawratuhu fī al-jaḥīm*, Cairo, 1968.
17 The best edition, the sixth, was published in Cairo in 1958.
18 On this, see Jayyusi, *Trends and Movements*, pp. 193–7.
19 Sāmī al-Kayyālī, *al-Adab al-'Arabī al-Mu'āṣir fī Sūriyya*, pp. 78–80. On neo-classicism in Syria and Lebanon, see Jayyusi, *Trends and Movements*, pp. 206–70.
20 *Anā wa-al-shi'r*, Cairo, 1959 and *Anā wa-al-nathr*, Cairo, 1960.
21 For a fuller discussion, see Jayyusi, *Trends and Movements*, pp. 210–27.
22 The term was originally applied to persons living in the *Jāhiliyya* (period before Islam) and into the times of Islam. See *EAL*, s.v.
23 For which, see Chapter 5 below, and Moreh, *Modern Arabic Poetry, 1800–1970*, pp. 137–8, 178–94.
24 After the classical Arabic poet. See Jayyusi, *Trends and Movements*, 246–60.

25 Ibid., pp. 246–7.
26 As used in modern Arabic, *zajal* denotes various types of poems composed in colloquial. See *EAL*, s.v.
27 Jayyusi, *Trends and Movements*, pp. 260ff.
28 For whom, see below, Chapter 5, p. 76.

4

Romanticism in Arabic poetry

Like those of the Arabic neo-classical movement discussed in the previous chapter, the boundaries of the Romantic movement in Arabic poetry are somewhat difficult to define. Arabic Romanticism emerged gradually from neo-classicism during the early years of the twentieth century and enjoyed its greatest vogue in the period between the two world wars, but no clear break separates the two movements, either chronologically or stylistically. Many poets whose verse is characterised by the attitudes of the Romantic school continued to use mainly or exclusively traditional poetic forms and, as we have seen in the preceding chapter, neo-classical poetry continued to be written, particularly in Iraq, until the last third of the twentieth century. The 'incremental' nature of the shift from neo-classicism to Romanticism is evident from the use by many critics of the term 'pre-Romantic' to describe poets whose work exhibits features of both movements.

Despite these *caveats*, the term 'Romanticism' (usually Arabicised as *al-rūmanṭīqiyya*)[1] appears to be a universally accepted one, employed by critics and literary historians to define a set of attitudes and poetic conventions that mirror (though they may not always precisely correspond to) those of the Western Romantics. The attitudes in question have been well summarised by Robin Ostle as follows:

> (a) the desire not to conform to traditional social norms or institutions; (b) the celebration of scenes of natural beauty and intense emotional identification with such scenes, along with a tendency to regard towns and cities as centres of evil and corruption; (c) deep emotional introspection and a tendency to glorify in the isolated state of the poet who, like the prophet without honour, is shunned by his contemporaries; (d) a strong sense of the neo-platonic duality of body and soul; (e) a tendency to write amatory poetry which is ethereal and spiritual rather than physical.[2]

It will of course be immediately obvious that not all of the characteristics identified by Ostle are exclusive to Romanticism: the Arab tradition of the *ṣu'lūk* ('outcast' or 'brigand') poet reaches back into pre-Islamic times, and the 'Udhrī poetry of the Umayyad period in particular is rich in examples of poets pining for a sweetheart beyond their reach. For a number of reasons, however, these attitudes proved particularly attractive to Arab poets during the inter-war years – years characterised on a political level by a sense of frustration that the hopes of national fulfilment engendered by the break up of the Ottoman Empire had not been realised, and that many parts of the region had simply witnessed the replacement of the Ottomans by a new set of masters in the form of Western, European powers.

An important factor in the genesis of Arab Romanticism was the existence of the various groups of 'Mahjar' poets and writers who had emigrated from Syria and Lebanon to North and South America from around 1850 onwards. Although some of the 'Mahjar' writers can no doubt be classed as 'economic migrants', an important motivation for many was the need to escape from political and religious persecution; in this context, it is significant that the overwhelming majority of the emigrants were Christian. These emigration movements represented a phenomenon parallel to the periodic migrations of intellectuals from Syria and Lebanon to Egypt which played such an important part in the development of the Egyptian press and theatre; in contrast to the movements to Egypt, however, the chief contribution of the 'Mahjar' intellectuals to Arabic literature generally lay in the field of poetry. This is therefore a convenient point at which to summarise some of the main features of Mahjar literature – a subject that not only forms an essential part of the background to the Arabic Romantic movement but which may also be regarded as a topic of both literary and sociological fascination in its own right.

Mahjar literature

Although Arabic literature was produced by Mahjar communities in both North and South America, it is the North American contribution that is better known in the English-speaking world (and indeed, the West generally), largely through the works of Jubrān Khalīl Jubrān – many of whose works were indeed originally written in English rather than Arabic. Interesting poetry was, however, produced not only in North but also in South America, particularly in Argentina and Brazil, and indeed, although literary activity in the Mahjar communities of North and South America initially developed at much the same time, the South American tradition in some respects seems to have been longer lasting.

In both continents, newspapers, periodicals and 'literary circles' of various kinds played an important part in sustaining the identities of the Arab communities involved. In North America, the first Arabic newspaper, *Kawkab Amīrkā*, was founded in New York in 1892, and some 135 newspaper and periodical titles are recorded as having appeared in the United States and Canada between that date and 1980.[3] Among the best known of these publications were the comparatively short-lived *al-Funūn*, founded by Nasīb 'Arīḍa, which appeared between 1913 and 1918 and which served as an outlet for authors such as Mikhā'īl Nu'ayma, Amīn al-Rīḥānī and Īliyā Abū Māḍī, as well as Jubrān Khalīl Jubrān himself; *al-Sā'iḥ*, founded by 'Abd al-Masīḥ Ḥaddād, which ran from 1912 to 1957; and Abū Māḍī's own *al-Samīr*, which ran from 1929 until 1957. In South America, the first Arabic newspaper, *al-Fayḥā'* appeared in São Paulo in 1895, and some 127 newspaper and periodical titles are recorded as having been produced in São Paulo between that date and 1980.[4] In addition, many prominent books in Arabic were published in both continents, beginning in 1895, and including works by Jubrān, Amīn al-Rīḥānī and Īliyā Abū Māḍī, among others.

The first Mahjar literary circle, the 'Riwāq al-Ma'arrī', had been founded in South America in 1900, but it was the city of New York that not only served as the main publishing centre for Arabic works in North America but was also home to the most important literary circle of the Mahjar, 'al-Rābiṭa al-qalamiyya' [Arrabita]. The name of the circle, which brought together poets and writers including Jubrān, al-Rīḥānī and Abū Māḍī, Mikhā'īl Nu'ayma and Nasīb 'Arīḍa, dates from 1916, but though the name was used sporadically during the next few years, the official founding session of the group did not take place until April 1920. According to the group's constitution, members of the group were to be divided into three categories: 'workers', i.e., authors and poets living in New York; 'sponsors', who supported the group; and 'correspondents', i.e., authors and poets living outside New York. Although the group's publication and translation ambitions were only achieved to a limited extent, it survived until the beginning of the 1930s, folding only with the death of Jubrān in 1931 and the return to Lebanon of Mikhā'īl Nu'ayma the following year. Other literary circles – that continued to play a part in Mahjar literary life until well after the Second World War – included 'al-'Uṣba al-andalusiyya', founded in São Paulo in 1933, which published an important literary journal *al-'Uṣba*.

It is difficult to overestimate the importance of the contribution made by the Mahjar writers to the development of modern Arabic poetry. Shielded from many of the more traditionalist Middle Eastern attitudes to literature both by their geographical distance and by their Christian upbringing, the Mahjar writers were directly exposed to Western writers and poets ranging from the European Romantics to contemporary American poets such as Walt Whitman. The result can be seen not only in the development of new strophic poetic forms, which rejected the metrical conventions of medieval Arabic poetry, but also in a radical shift in the language towards a simpler and more accessible vocabulary, less remote from the language of everyday use, which could serve as a vehicle for the expression of a personal vision and individual feelings. The Mahjar writers also pioneered attempts to bridge the gap between prose and poetry through the development of various types of 'prose poetry' (*shi'r manthūr*),[5] inspired in these efforts not only by Western models but also by Arabic translations of the Bible and by Christian liturgical literature.

Space forbids detailed discussion of more than a few of the most significant writers of the Mahjar. Of the Mahjar writers in North America, the name of Jubrān Khalīl Jubrān (1883–1931) has acquired almost cult status in some Western circles, largely through his best known work *The Prophet* and other similar works, in which a central theme is reincarnation and the migration of the human soul. Indeed, this work, originally written in English,[6] has been claimed, somewhat improbably, to have been 'the most widely read book of the twentieth century'.[7] Be that as it may, Jubrān, born in Bishirri (Lebanon), emigrated to the United States with his mother and other members of his family in 1895 and remained there for most of his life, with occasional visits to his native Lebanon, and a spell in Paris between 1908 and 1910, during which he became acquainted with the works of Nietzsche, which made a considerable impression on him. His mother, sister and step-brother died from tuberculosis in 1902 and 1903 and Jubrān was at first forced to live on money earned as a seamstress by his other sister, Marianna, until in 1907 he found a protectress in Mary Haskell, the owner of a private girls' school, who admired his painting as well as his writing and who encouraged him to go to Paris to study modern art.

It is difficult to arrive at a definitive evaluation of Jubrān's contribution to the development of modern Arabic literature: not only was much of his work written in English rather than Arabic, but his 'cult status' in some Western circles has seemed at times to distort critical judgement. Much of his work is marred by an at times almost mawkish sentimentality, but there is no doubt that he played an important, indeed a crucial, role in familiarising Arab readers with the ideas and ideals of Romanticism. Moreover, Jubrān was a genuine innovator (albeit an uneven one), and though it is tempting to dismiss him as a marginal figure, the fact is that despite his geographical isolation, he was in close contact with members of the Arabic literary establishment in the Middle East, not least through his extended literary and amorous correspondence with the poetess Mayy Ziyāda.

If Jubrān's literary reputation seems, perversely, at times more secure in the West than in the East, the opposite is true of his close colleague and biographer, Mikhā'īl Nu'ayma (1889–1989). Nu'ayma's training and early career is of considerable interest in the context of the transmission of Western ideas to Middle Eastern society: after attending the Russian school in Nazareth, he was sent to the Diocesan Seminary in Poltova, Ukraine, where he became acquainted with the works of Tolstoy and other modern Russian writers, and developed an admiration for Tolstoy's social ideas. At school, he had been the school mate of another Mahjar poet-to-be, Nasīb 'Arīḍa (1889–1946), the future publisher in New York of *al-Funūn*, and the early link formed between the two men provided one of the bases for the formation of 'al-Rābiṭa al-qalamiyya' in 1920. He emigrated to the United States in 1911 and after taking a law degree at the University of Washington, Seattle, was drafted into the United States army, reaching the front line in France a few days before the armistice of 11 November 1918. For much of the following decade he worked as a travelling salesman, returning to Lebanon in 1932, following Jubrān's death the previous year, and devoted the remainder of his life to writing.

Mikhā'īl Nu'ayma was a prolific writer, producing more than thirty volumes of poetry, prose, drama, biography, autobiography, essays and literary criticism. His frank biography of Jubrān,[8] which followed the style of the *biographie romancée*, was interpreted by some as an attack on his friend; and his own autobiography, *Sab'ūn*,[9] is an equally interesting work, not least for its account of his early years in Biskinta, Nazareth and Poltova. His reputation, however, rests above all on his literary criticism, in particular *al-Ghirbāl* (1923), which brought together his critical essays in which he denounced traditional Arabic prosody for restricting the free expression of emotion that he regarded as essential for contemporary poetry. This work may be regarded as one of the most important statements of the poetic principles underlying Mahjar, and indeed, Arabic Romantic poetry generally. His own poetic output was surprisingly small, most of his poems being published in a slim volume entitled *Hams al-Jufūn* in 1943, but despite that it quickly acquired a reputation as a distinctive contribution to contemporary verse; his poem 'Akhī' in particular was hailed as an example of a new, understated[10] style of poetry, and critics such as the Egyptian Muḥammad Mandūr[11] ensured that the ideas of Nu'ayma and his colleagues quickly became widely dispersed through the Arab world.

The 'Pre-Romantics'

If the experiments of the Mahjar writers provided one stimulus for the growth of the Arabic Romantic movement, this could clearly only have been because the new outlook was in some way responding to the needs of poets writing in the Middle East itself, for whom the assumptions of the neo-classicists seemed already to be becoming outmoded. Not for the first time, a Lebanese emigrant to Egypt seems to have played a key part in sparking a shift in literary attitudes. As with most literary developments however, the shift was a gradual rather than an instant one – a feature that has given rise to the use of the term 'pre-Romantics', for writers whose work exemplifies features of both literary groupings.

The first of these so-called 'pre-Romantics', Khalīl Muṭrān (1872–1949), was born in Baalbek and educated in the Catholic seminary in Beirut. Like several of his fellow countrymen before him, he subsequently became involved in anti-Ottoman political activities that led to his fleeing the country, and he at first found a haven in Paris, where he developed his knowledge of French literature. In 1902, however, he settled in Egypt, where he remained for the rest of his life, thereby earning himself the sobriquet *Shā'ir al-Quṭrayn* ('poet of the two regions', i.e., Egypt and the Levant). Like many of his contemporaries, Muṭrān was a man of many parts, being active not only as a poet but also in the fields of journalism and commerce; as well as writing poems, he translated several works into Arabic, including several of Shakespeare's plays.

Muṭrān's first volume of published verse, *Dīwān al-khalīl* (1908), included a preface in which he sought to distance himself from traditional Arab concepts of poetry by laying a new emphasis on the structural unity of the poem and on the primacy of the imagination of the individual artist. The extent to which these principles can be discerned in his own poetry is, however, extremely variable. The first volume of his *Dīwān* contains several poems that seem to mirror the attitudes of the European Romantics in their introspection and empathy with the poet's natural surroundings. His poetry, however, also continued the neo-classical tradition of using verse as a vehicle for political, often anti-imperialist, propaganda, and as time went on, the more conventional neo-classical aspects of his poetic talent appear to have become dominant. For whatever reason, his subsequent poetry[12] failed to develop the promise of the first volume of his *Dīwān* to any significant degree and it was left to others to build on the principles outlined in his early 'manifesto' and develop more fully the Romantic trends that he had hinted at in his early poems.

It is at this point that we see emerging in Egypt a phenomenon that parallels the literary groupings of the Mahjar – the emergence of groups of poets, usually centring on a literary periodical, forming the focus for the development of particular trends. The first of these groupings, the so-called Dīwān Group, was a somewhat short-lived and stormy affair, centring on three men, 'Abbās Maḥmūd al-'Aqqād, Ibrāhīm 'Abd al-Qādir al-Māzinī, and 'Abd al-Raḥmān Shukrī (1886–1958). The first two of these also played a leading role in the development of Arabic prose forms in Egypt and will be further encountered in Chapter 7 below; indeed, of the three, only 'Abd al-Raḥmān Shukrī is today remembered primarily for his poetry. Born in Port Said, Shukrī received his primary and secondary education in Alexandria and like al-Māzinī, was a student at the Teachers' Training College in Cairo. He published his first collection of poetry in 1909, but the distinctive formative influence on his poetry was the three-year period that he spent in England between 1909 and 1912, studying history and English at Sheffield University College. While there, he acquired a wide ranging knowledge of English poetry and the English tradition of literary criticism, and developed a particular empathy for English poetry of the eighteenth and nineteenth centuries, the influence of which is evident not only in his own later poetry but also in his essays and literary criticism. Many of his ideas and poetic practice can be traced back directly to poets of the English tradition such as Wordsworth and Keats and to critics such as Hazlitt and Coleridge, and his work exemplifies many of the 'classic' traits of Romanticism, as described by Robin Ostle:[13] these included the insistence on the overriding importance of feeling, the tension between the physical and spiritual aspects of love, and the idea of the special status of the poet. His *Dīwān* was published in seven volumes between 1909 and 1919, later poems appearing in periodicals; his complete works were published posthumously in Alexandria in 1960.

Temperamentally, Shukrī was a very different character from al-ʿAqqād and al-Māzinī, the other two members of the so-called Dīwān Group; he showed little enthusiasm for public life and, on his return from England in 1912, opted instead for a career in education, as a teacher and official in the Ministry of Education. Although his friendships with al-ʿAqqād and al-Māzinī had already been formed before his departure for England in 1909, the three men's association did not come to full fruition until after his return, and the name 'Dīwān Group' indeed dates only from the early 1920s. The appropriateness of this title has indeed been questioned by critics. The three men had originally come together on an informal basis to share their interests in poetry and literary criticism, and the association at first seemed promising, but a furious quarrel erupted when Shukrī drew attention in print to al-Māzinī's 'borrowings', and when in 1921 al-ʿAqqād and al-Māzinī produced their seminal work of criticism entitled *al-Dīwān: kitāb fī al-adab wa-al-naqd*, which included a bitter attack on Shukrī, the group's disintegration became inevitable. Al-Māzinī subsequently expressed his regret for this attack on his former colleague and expressed his indebtedness to him.

In terms of their poetic output, al-ʿAqqād and al-Māzinī are less significant figures than Shukrī. Al-Māzinī's *Dīwān* appeared in two volumes in 1914 and 1917 respectively, and he also published, in 1915, a study of the poetry of Ḥāfiẓ Ibrāhīm, but he subsequently devoted most of his literary activities to prose writing, including a significant contribution to the development of the Egyptian novel, through works such as *Ibrāhīm al-kātib* (1931).[14] For his part, al-ʿAqqād continued to produced volumes of poetry through his long career, beginning with *Yaqẓat al-ṣabāḥ* (1916) and including also, for example, *Hadiyyat al-karawān* (1933), *ʿĀbir sabīl* (1937) and *Aʿāṣīr maghrib* (1942). He also wrote a long study on the classical Arabic poet Ibn al-Rūmī, in whom he had a particular interest. Not all of al-ʿAqqād's poetry lived up to the expectations generated by his critical pronouncements, however, and in general it is probably not unfair to suggest that the significance of the Dīwān Group derives more from their critical pronouncements than from their actual poetry. These pronouncements were at times focused on a rejection of the immediate past on an arguably excessively personal level – not least, al-ʿAqqād's attacks on the verse of the neo-classicist Aḥmad Shawqī for its lack of poetic unity. Significantly, however, the group was notable for having derived many of their ideas of Western literature from English rather than French poets and critics: all three were familiar with Palgrave's *The Golden Treasury*, and it was the English poets of the eighteenth and nineteenth centuries, together with the poets of the ʿAbbasid era, that provided their main inspiration.

The approach of the Egyptian 'Dīwān Group' to questions such as poetic unity and their emphasis on the primacy of the poet's experience were echoed elsewhere in the Arab world, for example in the work of the Lebanese poet Bishāra ʿAbd Allāh al-Khūrī (1890–1968), usually known by his pen-name of al-Akhṭal al-Ṣaghīr, a name adopted early in his career as an emblem of his Arab nationalism.[15] As already noted in the previous chapter, most of Bishāra al-Khūrī's poetry was published rather late in his career (his first volume, *al-Hawā wa-al-shabāb*, appeared in 1952) and his poetry therefore appears sometimes anachronistic in the context of later developments, but his influence on later poets of the Romantic school has been acknowledged by many critics, and his poetry – which includes a number of poems using the *muwashshaḥ* form of Islamic Spain – arguably deserves to be better known.

If the 'Dīwān Group' had laid the foundations for a radical shift away from the assumptions and style of the neo-classicists, it was left to another Group, the Apollo Group, to carry forward their ideas and to establish Romanticism as the dominant poetic trend in the inter-war period. Like the 'Dīwān Group', the Apollo Group was based in Egypt, but unlike the earlier group, which had consisted of no more than three people at best, the Apollo Group was 'inclusive' in its outlook, embracing not only a variety of poetic styles and approaches, but also a wide range of nationalities, including poets from as far afield as Tunisia, Sudan, Iraq and the Mahjar, as well as Egypt itself.

Like many of the literary associations of the Mahjar, the Apollo Group revolved around a periodical, itself called *Apollo*, and both the Society and the periodical were the creation of one man, Aḥmad Zakī Abū Shādī (1892–1955). The use of the name of the Greek god Apollo – associated not only with beauty and art but also with philosophy and other manifestations of higher civilisation – was emblematic of a group that not only deliberately sought links with the classical civilisations of the West, but also adopted a forcefully cosmopolitan approach to contemporary writing and art. Indeed, in this regard, the *Apollo* phenomenon may perhaps be regarded as a contribution to the contemporary debates raging among Egyptian intellectuals about the nature of Egyptian civilisation, a debate that pitched a 'pharaonic' trend, most forcefully articulated by Tawfīq al-Ḥakīm,[16] against the 'Mediterranean' viewpoint propounded by Ṭāhā Ḥusayn in *Mustaqbal al-thaqāfa fī Miṣr* (1938) and elsewhere.[17]

Be that as it may, Abū Shādī's contribution to the development of modern Arabic poetry, and to the Romantic movement in particular, is assured, both through his own prodigious poetic output and through the monthly *Apollo* magazine, which he founded, edited and supported financially. Born in Cairo, Abū Shadī had spent ten years in England between 1912 and 1922, studying medicine in London, where he specialised in bacteriology, at the same time (like 'Abd al-Raḥmān Shukrī before him) acquiring an extensive knowledge of English literature. On his return to Egypt, he combined his literary interests with a distinguished scientific career, which culminated in an appointment as Professor of Bacteriology at the University of Alexandria in 1942; in addition to his professional interests, he was also an enthusiastic amateur painter and bee-keeper.

Abū Shādī's own poetry is of uneven quality – unsurprisingly, perhaps, given that he produced some nineteen collections of verse, as well as half a dozen verse plays, or 'operettes', translations and literary criticism. Although best known for his nature poetry and love poetry, both of which exemplify the characteristic Romantic features summarised by Ostle above,[18] he seems to have had the ambition 'to translate into poetry the whole human experience',[19] but his talent, though considerable, was clearly unequal to this task – not least, it has been suggested,[20] because his education had been largely in English and he lacked a thorough grounding in the Arabic language and literary heritage. He was, however, an innovative poet, not only in terms of his themes (he was among the first to make use of classical Greek and Egyptian mythology in his poetry, in which by his own admission he was indebted to Khalīl Muṭrān), but also in formal terms, experimenting with various forms of blank verse and free verse – even though these experiments, in the event, largely came to nothing.

The *Apollo* magazine itself, the first such magazine in the Arab world to be devoted solely to poetry, was a comparatively short-lived publication, of which no more than twenty-five monthly issues appeared between 1932 and 1934. Although subsequently associated primarily with the Romantic movement, the magazine in fact embraced a number of poetic approaches, sometimes publishing highly traditional poetry side by side with radical experimental verse. The aim of the magazine, and of the group, was indeed not so much to promote one poetic outlook in particular as to provide a forum for any poet prepared to accept the need for revitalisation of contemporary Arabic poetry; and to provide them with both moral and material support. Its inclusive nature can be seen from the fact that the first president of the group was not one of the *avant-garde* poets coming into prominence at the time but the neo-classical poet Aḥmad Shawqī, a representative of the 'old school'; when he died in 1932, he was succeeded by Khalīl Muṭrān, a 'pre-Romantic' of an essentially conservative disposition.

For the two years of its publication, the *Apollo* magazine epitomised the aspirations of writers not only in Egypt but also in the wider Arab world, eager not only to cast off the traditional literary conventions but also to escape from the oppressive political climate of the day. In addition to original poetry, the magazine also published translations, mainly from English, but also from French, with Romantic poets such as Wordsworth and Keats occupying a prominent position. Its literary contents were complemented by reproductions of Western painting and sculpture, including scenes from Greek and Egyptian mythology that both reflected the cosmopolitan tastes of Abū Shādī and his associates, and mirrored the themes of the poetry contained in the magazine. Perhaps the most striking feature of the magazine, however, was its geographical reach, enabling the ideas of the Romantic school to be diffused widely throughout the Arab Middle East and providing an outlet for poets as far afield as Iraq, North Africa, Sudan, and the Mahjar, in addition to Egypt itself. As such, it has a justified claim to be regarded as the leading *avant-garde* Arabic literary periodical of the day.

Despite its intrinsic importance and high reputation – a reputation that continues in retrospect until this day – the *Apollo* magazine was a short-lived phenomenon, which lasted for no more than twenty-five issues. The reasons for its collapse were complex, but included not only a lack of financial support, but also political opposition from the Wafd party and others, not least on the part of ʿAbbās Maḥmūd al-ʿAqqād.[21] Abū Shādī's subsequent literary career was marked by disappointment: neither of the two literary periodicals that he edited, *al-Imām* and *al-Hudā*, achieved the same reputation as *Apollo*, and in 1946, following the death of his English wife, and apparently disillusioned by the lack of recognition accorded to him in his native Egypt, he emigrated to the United States, where he founded another literary society, the Minerva Society, and from where he published a final collection of poems, *Min al-samāʾ*, in 1952.

A particularly intriguing feature of Abū Shādī's own work is the number of poems inspired by paintings – an indication, as Robin Ostle has observed, of 'how universal the author intended the cultural mission of the Apollo Society to be'.[22] (Similar manifestations of this liberal vision of Arab culture can be seen, for example, in the sculpture of Maḥmūd Mukhtār and the painting of Muḥammad Nājī.) The poet's importance lies not so much in his own verse, which as already noted is somewhat difficult to evaluate, as in his role in bringing together a number of talents who were to form the heart of the romantic movement in Arabic not only in Egypt but also elsewhere. The list of those included many household names – not only romantic poets such as Ibrāhīm Nājī (1898–1953), ʿAlī Maḥmūd Ṭāhā (1902–49), the Tunisian Abū al-Qāsim al-Shābbī (1909–34), the Lebanese Ilyās Abū Shabaka (1903–47) and the Sudanese Muḥammad Aḥmad al-Maḥjūb (1910–76), but also Mahjar poets such as Īliyā Abū Māḍī, Shafīq al-Maʿlūf and Shukr Allāh al-Jurr, and a number of poets who had no claim at all to be regarded as 'Romantics' including Aḥmad Shawqī and Muṣṭafā Ṣādiq al-Rāfiʿī.

Clearly, any attempt to list the Egyptian poets (or indeed, those of any other Arab nationality) with a claim to be labelled as 'Romantics' would be unproductive. Not only did the quality of their work vary widely, but the term 'Romantic' itself is an imprecise and fluid one. Critics seem generally agreed, however, that in Egypt itself, despite a number of other obviously gifted poets such as Ṣāliḥ Jawdat and Muḥammad ʿAbd al-Muʿṭī al-Hamsharī (1908–38),[23] the achievements of Romanticism reached their high point with the work of two poets, ʿAlī Maḥmūd Ṭāhā (1901–49) and Ibrāhīm Nājī (1898–1953).

The names and careers of ʿAlī Maḥmūd Ṭāhā and Ibrāhīm Nājī are so intertwined that at times it seems difficult to separate them, though of their immense reputation, there can be no doubt. Indeed, the reputation of ʿAlī Maḥmūd Ṭāhā[24] probably surpassed that of any other contemporary poet not only in the period between the two world wars but also into the 1940s; this was due not only to his verse as such, but also to the fact that much of it had acquired a 'popular' feel through being set to music. Born in Mansoura, Ṭāhā graduated as an engineer, combining – like innumerable other Arab writers and poets – his literary activities with professional employment in a completely different field. He travelled widely in Europe, visiting Italy, Germany and Switzerland (visits that often found direct echoes in his poems), and quickly acquired the reputation of a rebellious bohemian – a reputation that was subsequently given added weight by his early death. His first collection, *al-Mallāḥ al-tā'ih* (1934), set the tone for much of his subsequent work, being characterised by a typically Romantic introspection and sense of alienation – characteristics that were somewhat redeemed by an attractive streak of rebellion and an undisguised sensuality. His first collection, *al-Mallāḥ al-tā'ih*, was followed by *Layālī al-mallāḥ al-tā'ih* (1940), *Zahr wa-khamr* (1943), and *al-Shawq al-ʿā'id* (1943). In addition to conventional poetry, he also composed a number of poetic dramas, including *Arwāḥ wa-Ashbāḥ* (1942), in which he derived his inspiration from Greek legend, and from the Old Testament, and *Ughniyat al-riyāḥ al-arbaʿ* (1943).

For his part, Ibrāhīm Nājī,[25] born in Cairo, had graduated from medical school, subsequently combining his literary activities with a career as a doctor. Like Abū Shādī himself, he was an admirer of the 'pre-Romantic' poet Khalīl Muṭrān, and he served as vice-president of Abū Shādī's Apollo Society. Nājī produced three collections of poetry: *Warā' al-ghamām* (1934), *Layālī al-Qāhira* (1944), and *al-Ṭā'ir al-jarīḥ* (posthumous, 1957); his work reveals an acquaintance with a wide range of European literature – English, French and German – but his major interest was clearly in French Romantic poetry, the influence of which is particularly apparent in his second collection, *Layālī al-Qāhira* – as well as in, for example, his translation of Baudelaire's *Fleurs du Mal*. Nājī's particular speciality and forte, however, was amatory poetry, in which he succeeded in marrying the tradition of classical Arabic love poetry and the spirit of the European romantics in a quite unique way; his love poems range in scope from short poems, after the style of the classical *qiṭ'a*, to considerably longer and more complex poetry. The editions of his works, like those of other Romantic poets, were often suggestively illustrated. Perhaps the most notable feature of his talent, however, was his ability to indulge in a creative dialogue with tradition – a characteristic that was not widely in evidence in the Arabic romantic poets, though it had been deliberately cultivated by the neo-classical poets before them. Nājī's poem 'al-'Awda', for example, which describes the return of the poet to a house formerly inhabited by his beloved, is a skilful reworking of the classical tradition of the poetic *nasīb*, effortlessly transported to modern Cairo.

The role of the Apollo Society and its periodical *Apollo*, in forging a tradition of Romanticism that transcended state boundaries can perhaps be best seen in the case of the Tunisian poet al-Shābbī, whose promise was cut short by an early death from a heart disease that is presaged in some of his poems. Al-Shābbī, the son of a *qāḍī*, came from a traditional family and received a conservative Islamic education at the Zaytouna Mosque in Tunis before enrolling at the Tunisian law school. Unlike most of his Egyptian counterparts, he knew no foreign languages, and his acquaintance with Western literary models was therefore entirely derived from his reading of Arabic translations of Western articles and literary criticism, and through his reading of other Arabic poets, including those of the Mahjar, who had themselves been influenced by Western Romantic models.

His poetry apart, al-Shābbī is perhaps most famous, or perhaps notorious, for an iconoclastic lecture that he delivered in 1929 at the Khaldūniyya Institute, in which he questioned the assumptions underlying the entire literary heritage of classical Arabic; the lecture was subsequently published under the title *al-Khayāl al-shi'rī 'inda al-'Arab*, and reviewed in the March 1933 issue of *Apollo* magazine itself. The main themes of his poetry are typically romantic ones – love, death, light and darkness – but he seemed to have an especial fondness for the image of the new dawn, which occupies a central position in his imagery; themes such as this are given added poignancy by his own illness, the first symptoms of which had become apparent in 1929, and by the awareness of his own impending death. An additional dimension is given to his poetry, however, by the fact that these themes are often transposed to the Tunisian people as a whole, at a time when the country remained under the firm, and sometimes oppressive, control of the French occupying power; as a result, al-Shābbī's romanticism quickly became inextricably associated with Tunisian nationalism, and indeed with Arab nationalism more generally, in a way which echoes that of some Romantic poets in nineteenth-century Europe; adopted as Tunisia's 'national poet', his nationalist poems quickly found echoes all around the Arab world, and he remains by far the best known North African poet of modern times.

In Sudan, equivalent voices are to be found in the likes of al-Tijānī Yūsuf

Bashīr and Muḥammad Aḥmad Maḥjūb (1910–76). Like many of the Egyptian poets just discussed, Maḥjūb had a career outside literature, qualifying in both law and engineering; he worked at various times as an engineer, judge and lawyer, and even served as Prime Minister of Sudan after independence in 1956. A member of the 'Fajr' group, he published several books of prose and poetry, which reveal a deep consciousness of hybrid cultural identity.

For his part, al-Tijānī[26] is often compared with the Tunisian al-Shābbī, for like al-Shābbī, he had had a conservative, religious education, knew no Western languages, and died tragically young, from consumption. Al-Tijānī was born into a religious family with Sufi connections (from which he derived his name), and studied at a *khalwa* and at the al-Ma'had al-'Ilmī in Omdurman; like Maḥjūb, however, he later started an association with the so-called Sudanese 'Fajr' school, which published a magazine of the same name from 1934. Suffused with the Sudanese mystical tradition, he may perhaps be viewed as a sort of 'Sufi Romantic'; his poetry incorporates a sense of mysticism as a refuge from the harsh world around us, but is nonetheless tinged with a sense of religious doubt, as well as a keen sense of beauty. Significantly, his collected poetry was entitled *Ishrāqa* ('Illumination').

In Syria, the most prominent representative of the Romantic movement was 'Umar Abū Rīsha (1910–).[27] Born in Aleppo, he studied chemistry in Beirut and Manchester, and though he did not complete his course, this period of study was undoubtedly responsible for the obvious influence of the English rather than the French romantics in his work – though in addition to poets such as Shelley, Keats and Byron, he was also an admirer of Baudelaire. After working for a time as a librarian in Aleppo, Abū Rīsha embarked on a career that combined politics and diplomacy with his literary interests, serving at various times as Syrian cultural attaché to the Arab League and as Syrian ambassador in Brazil and India. In addition to his four collections of poetry (*Shi'r*, 1936; *Min 'Umar Abū Rīsha: Shi'r*, 1947; *Mukhtārāt*, 1959; and *Dīwān 'Umar Abū Rīsha*, 1971), he also composed four verse dramas. Much of his poetry, which strikes one as rather conservative by the standards of his fellow Romantics, is preoccupied with the dualism of physical passion vs platonic love, but like the Tunisian al-Shābbī and others, he was also concerned with social and political issues, and poems such as 'Nisr' show a keen awareness of the sorry state into which the Syrian nation and Arab nationalism had been reduced, following a series of defeats and disappointments.

Abū Rīsha's Lebanese counterpart, Ilyās Abū Shabaka (1903–47) was actually born in New York of Christian Lebanese parents, but left the US at an early age. Largely self-taught, he developed an early passion for French literature, which is reflected in his translations from French of works by Molière, Voltaire and Lamartine among others, and in his critical studies of Lamartine, Baudelaire and Oscar Wilde. His early work *al-Qīthāra* (1926) shows the influence of classical Arab poets such as Abū Nuwās; it was followed by a number of collections (some of which contain narrative poems), including *al-Marīḍ al-ṣāmit* (1928); *Afāʿī al-Firdaws* (1938) and *Ghalwā'* (1945, though written earlier); of these, the last-mentioned was inspired by the poet's fiancée Olga and has been described by Ostle as 'undoubtedly one of the most accomplished narrative poems in modern Arabic'.[28] Obsessed with the need for honesty in sexual matters, much of Abū Shabaka's poetry revolves around themes of love, sexuality, guilt and sin, in the course of which he draws on biblical stories, including that of Sodom and Gomorrah, as a way of illustrating his themes. In his later collections, which include *al-Alḥān* (1941), *Ilā al-abad* (1944), *Nidā' al-qalb* (1944) and the posthumous *Min ṣaʿīd al-āliha* (1958), the poet's inner struggles seem to be abated somewhat, and the poet seems to have achieved some sort of harmony and found a *modus vivendi* with himself.

Symbolism in modern Arabic poetry

Another important representative of Romanticism in Lebanon, Ṣalāḥ Labakī (1916–55), originally born in Brazil but brought up in Lebanon, combined Romantic with symbolist influences in his five collections of poetry published between 1938 and 1961. As Jayyusi notes,[29] the rise of symbolism in modern Arabic poetry is a less easily explicable phenomenon than the rise of Romanticism (with which, in chronological terms, it roughly coincided) – for while the factors leading to the rise of Romanticism in the European tradition can be at least partly paralleled in Arabic literature, in the case of symbolism no such obvious parallels can be drawn. Be that as it may, the two movements are clearly connected, and symbolist elements – with their emphasis on musicality, suggestiveness and beauty for its own sake – are apparent in a number of poets discussed above who are almost without exception classified as 'Romantics', including the Mahjar writer Jubrān, the Tunisian al-Shābbī, and the Egyptian al-Hamsharī. The more explicit use of symbolist techniques[30] appears to be primarily a Lebanese phenomenon, however – the first mature symbolist poetry as such in Arabic being usually credited to Adīb Maẓhar (1898–1928). After reading the poetry of French writers such as Baudelaire and Pierre Saman, Maẓhar, a member of the well-known al-Maʿlūf family, began composing symbolist poems in Arabic in the 1920s; his poems – the first of which, *Nashīd al-sukūn*, is often counted the first symbolist poem in Arabic – clearly show an acquaintance with the work of Baudelaire, and are marked by an almost mystical obsession with death.

Maẓhar's promising poetic career was brought to an early end by his premature death, but the interest in symbolist techniques and attitudes was continued by a number of other poets, including Yūsuf Ghuṣūb (1893–1971), and Sa'īd 'Aql (1912–). Like that of Ṣalāḥ Labakī, the work of Ghuṣūb, intriguingly described by Jayyusi as a 'mild symbolist',[31] crosses the boundaries between Romanticism and symbolism; like the symbolist poets generally, Ghuṣūb's work is characterised by a strong desire on the part of the poet to detach himself from social and public themes, and indeed, he is credited by Jayyusi[32] with being 'the first poet to begin the tradition of art for art's sake, not only in Lebanon, but in Arabic poetry on the whole [*sic.*]'; this is a strong claim, which perhaps deserves further investigation.

Better known than either Ghuṣūb or Maẓhar is the work of Sa'īd 'Aql, whose reputation rests on his position as the leading Arabic symbolist poet of his day, if not indeed of the entire early symbolist movement in Arabic. As a Christian who had nonetheless studied the Qur'ān for its literary merits, if not its ideas, Sa'īd 'Aql was continuing a tradition that had roots among the nineteenth-century Lebanese Christian proponents of the *nahḍa*. His works, some of which are in dramatic form, show the influence of nineteenth-century French poets such as Mallarmé and Paul Valéry. 'Aql's most important work, *al-Majdaliyya* (1937), based on the story of Mary Magdalene's meeting with Christ, was written at an early stage of his career; but although his reputation survived the 1940s, the attitude of artistic detachment and emphasis on poetic beauty for its own sake that was inherent in the symbolist philosophy quickly began to sound out of place in the new literary and political atmosphere of the period following the Second World War, and none of his later poetry (which included, for example, the poems of *Rindalā*, 1950, or *Ajmalu minki? Lā*, 1960) had the impact of *al-Majdaliyya*. Despite the typically symbolist emphasis on love and beauty in much of his work, Sa'īd 'Aql was also on occasions a spokesman for Lebanese nationalism, for example in his verse play *Qadmūs* (1944). He also experimented with colloquial poetry in *Yārā* (1960), which used a modified form of the Roman script as a means of writing Arabic, but his orthographically awkward system is today nothing more than a curiosity. Other poets who arguably belonged to the same trend include the Egyptian Bishr Fāris (1907–63) and the Syrians Urkhān Muyassar (1911?–1965) and 'Alī al-Nāṣir, who in 1947 published a volume of prose poetry entitled *Siryāl*, described by Jayyusi as 'probably the most avant-garde poetic experiment in modern Arabic poetry before the movement of free verse at the end of the forties'.[33]

The interest in French symbolism on the part of these early Arabic symbolist poets such as Ghuṣūb, Maẓhar and Sa'īd 'Aql were to find echoes in the period after the Second World War, when major poets such as Yūsuf al-Khāl, Khalīl Ḥāwī and Adūnīs ('Alī Aḥmad Sa'īd) were to rediscover the French sources in a different structural context, following the introduction of free verse and the renewed interest in prose poetry. These poets' efforts belong to a later period, however, and will therefore be considered in the following chapter. In the meantime, it is tempting to suggest that, by comparison both with the mainstream and Mahjar Arab Romantics, and with the work of the later writers of free verse, the work of the early symbolists such as Sa'īd 'Aql has been under-researched and is ripe for reappraisal.

Late Romanticism and the move to Modernism

Despite the desire of many adherents of the Romantic movement to break away from the classical Arabic poetic traditions, much romantic poetry continued to adhere fairly closely to traditional structures of metre and rhyme. Even where stanzaic forms were employed in imitation of European models, these were usually marked by a regularity of structure that was essentially conservative – giving a sense of order and control. In language and imagery, however, a major change from the old habits of neo-classical thought can clearly be observed. In the hands of the most gifted poets, the new trend produced a number of works in which a new lyricism and simplicity of language is deployed to considerable effect. At the same time, in the hands of less gifted poets, the introspection associated with the new style led to a host of publications in which the poet's isolation, feelings of nostalgia, and concepts such as *al-majhūl* ('the unknown') produce a sense rather of literary escapism.

To what extent the phenomenon of Arab Romanticism was a direct imitation of western Romanticism and to what extent it arose as a direct result of the political and cultural changes occurring in the Middle East in the period following the First World War is a question much debated. What is not in doubt, however, is that Romanticism in a general sense perfectly mirrored the political realities of the age. The First World War had been quickly followed by the dissolution of the Ottoman Empire, but in most parts of the Arab world, Western colonialism had continued to hold sway, and Arab nationalist sentiments had as yet been unable to find real expression. The search for new means of expressing an Arab identity provided a natural stimulus for authors to seek new means of expression, and the literature of European Romanticism – itself a product of the tension between the individual and the society around him – provided a natural focus for writers anxious to cast off the literary conventions that the neo-classicists had largely maintained.

The personal agony of the inter-war Arabic Romantics, with their desire to seek a 'realm behind the clouds', thus echoed the apparent impotence of the region's political leaders. The experience of the Second World War, however, and the various dramatic changes in the Arab world that accompanied the loss of Palestine in 1948 and the end of the Egyptian monarchy in 1952, appear to have quickly led to signs of impatience with the sort of escape into unreality that the Romantic movement seemed to be promising. Lūwis 'Awaḍ pointed out, for example, that the English poet Shelley was not only a Romantic but also a political reformer.

As we shall see in the following chapter, the new mood of political 'engagement', often involving a shift in focus towards something that might be termed 'social realism', was accompanied by radical structural changes in verse expression and by a new mood of experimentation with various types of 'free verse' and prose poetry, expressing in poetic form the need for new structures in Arab society and culture. Despite the radical nature of the changes that were sweeping the Arabic poetic scene, however, the fall of romanticism was a gradual process rather than a 'clean break'. Instead, the influence of the Romantic movement continued to be visible in the early works of poets who were later to be hailed as pioneers of the new free verse movement; these included, for example, the Iraqis Badr Shākir al-Sayyāb, 'Abd al-Wahhāb al-Bayātī, Nāzik al-Malā'ika and the Palestinian Fadwā Ṭūqān, the sister of the neo-classical poet Ibrāhīm Ṭūqān mentioned above.[34] For this reason, some critics, including Mustafa Badawi, identified a separate class of 'late Romantics',[35] including not only Nāzik al-Malā'ika and Fadwā Ṭūqān, but also such names as the Egyptian Kamāl Nash'at (1923–), the Palestinian poet and critic Salmā al-Khaḍrā' Jayyūsī and, most interestingly, the Syrian Nizār Qabbānī (1923–98).

Of these, it is the last-mentioned, Nizār Qabbānī, almost certainly the most popular of contemporary Arabic poets, who provides perhaps both the best example of the phenomenon of late Romanticism, and the most instructive guide to its eclipse. Born in Damascus in comfortable circumstances, Qabbānī graduated in law and for some twenty years worked as a diplomat in the Syrian foreign service, before resigning in 1966 to devote himself to literature and journalism; based in Beirut, he subsequently established his own publishing house to publish his own works. Already, from his first collection of poems, *Qālat lī al-samrā'* (1944), Qabbānī had begun to establish a reputation as a love poet, employing a straightforward but vivid language to describe the beauty of the female in a way that struck an immediate chord with readers across the Arab world. Later collections of verse, including *Anti Lī* (1950), *Qaṣā'id* (1956), *Ḥabībatī* (1961) and *al-Rasm bi-kalimāt* (1966) show a progressive refinement of this initially somewhat 'adolescent' vision towards a more mature view of love and the relationship between the sexes – a relationship that in his later poems appears indeed as a relationship of equals. Behind this evolving vision, however, lurked a social and political consciousness that occasionally found expression in poems such as 'Khubz, ḥashīsh wa-qamar' (1955), in which he attacked the daydreaming of contemporary Arab society; following the 1967 Arab defeat in the Six-Day War with Israel, however, he embarked on a radical change of direction, publishing a series of poems, of which 'Hawāmish 'alā daftar al-naksa' is the best known, angrily attacking the corruption and hypocrisy of the ruling

Arab elites – a political commitment that subsequently found further material in the Lebanese civil war of 1975–90 and in the Palestinian *intifāḍa* against the Israeli occupation.

It is difficult to think of any clearer indication than Qabbānī's 'conversion' to 'committed literature' of the fundamental shift in literary and cultural attitudes brought about by the enormity of the 1967 defeat – a shift which, as we shall see in subsequent chapters, found expression not only in poetry, but also (and perhaps, even more obviously) in prose fiction. By this time, however, the metrical and structural conventions of modern Arabic poetry had themselves undergone radical change with the spread throughout the Arab world of 'free verse' – a phenomenon to which we shall turn in the following chapter.

Notes

1 The form *al-rūmansiyya* is also sometimes used in this sense.
2 *EAL*, volume 2, p. 828, s.v. 'poetry, modern'.
3 See Fawzī 'Abd al-Razzāq, 'Bāqāt min al-maṭbū'āt al-'arabiyya al-ṣadira fī al-Amrīkatayn', *'Ālam al-kutub* 4 (4) (1991), pp. 546–76.
4 Ibid.
5 Other terms used for this technique include *shi'r ḥurr, muṭlaq* and *ṭalīq*. See also below, pp. 79–81.
6 1st edn, New York, 1923. Disentangling Jubrān's works written in English and subsequently translated into Arabic from those written in Arabic and translated into English is not always easy. For a list, see S. Bushrui and J. Jenkins, *Kahlil Jibran: Man and Poet*, Oxford, 1998.
7 See, for example, the dustjacket ibid.
8 *Jubrān Khalīl Jubrān*, Beirut, 1932; English version, *Kahlil Gibran*, New York, 1950.
9 Beirut, 1959–60.
10 *shi 'r mahmūs* ('whispered poetry').
11 For whom, see David Semah, *Four Egyptian Literary Critics*, Leiden, 1974.
12 His complete *Diwan* in four volumes was published in Cairo, 1948–9.
13 See above, p. 60.
14 For which, see below, pp. 103–5.
15 Al-Akhṭal himself was an Umayyad poet (c. 640–c. 710), famous for his *naqā'iḍ* ('flytings').
16 For example in the novel *'Awdat al-rūḥ* and play *Ahl al-kahf*, both published in 1933. See below, pp. 115–16 and 180.
17 For a discussion, see Pierre Cachia, *Taha Husayn*, London, 1956.
18 See above, p. 60.
19 Jayyusi, *Trends and Movements*, p. 381.
20 Ibid.
21 For whom, see David Semah, *Four Egyptian Literary Critics*, Leiden, 1974, pp. 3–65; J. Brugman, *An Introduction to the History of Modern Egyptian Literature in Egypt*, Leiden, 1984, pp. 121–38, etc.
22 See Robin Ostle, 'Modern Egyptian Renaissance Man', *Bulletin of the School of*

Oriental and African Studies, 57 (1994), pp. 184ff.

23 For whom, see Jayyusi, *Trends and Movements*, pp. 388–94.

24 For a longer discussion, see Badawi, A *Critical Introduction*, pp. 137–45.

25 For a longer discussion, see Badawi, A *Critical Introduction*, pp. 129–37.

26 For whom, see Jayyusi, *Trends and Movements*, pp. 452–74.

27 See Badawi, A *Critical Introduction*, pp. 172–8.

28 *EAL*, s.v. 'Abū Shabaka, Ilyās'.

29 Jayyusi, *Trends and Movements*, p. 475.

30 Symbolism, which also found expression in painting and in the theatre, in Europe reached its high point in the 1890s; it is characterised by a desire to liberate poetry from convention through devices such as the complex use of often highly personalised metaphor, and synaesthesia (the expression of one sense impression in terms of another).

31 Jayyusi, *Trends and Movements*, p. 481.

32 Ibid., p. 486.

33 Ibid., p. 514.

34 See above, p. 57.

35 Badawi, M. M., *An Anthology of Modern Arabic Verse*, Beirut, 1969, pp. xxxiv–xxxv.

5

Poetry: the Modernists

Continuing the account of the previous chapter, this chapter will discuss the main thematic, technical and stylistic developments in Arabic poetry after the Second World War; as with most previous developments in modern Arabic poetry, these changes have to be seen against the background not only of developments in contemporary Western poetry, but also of social and political developments in the Middle East itself.

As has already been noted in the last chapter, although many Romantic poets remained essentially conservative in their attitudes to poetic structures, the movement had witnessed a degree of experimentation in regard to poetic forms, in particular in relation to the use of various forms of stanzaic structures, usually modelled on Western originals. A number of poets had also experimented with different forms sometimes (perhaps misleadingly) called 'free verse',[1] and with different types of 'prose poetry'. Despite this, even when departing from the norms of classical Arabic monorhyme and monometer, most Romantic poetry is marked by an essential regularity of structure; even a poem such as Mīkhā'īl Nu'ayma's 'Akhī', for example, in which lines of different length are used, is characterised by a very tightly drawn structure, in which the stanzas conform to a regular pattern.

Despite the experiments of some earlier pioneers, then, it was not until after the Second World War that these patterns of poetic structure were broken, with the introduction of 'free verse' (*shi'r ḥurr*) in the true sense of the term, and with the widespread adoption of prose poetry as a means of poetic expression. Although the two phenomena are essentially separate, it is difficult to discuss them in isolation, since many of the leading innovative poets of the post-war period used both techniques; in this chapter, I will first discuss the phenomenon of 'free verse', before moving on to a discussion of the 'prose poem'.

Free verse

The essential characteristic of 'free verse' in Arabic is that, while preserving the basic patterns of the metrical 'foot', as codified by al-Khalīl ibn Aḥmad (c.

718–91),[2] it allows the poet to vary the number of feet in the line, thus freeing him (or, less usually, her) from one of the main constraints of the traditional verse pattern; at the same time, the constraints on rhyming patterns, which the Romantic poets had already begun to demolish, were removed altogether, allowing poems to be composed with varying rhyme patterns, or indeed with no rhyme at all.

Not for the first time in the history of modern Arabic literature, a period of rapid literary development is popularly associated with radical political and social change. The period following the Second World War saw rapid changes in the Middle East, some positive, or even 'progressive' (most notably the Free Officers' Revolution and the emergence of the Nasserist regime in Egypt in 1952–4), others, from an Arab viewpoint, essentially negative – most notably, the loss of Palestine and the establishment of the state of Israel following the Arab–Jewish War of 1948.

If it was Egypt and the Mahjar, however, that had provided the focal points for many of the developments associated with the Romantic movement, it was Iraq that was to assume this role in the immediate aftermath of the Second World War. The credit for the radical developments of the free verse movement, which at first provoked controversy but which quickly swept through most parts of the Arab world, is almost universally given to two Iraqis, Badr Shākir al-Sayyāb (1926–64) and the poetess Nāzik al-Malā'ika (1923–), who within a few months of each other in 1947 had published verse in the new style and who, despite the dozens of imitators who quickly followed the new formula, continued to hold a leading position and retain their reputation as pioneering practitioners of the modernist trend.[3]

It is important to stress that, as in the case of Romanticism, the new verse forms did not emerge from a vacuum, nor can they be viewed in isolation from the new attitudes which many of them embody. The new movement is associated with the spread of a number of attitudes, some mainly literary, others rather political or social, which interacted in sometimes complex ways and which had their roots in the inter-war period.

On the literary level, the main new influence was an increasingly widespread knowledge among the Arab intelligentsia of modernist Western poets, mainly but not exclusively English and French, among whom the name of T. S. Eliot occupies a prominent position, not least for his *The Wasteland*, originally published in the aftermath of the First World War in 1922, which established him as a spokesman for a disillusioned generation. For all the differences in the political and social circumstances of the Arab world and the contemporary West, this work of T. S. Eliot appears to have struck an immediate and powerful chord with many Arab *literati*. Indeed, the first references to Eliot's work can be found in two articles by the Sudanese Mu'āwiya Nūr as long ago as the early 1930s.[4] The credit for introducing Eliot to the wider Arabic-reading population, however, almost certainly belongs to the Egyptian critic Luwīs ʿAwaḍ (1915–90), whose articles, translations and creative writing over a period of more than fifty years established him not only as one of the most influential figures in Egyptian cultural life, but also (because of his Marxist leanings) as one of the most controversial. Creative writer as well as critic, ʿAwaḍ's volume of verse entitled *Plutoland wa-qaṣā'id ukhrā* (1947) is remarkable not only for the inclusion of a number of poems in colloquial Arabic but also for the undeniable allusions to Eliot's style, which combines a preoccupation with tradition with a liberating spirit of modernism – a combination which seems to have perfectly suited the mood of Arab intellectuals in the period following the Second World War.

Like those of al-ʿAqqād and al-Māzinī, or of Shawqī and Ḥāfiẓ Ibrāhīm, the careers of the two Iraqi pioneers of the 'free verse' movement, al-Sayyāb and Nāzik al-Malā'ika, are a study in similarities and contrasts. Born in the village of Jaykūr, in southern Iraq, Badr Shākir al-Sayyāb was educated in Basra before entering the Teachers' Training College in Baghdad, from which he graduated in 1948. He worked as a teacher, journalist and civil servant, but suffered persecution for his Marxist and nationalist leanings, leading to periods of self-exile in Iran and Kuwait, where he died in 1964. His home village of Jaykūr remains a central anchor point in many of his poems. In addition to political persecution, the latter years of his life were marked by ill health caused by a degenerative disease of the nervous system, giving his poetry (like that of the Romantic poet al-Shābbī before him) a certain quality of urgency that it might otherwise not have had.

As already noted, some experimentation with a somewhat different kind of free verse based on mixed metres had earlier been attempted by the Egyptian Romantic poet Abū Shādī and further developed by Muḥammad Farīd Abū Ḥadīd[5] and the Mahjar poet Īliyā Abū Māḍī;[6] but these experiments proved something of a blind alley, and it was not until after the Second World War, with the widespread adoption of 'free verse' proper, that the technique began to acquire momentum, effectively displacing the traditional Arabic rules of metre and rhyme as the norm among leading poets. The new style of 'free verse' was based on metres using only one pattern of foot, with irregular rhyme schemes (or none at all) and irregular line lengths that use as many feet per line as the thought requires. Both types of free verse are to be distinguished from 'blank verse' (*shiʿr mursal*), employing regular metres but no rhyme, which had also been the subject of experiments by Abū Shādī and others, and used by the dramatist ʿAlī Aḥmad Bākathīr for a translation of Shakespeare's *Romeo and Juliet*; this technique, however, like that of the 'Egyptian school' of free verse, also proved to be something of a dead end and, despite its occasional use by poets such as Yūsuf al-Khāl, it has today effectively died out.[7]

For her part, Nāzik al-Malā'ika, the daughter of a wealthy Baghdad family with literary connections, also attended the Teachers' Training College in Baghdad, graduating in 1944. She subsequently completed an MA in comparative literature in the United States, before returning to Iraq, where she lectured at the Teachers' Training College; from 1970 until her retirement in 1982 she taught at the University of Kuwait.

Although rightly revered as pioneers of modernism, the early poetry of both al-Sayyāb and Nāzik al-Malā'ika in fact shares many of the characteristics of Romanticism as exemplified in the Arab poets of the inter-war years. Al-Sayyāb's early collections *Azhār Dhābila* (1947) and *Asāṭīr* (1950), for example, show the influence of English and French poets such as Wordsworth and Baudelaire, as well as Egyptian Romantic poets such as ʿAlī Maḥmūd Ṭāhā and others. Love and nature occupy a prominent position in his poetry of this period, as also in al-Malā'ika's earliest collection of poems *ʿĀshiqat al-Layl* (1947). Al-Malā'ika's admiration for the English Romantic poets is demonstrated in her poem entitled 'Ilā al-shāʿir Keats', her early poetry being characterised by a profound pessimism and fear of death – characteristics which are indeed features of much of her later poetry also.

It was not so much for their sentiments, however, that the early poems of al-Sayyāb and al-Malā'ika were remarkable as for their revolutionary attitude to technical innovation and the need to regenerate the Arabic poetic tradition. The new verse form was employed for the first time by al-Sayyāb in one poem in *Azhār Dhābila*, but more particularly in *Asāṭīr*; while for her part, Nāzik al-Malā'ika included nine poems in free verse in her second collection *Shaẓāyā wa-Ramād* (1949), prefacing the work with an introduction in which she argued that the traditional Arabic monorhyme had impeded the development of Arabic poetry by comparison with other world literatures.

Although both al-Sayyāb and Nāzik al-Malā'ika have some claim to be accounted among the leading Arab poets of the second half of the twentieth century, it was undoubtedly al-Sayyāb who had the greater influence of the two. Indeed, compared with that of al-Sayyāb, Nāzik al-Malā'ika's later poetry strikes the reader as rather conservative, for the revolutionary attitudes expressed in the preface to *Shaẓāyā wa-Ramād* seem never to have been developed in any radical way, and much of her poetry is best regarded as an expression of a 'late romanticism', marked by the same deeply pessimistic attitude to life that had marked her early poems. This attitude is most dramatically illustrated, perhaps, by both the contents and the title of her longest poem *Ma'sāt al-Ḥayāt*, a long poem of more than a thousand lines in rhyming couplets originally written in 1945 and 1946, and completed when the poetess was only twenty three years old.[8]

By comparison with Nāzik al-Malā'ika, al-Sayyāb's influence was considerably more far-reaching. Most importantly, it was largely through al-Sayyāb that the 'strangely powerful influence of T. S. Eliot'[9] that had already began to make its presence felt through the writings of Luwīs ʿAwaḍ seems to have acquired its status among contemporary Arab writers and poets. In particular, the Tammuz or Adonis resurrection myth, expounded by Sir James Frazer in *The Golden Bough*,[10] and which underlies much of Eliot's *The Waste Land*,[11] makes its first appearance in Arabic through al-Sayyāb's work, which embodies the themes of faith, sacrifice, death and resurrection. The Tammuz myth quickly struck a chord with other leading contemporary Arab poets, and the theme became central to much Arabic poetry of the 1950s and 1960s, through its adoption by the so-called 'Tammuzi poets' – a loosely constituted group comprising five leading poets (Yūsuf al-Khāl, Khalīl Ḥāwī, Jabrā Ibrāhīm Jabrā, Adūnīs, and al-Sayyāb himself), who exercised a leading role in modern Arabic poetry from the 1950s until al-Sayyāb's death in 1964. Many of the central ideas of this trend can be seen in al-Sayyāb's most important collection *Unshūdat al-maṭar* (1960): the title poem of this collection, originally written in 1956, also exemplifies al-Sayyāb's fondness for the imagery of water – a constant preoccupation in the arid Middle East, but whose life-giving properties may also, of course, be tinged with menace – while another poem from almost the same date, *al-Masīḥ baʿd al-Ṣalb* (1957) is a vivid illustration of the inclusive attitude of this group of poets towards the stories and myths of other religions – the most successful attempt, in my view, by a Muslim writer anywhere to 'empathise' with one of the central tenets of the Christian faith. In al-Sayyāb's poetry, as in that of other members of this school, the use of such religious imagery is not a mere intellectual exercise, however, but is closely bound up with a vision of the contemporary Arab world and its potentiality for rebirth – a vision which led al-Sayyāb from an early belief in Marxism through Arab nationalism to a broader humanism, tinged towards the end of his life with a despair born of his own physical suffering.

As already mentioned, the early free verse experiments of al-Sayyāb and Nāzik al-Malā'ika quickly found imitators in almost every part of the Arab world, not least in Iraq itself. The technique was eagerly espoused by yet another graduate of the Baghdad Teachers' Training College, ʿAbd al-Wahhāb al-Bayātī (1926–99), whose name is often linked with that of al-Sayyāb; more importantly, perhaps, al-Bayātī has come to be regarded by many critics as the most prominent spokesmen for the 'social realist' movement in modern Arab poetry. Born in Baghdad, al-Bayātī worked for a time as a teacher and journalist, but was imprisoned for his political views and spent much of his life in exile in Cairo and Beirut, as well as in Eastern Europe and the Soviet Union. During a short period of rehabilitation, he briefly served as Cultural Attaché in the Iraqi Embassy in Moscow and lectured in the University there.

Like al-Sayyāb, al-Bayātī started his career writing poems with a 'Romantic' flavour, as may be seen in his first published volume, *Malā'ika wa-Shayāṭīn* (1950). His 'social realist' orientation, however, quickly became evident with his second volume, *'Abārīq muhashshama* (1954), a protest against the oppression of the poor that both idealises and graphically describes the wretched life of the peasantry, while simultaneously portraying the city as a place of misery and corruption. Many of these themes were subsequently taken up and developed by other poets of similar outlook, not only in Iraq but also elsewhere in the Arab world. Other themes prominent in his work include, unsurprisingly, the misery of exile, his home city of Baghdad, friendship and love. Above all, however, it is his commitment to the ordinary people that most shines through his work. While he remained a committed Marxist, al-Bayātī's later published volumes also show a preoccupation with Christian imagery – Christ the saviour being seen as a liberator of the oppressed and a bringer of social justice. In this, as in much else, he was no doubt influenced by his wide reading in European literature: he translated work by Paul Eluard and Louis Aragon, and formed a friendship with the Turkish poet Nazım Hikmet, to whom he addressed a letter calling the Iraqi Qāsim regime to account.

Among other prominent Iraqi poets of this generation writing in a similar style and with a similar outlook, mention should also be made of Būland al-Ḥaydarī (1929–96), born into a Kurdish family, whose artistic career began with a group calling itself the 'Lost Time Group', and whose communist sympathies again led to his spending a substantial proportion of his life outside his native country: from 1963 to 1976 he lived in Beirut, where he edited the journal *al-'Ulūm*, and he later spent a period in London.

It was not only Iraqis, however, who were inspired to follow the lead of al-Sayyāb and al-Nāzik al-Malā'ika. Outside Iraq also, the ideas of the free verse movement quickly gained popularity. In Egypt, the early social realism of Ṣalāḥ 'Abd al-Ṣabūr (1931–81), widely regarded as the most significant Egyptian poet of the post-Second World War period, echoed that of the Iraqi al-Bayātī with its realistic portrayals of village life. Educated at Cairo University, 'Abd al-Ṣabūr was influenced by Luwīs 'Awaḍ, who had done much to introduce T. S. Eliot and other Western poets to the Arab world. Like many writers and poets in the Arab world, he also worked as a journalist, serving for a time as assistant literary editor of *al-Ahrām*. In addition to his poetry, he produced a large amount of literary criticism, some translations, and a partly autobiographical work *Ḥayātī fī al-shi'r* (1969) in which he expounded his personal approach to poetry. Despite the considerable impact made by his first volume of collected poems, *al-Nās fī Bilādī* (1957), however – the title poem of which had originally been published in 1954 – 'Abd al-Ṣabūr's subsequent creative work in practice seems to have moved away from the 'social commitment' of his earlier work towards a more personal vision, at times verging on mysticism, and tinged with a sense of disillusion; these trends are evident not only in his poetry, but also in his verse drama, *Ma'sāt al-Ḥallāj* (1965),[12] which revolves around the suffering of the tenth-century Islamic mystic crucified in AD 922.

Other prominent Egyptian and Sudanese poets writing in 'free verse' who may be classed as 'social realists' include the Egyptian Aḥmad 'Abd al-Mu'ṭī Ḥijāzī (1935–), the half-Sudanese Muḥammad Miftāḥ al-Faytūrī (1930–), and the Sudanese Tāj al-Sirr Ḥasan (1930–) and Jīlī 'Abd al-Raḥmān (1931–). The verse of all these poets reflects their own varied upbringings and experiences, which nonetheless drew them all to Cairo, usually in search of work or education. The verse of Aḥmad 'Abd al-Mu'ṭī Ḥijāzī, beginning with *Madīna bilā Qalb* (1959), represents another variation on a theme already prefigured by al-Bayātī and 'Abd al-Ṣabūr – the alienation of the villager drawn to the big city in search of a livelihood – and as such reflects his own origins in a small village in Lower Egypt; similar themes pervade the poetry of Jīlī 'Abd al-Raḥmān, forced to emigrate from Sudan to the slums of Cairo with his father in search of a livelihood. The most distinctive of these poets is, however, perhaps Muḥammad Miftāḥ al-Faytūrī, born in Alexandria to a Sudanese father and an Egyptian mother, who first moved to Cairo, but who later became a Libyan citizen and worked as a Libyan official. He achieved instant recognition with his first volume of verse entitled *Aghānī Ifrīqiyā* (1955), which he followed with further volumes entitled *Aḥzān Ifrīqiyā* and *'Āshiq min Ifrīqiyā*: much of al-Faytūrī's early work in particular is permeated by themes of colour and racism (not, as such, a dominant theme of modern Arabic poetry in general),[13] and his verse raises questions about the relationship of the 'Arab' to the 'African' that are curiously (and perhaps not entirely coincidentally) reminiscent of some of the political leader Mu'ammar al-Qadhdhāfī's musings on the subject.

For all that Egyptian writers had arguably dominated most areas of literary activity in the first half of the twentieth century, their contribution to the development of modern Arabic poetry in the years following the Second World War was undoubtedly surpassed by the achievements of poets from the Levant, a number of whose names have already been mentioned in the context of the so-called 'Tammūzī' group of poets. Three poets in particular deserve attention in some detail: the Syrians Adūnīs (the pen name of 'Alī Aḥmad Sa'īd, 1930–) and Yūsuf al-Khāl (1917–87), and the Lebanese Khalīl Ḥāwī (1919–82).

The first-named of these three poets, 'Alī Aḥmad Sa'īd, is widely acknowledged not only as one of the most important Arab poets of the twentieth century but also as one of the most influential figures in modern Arabic literature generally. Born in Qassabin, Syria, he acquired a deep knowledge of classical Arabic literature and thought from his father at an early age, then read philosophy at the University of Damascus, from where he graduated in 1954. He subsequently studied at the Université St Joseph in Beirut and was later awarded a scholarship to study in Paris for a year in 1960–1. His early career in Syria was marked by political involvement, including a six-month term of imprisonment in 1955 for membership of the Syrian National Socialist Party; his views at this stage were heavily influenced by those of Anṭūn Saʿāda,[14] and these left a distinctive mark on his early poetry. He adopted the pen-name 'Adūnīs' (with its obvious overtones of death and resurrection)[15] early in his career. From 1956 to 1985, Adūnīs lived and taught mainly in Beirut, taking Lebanese citizenship, but with short periods as Professor in Damascus and Paris; since 1985, he has lived mainly in Paris.

The importance of Adūnīs derives not only from his own poetry, but also from his extensive theoretical and critical writing and from his role as founder and editor of two literary periodicals that provided an outlet for many writers both of his own and of a younger generation: *Shiʿr*, which he co-founded with Yūsuf al-Khāl in Beirut in 1957, and which played an analogous role for the modernist movement to that played by *Apollo* magazine in the 1930s for the Romantic movement; and *Mawāqif*, which ran from 1968 to 1994. In addition to his original and critical writing, he has also translated a number of writers into Arabic, most notably the poetry of St John Perse.

Adūnīs's early verse, including *Qālat al-Arḍ* (1945), *Qaṣā'id ūlā* (1957) and *Awrāq fī al-Rīḥ* (1958) shows the influence not only of the politician Saʿāda but also of Arabic writers and poets such as Jubrān and Ilyās Abū Shabaka. There is general agreement among the critics, however, that it was with his volume of poetry *Mihyār al-Dimashqī* (1961) that Adūnīs first established himself as an entirely distinctive voice in modern Arabic poetry; indeed, in the view of some critics, the lyricism and coherence of this collection, in which the author adopts the *persona* of the medieval poet Mihyār to articulate his personal vision of the world, has never been surpassed. Subsequent works have been marked by a continuing spirit of adventure and experimentation that have earned him a continuing place in the vanguard of contemporary Arabic literature and ensured that his work will continue to be read by the younger generation of poets, but the results have not made for easy reading: works such as *al-Mufrad bi-ṣīghat al-jamʿ* (1975) and *al-Kitāb* (1995), are more immediately notable for their complexity than for any other literary quality; the pages of *al-Kitāb*, for example – the name of which deliberately evokes that of the Qur'ān – are divided into four sections, each representing a different voice and a different aspect of Islamic history. This sort of extreme complexity has indeed prompted one literary critic to wonder whether Adūnīs's work does not in fact represent 'a dead end, which if universally followed could spell the end of Arabic poetry'.[16] By contrast with the complexity and apparent prolixity of works such as *al-Mufrad bi-ṣīghat al-jamʿ* and *al-Kitāb*, Adūnīs's name has also been associated with a revival of interest in the small-scale poem, or *qitʿa*;[17] his poem 'A stranger arrived. / The minaret wept. / He bought it and topped it with a chimney'[18] may perhaps be regarded as one of the most succinct comments ever made on the state of contemporary Arab society.

Be that as it may, Adūnīs's poetry cannot sensibly be considered in isolation from that of his contemporaries such as al-Sayyāb and al-Bayātī, with whom indeed it shares many common features – not least, its openness to the symbols and personae of other religious and mystical traditions. Much of Adūnīs's work, in addition to its revolutionary political content, is suffused with a spirit of mysticism, partly derived from the writings of the Sufi poets, which is fused with symbolist elements akin to those of some twentieth-century French poets. The Islamic heritage is mingled with other traditions so that Mihyār, for example, is identified with figures from the Bible and Greek mythology such as Noah and Ulysses.

Throughout his poetic development, Adūnīs has remained faithful to two fundamental projects: to recreate Arab society and to transform the Arabic language – these two projects being so intertwined in his eyes that it is impossible to separate the one from the other. The starting point for his views on both is essentially the same: a sense that both the society in which he lives and the language in which he writes have stagnated. As such, Adūnīs's name has become almost inseparably linked with the concept of *ḥadātha* ('modernity') in modern Arabic poetry, a concept that he has not only vividly expressed in his own verse but has also elaborated at length in his own critical writings. Like those of many other Arab writers, of both prose and verse, his views on 'modernity' were profoundly shaken by the Arab defeat in the 1967 Arab–Israeli War; unlike some, however, the defeat does not appear to have dented the constant sense of enquiry and adventure that he brings to everything he writes.

An Introduction to Arab Poetics, a series of four lectures originally delivered at the Collège de France in 1984, and admirably translated into English by Catherine Cobham,[19] provides a convenient summary of his views on some of the main topics with which he has been concerned in the course of 'over a quarter of a century's research into Arabic poetry and Arab culture', including 'Poetics and orality in the *Jāhiliyya*', 'Poetics and the influence of the Qur'ān', 'Poetics and thought' and 'Poetics and modernity' – the last mentioned being of particular interest in the present context. Any overall assessment of Adūnīs's work is undoubtedly premature, however, complicated by the fact that he has tended constantly to revise his own works between editions, and by the sense one has, reading his work, that at the age of seventy five, he still has the capacity to shock and surprise us.

Many of the attitudes and trends discernible in the poetry of Adūnīs may also be seen in the verse of Khalīl Hāwī and Yūsuf al-Khāl, each of whose work has its own distinctive flavour, while at the same time illustrating the extent to which the modernist movement in Arabic poetry has transcended religious and sectarian boundaries. Yūsuf al-Khāl, whose role as founder of *Shi'r* magazine has already been mentioned, was born in Syria but brought up in Tripoli, north

Lebanon, where his father was an Evangelical minister. He graduated from the American University of Beirut with a degree in literature and philosophy, then worked abroad in New York, in the United Nations' Office of Press and Information, and in Libya, before returning to Lebanon in 1955. In 1957 he founded *Shi'r* magazine, which ran from 1957 to 1964 and again from 1967 to 1969, during which period it served as the main rallying point for modernist poets in Arabic and as a forum for the discussion of modernist ideas on poetry and literature generally. In 1961 he established another periodical, *Adab*, which closed in 1963. In addition to his own poetry, Yūsuf al-Khāl also worked on a new version of the Arabic Bible (though he died before completing it) and translated a large number of works into Arabic, including verse by T. S. Eliot, Walt Whitman and Ezra Pound, the influence of whom on his own poetry is evident from the collection entitled *al-Bi'r al-mahjūra* (1958), which opens with a poem bearing Pound's name. Yūsuf al-Khāl was also heavily involved during his lifetime both in publishing and with a modern art gallery, Gallery One, in Beirut.

Like Adūnīs, Yūsuf al-Khāl had been an early follower and admirer of the Syrian nationalist Anṭūn Sa'āda, though his membership of the Syrian National Socialist Party did not last beyond his youth. Although Sa'āda's philosophy left some impression on al-Khāl's poetry, however, a more lasting influence was undoubtedly his strongly Christian religious background, linked to his family upbringing. His first volume of verse, *al-Ḥurriyya*, was published as early as 1944, and shows the influence of the Lebanese symbolist poet Sa'īd 'Aql (1912–), but it was his two collections entitled *al-Bi'r al-mahjūra* (1958) and *Qaṣā'id fī al-Arba'īn* (1960) that contain his most significant experimental, 'modernist' verse. Compared with that of many of his contemporaries, his verse has a more metaphysical, contemplative quality, rich in the imagery of the Bible (unsurprisingly, in view of his background) as well as that of other spiritual traditions. Distinctively, however, and unlike the other poets of the so-called 'Tammuzi' tradition, al-Khāl's Christian imagery is not merely a literary conceit, or an attempt to relate the Christian story to the contemporary Arab world, but springs from a deep and genuine Christian belief that at times indeed identifies the poet with Jesus and the poet's suffering with the suffering of Christ. In this respect, his outlook had much in common with that of the Mahjar writer Jubrān Khalīl Jubrān[20] and it is, perhaps, not surprising that he should emerge as the translator of Jubrān's *The Prophet* (originally written in English) into Arabic. In addition to his poetry and his many translations, al-Khāl also produced a verse drama, *Hīrūdiyā* (New York, 1954), a further three plays (*Thalāth masraḥiyyāt*, 1959) and some elegant writing in prose, of which the late *Rasā'il ilā Don Kishūt*, with their mystical tone, are perhaps the most distinctive.

The poetry and outlook of the Lebanese Khalīl Ḥāwī (1925–82) has much in common with that of Yūsuf al-Khāl. Born in al-Shuwayr, Ḥāwī was, like

Adūnīs and Yūsuf al-Khāl, influenced as a young man by the teachings of Anṭūn Sa'āda, but later abandoned his doctrines; he studied at the American University of Beirut, then in Cambridge, England, where he presented a thesis on Jubrān Khalīl Jubrān; he subsequently published his study of Jubrān under the title *Khalil Gibran: his background, character, and works* (1963). For much of his working life, he taught at the American University of Beirut and at the Lebanese University.

Khalīl Ḥāwī's first poetic productions were in colloquial Lebanese, but he soon turned to Modern Standard Arabic, and published a number of collections, including *Nahr al-ramād* (1957), which made an immediate impact on its publication; *al-Nāy wa al-Rīḥ* (1961); *Bayādir al-jū'* (1965) and *al-Ra'd al-jarīḥ* (1979). Symbol and myth are central to his poetic expression, which appears to have seesawed between pessimism and hope according to his personal circumstances and the political vagaries of the world around him. *Nahr wa-ramād*, his first mature collection, conveys a powerful sense of disillusion, to some extent dissipated in the more optimistic *al-Nāy wa al-Rīḥ*; like other writers of his generation, however, Ḥāwī was powerfully affected by political setbacks in the Arab world, and the collapse of the short-lived union between Egypt and Syria in 1961 had a powerful effect on him; his ultimate gesture of protest against the course of contemporary Middle Eastern politics was to shoot himself in his Beirut flat on 6 June 1982, two days after the Israelis had invaded Lebanon.

Prose poetry

Although the development and progressive adoption of 'free verse' in the period following the Second World War has usually been regarded as the essential characteristic of 'modernism' in contemporary Arabic poetry, this movement has also been characterised by the extensive use of various forms of 'prose poetry' – a form of expression which retains some at least of the characteristics of poetry, but in which there is no discernible or formal metrical scheme. This definition is arguably, of course, satisfied by many works of medieval or classical Arabic prose; partly for reasons associated with the need to maintain the doctrine of the *i'jāz*[21] of the Qur'ān, however, traditional Muslim critics have almost always drawn a clear distinction between poetry and prose. Discussion of the phenomenon of 'prose poetry' in a modern context, which clearly lags behind the study of 'free verse' itself, has not been helped either by the varied and confusing terminology[22] that has been used to describe it, nor by the fact that some conservative critics have denied that it can be classified as poetry at all.

Be that as it may, 'prose poetry' in a general sense may be regarded as tracing its origins to the almost entirely Christian Arab reformers of nineteenth-century Lebanon, inspired, as already noted in a previous chapter, by Arabic translations of the Bible and by Christian liturgical texts rather than by Western literature. During the early part of the twentieth century, the principal exponents of this type of expression – which essentially relies on a rhythm of thought as a substitute for formal metrical or rhyme schemes – were the Mahjar writers Jubrān Khalīl Jubrān and Amīn al-Rīḥānī; but their experiments, which were influenced by Western models such as Walt Whitman and the French Romantic poets, do not appear to have led directly to any significant further developments.

Despite the efforts of pioneers such as Jubrān and Rīḥānī, it was not until after the Second World War that the prose poem became invested with a new urgency in the work of such poets as the Palestinian Tawfīq Ṣāyigh (1924–71) and the Lebanese Unsī al-Ḥājj (1937–). Born in Khirba (southern Syria), Tawfīq Ṣāyigh[23] studied English at Harvard University and subsequently taught in both England and the United States; between 1962 and 1967, he edited the Beirut cultural review *al-Ḥiwār*. His own output, unsurprisingly influenced by English and American rather than by French models, is all in the form of prose poetry, and includes *Thalāthūn Qaṣīda* (1954), *al-Qaṣīda K* (1960) and *Mu'allaqāt Tawfīq Ṣāyigh* (1963); his enthusiasm for English- rather than French-language Western models is reinforced by the translations that he produced from the work of American poets, including a version of T. S. Eliot's *Four Quartets*. For his part, Unsī al-Ḥājj, who was closely associated with the *Shi'r* magazine founded by Adūnīs and Yūsuf al-Khāl, was influenced by French models such as Saint-Jean Perse and Rimbaud rather than the English-language writers drawn on by Tawfīq Ṣāyigh; he translated a number of French poems into Arabic, including verse by Breton and Artaud; his own collections include the seminal *Lan* (1960), *al-Ra's al-maqṭū'* (1963) and *Māḍī al-ayyām al-ātiya* (1965).

Despite the formal similarities, the mood and tone of Arabic prose poetry in the hands of poets such as Tawfīq Ṣāyigh and Unsī al-Ḥājj has little in common with the earlier efforts of Jubrān and his colleagues, and indeed, the new phenomenon was quickly marked by a change of terminology from *shi'r manthūr* to *qaṣīdat al-nathr*, a term used for the first time, according to Jayyusi, in 1960.[24] Be that as it may, the potential of the new medium as a means of revolt against the conventional Arabic literary tradition had already been identified by al-Ḥājj in the preface to his collection *Lan* (1960), and it was enthusiastically taken up by poets such as Yūsuf al-Khāl, Shawqī Abī Shaqra (1935–) and by Adūnīs himself, who with al-Ḥājj acknowledged his indebtedness to Suzanne Bernard's book *Le Poème en prose de Baudelaire jusqu'à nos jours* (Paris, 1959). By the early 1960s, it is probably fair to say that prose poetry in Arabic had been widely accepted as a legitimate form of poetic expression – though such acceptance has by no means been universal, and the prose poem has in any event not succeeded (and shows no signs of succeeding) in displacing poetry based on the single metrical foot, or even of more traditional forms of Arabic verse.

The 1967 defeat: a change of mood

The excitement and sense of discovery that had characterised much *avant-garde* Arabic poetry since the 1950s – finding expression in particular in the work of poets such as the Syrian Adūnīs, the Lebanese Yūsuf al-Khāl and Khalīl Ḥāwī, and the Egyptian Ṣalāḥ 'Abd al-Ṣabūr – was abruptly shattered by the catastrophic Arab military defeat in the 1967 war with Israel. As we shall see later, this catastrophe (almost invariably termed *naksa* in Arabic) is reflected not only in poetry, but also – perhaps even more obviously – in prose fiction. In poetry, its effects manifested themselves in a variety of ways, some of which may appear at first sight contradictory. First, as already noted in the last chapter, the defeat spelled a further blow to the 'Romantic' attitudes that had been the hallmark of much poetry in Arabic during the inter-war years, and indeed, into the 1940s and 1950s: this reaction found perhaps its best known and most public expression in the work of the Syrian 'late romantic' poet Nizār Qabbānī, whose subsequent poetry becomes marked with a new political 'edge'. At the same time, in what may appear to be a contradictory trend, the mood of excited 'commitment' (*iltizām*) that had marked much of the experimental poetry of the 1950s and early 1960s was replaced by a mood of self-doubt and of questionings about the nature of 'modernity' (*ḥadātha*), and its relationship to contemporary Arab society; although much of this debate took place among the so-called 'Tammuzi' poets discussed above, it was significantly also joined by a wider range of poets, including, significantly, a number of poets from Palestine itself. Thirdly, and most directly, in a development that coincides with the growth of Palestinian political and military resistance, we find the emergence of a new group of Palestinian poets who begin to be regarded, in what is almost a throwback to the function of the pre-Islamic 'tribal' poet, as spokesmen for their people – 'commitment', as it were, turned on its head under the pressure of contemporary events.

The output of this group of poets, generally known as 'resistance poetry' (*shi'r al-muqāwama*), forms a readily identifiable and arguably self-contained corpus of literature that has been much translated into other languages and is accordingly among the best known examples of modern Arabic writing to Western readers. The use of poetry as a means of propagating the Palestinian cause was not, of course, a totally new phenomenon: as already noted, a number of Palestinian poets, most prominently Ibrāhīm Ṭūqān, had been using poetry as an expression of support for the Palestinian cause since the 1920s and 1930s, and some at least of the new generation of so-called 'resistance poets' had published poetry well before the 1967 defeat; the events of that year, however, gave them for the first time a wider than purely local stage and a popularity that, as Badawi caustically observes, 'is not always related to their poetic merit'.[25]

The leading members of this group of 'resistance poets' include Maḥmūd Darwīsh (1941–), Samīḥ al-Qāsim (1939–), Ḥannā Abū Ḥannā (1928–), Mu'īn

Basīsū (1927–84) and Tawfīq Zayyād (1932–94). Of these, Maḥmūd Darwīsh is almost certainly the best known outside Palestine itself. Born in the village of al-Barwa, which was razed by the Israelis after 1948, he effectively lived for much of his life as an exile in his own country – an experience that is directly and vividly reflected in his several volumes of collected poems, beginning with *Awrāq al-Zaytūn* (1964) and *ʿĀshiq min Filasṭīn* (1966). Politically active in the Israeli Communist Party, Darwīsh for some time edited the Party's Arabic newspaper *al-Ittiḥād*, before leaving Israel in 1971 to live in Beirut, and later in Jordan, Paris and Tunisia. Darwīsh's poetry is distinguished by an appealing immediacy, which is often linked to the use of symbols. Although at times this symbolism seems rather too obvious, as in the link between the lover's yearning for a beloved and the poet's yearning for his homeland, he is also capable of exploiting old images, such as 'sand' and 'wind', to produce novel effects in a new context to considerable effect. A distinctive feature of his poetry, shared by many other Palestinian writers, is his willingness to draw on a wide range of sources for his symbols and motifs, including not only local Palestinian folklore but also Arab and Islamic history more generally, as well as mythological and religious material from other cultural traditions; although this characteristic is also, of course, a feature of much other modernist Arabic poetry, not least of that of Adūnīs and his associates, its use in the context of the Palestinian struggle appears, partly at least, deliberately designed as an attempt to universalise the significance of the struggle. Be that as it may, the clarity of Darwīsh's message, coupled with his obvious intellectual and political courage and his ability to link the Palestinian cause both conceptually and symbolically with liberation movements in other parts of the world, have led to his poetry being adopted at times almost as an emblem of the Palestinian struggle, and several of his poems have been set to music. In addition to his nationalistic poetry, he is rightly renowned for his powerful prose work *Dhākira li-l-nisyān*, a personal account of a day in the Lebanese Civil War, written under the heat of fire in war-torn Beirut.[26]

Many of Darwīsh's techniques and attitudes, which include a generally Marxist orientation, are shared by other prominent 'resistance poets', even though their individual personal circumstances may differ significantly from each other. Samīḥ al-Qāsim, for example, a close associate of Darwīsh, was born into a Palestinian Druze family in Zarqa, Jordan, but has remained resident in Israel for almost all his life, even at one stage being drafted into the Israeli army; for a time, he taught in an Israeli school, but was dismissed for his political activities, and has several times been imprisoned or suffered house arrest. Like Darwīsh, Samīḥ al-Qāsim began publishing poetry before the 1967 War (his first volume, *Aghānī al-Durūb*, appeared in 1964), but came to the notice of a wider public only later; he has since proved to be one of the most prolific of the 'resistance poets', with over half a dozen volumes of collected poetry to his name. In addition to his poems, Samīḥ al-Qāsim has also been greatly interested in the possibility of creating a Palestinian theatre,[27] and his interest in dialogue, and at times indeed in the use of local dialect, is apparent in a number of his poems. For his part, Muʿīn Basīsū, who was also interested in the possibilities offered by the drama for advancing the Palestinian cause, worked for much of his life for the Palestine Liberation Organisation in Beirut; while Tawfīq Zayyād, who was born in Nazareth and educated partly in Moscow, served as mayor of his hometown for several years; among Zayyād's other contributions to Arab intellectual life are translations of the Turkish writer Nazım Hikmet and a number of works of Russian literature.

Modernist poetry: later trends

Although the main trends, developments and themes of modernist poetry in Arabic for the first two decades or so following the spread of 'free verse' are fairly clear, the researcher attempting to find a clear pattern of trends over the last thirty years may well be tempted to give up in despair. This is not simply due to the inevitable fact that trends and patterns in literature, as in most other spheres of intellectual activity, become easier to see with the passage of time; it is also due to the fact that, unlike in the field of prose fiction, for example, few new obviously outstanding talents appear yet to have emerged to rival those of the modernist pioneers – a number of whom, like Adūnīs himself, are of course still alive and productive. A further factor, as Jayyusi points out,[28] is the uncomfortable fact that, for part at least of the period in question, Arabic poetry appeared to be in a state of 'chaos'; this was caused, at least in part, she suggests, by the tension between contemporary political developments, on the one hand, and, on the other, by the obsession with a linguistic 'modernity' that often expressed itself in progressively more incomprehensible productions. The poetry of this period, to quote Jayyusi again, 'aspired towards great complexity which, had it been artistically apt and mature, could anyway have been apprehended only by an elitist group of readers. As it was, much of it was apprehended by no one.'[29]

Given the inherent vigour of the Arabic poetic heritage and the wealth of poetic talent evident in most parts of the Arab world, it is hardly surprising that Arabic poetry quickly 'bounced back', albeit with a somewhat changed perspective and emphasis that appeared to be better suited to the climate of the times. The early modernists had peddled a vision of the world, or at least of the Middle East, in which the poet, relieved of the outcast role bequeathed to him by Romanticism, not infrequently himself aspired to play the part of leader and saviour. With the waning of what one critic has described as the 'ideological' phase of modern Arabic poetry, however,[30] the new mood was more low-key. Instead of self-glorification, optimism and high political ideals, the new poetry spoke of simplicity, of the mundane, of the everyday, often even of the poet as a victim – a mood that was reflected in a move away from the complex metaphorical language of Adūnīs and his associates towards a new simplicity of language.

The poets who best epitomised this new mood were not necessarily young or 'new': in some cases, they had been writing for several decades. Their voices, however, which had for a time been eclipsed by those of Adūnīs and his colleagues, now began to acquire a new authority and resonance. In Egypt, the poetry of Ṣalāḥ ʿAbd al-Ṣabūr, much of whose work exudes a sense of pessimism and creative doubt, seemed again to mirror the spirit of the times. In Syria, Muḥammad al-Māghūṭ (1934–), who despite his long association with Adūnīs and the *Shiʿr* group, had for a long time seemed a lone voice, began to make his influence felt anew, through a revival of interest in his poetry that powerfully reflects the anguish and yearning for justice of the deprived. Another influential model for the younger generation was the poetry of the Iraqi Saʿdī Yūsuf (1934–), whose poetry, some of which employs colloquial dialogue, directly reflects the repressive political situation of Iraq during much of the latter part of the twentieth century, but at the same time has acquired a universal significance; his several *dīwāns*, beginning with 51 *Qaṣīda* (1959), were collected and republished in a single volume in 1979. Saʿdī Yūsuf's poems, their lines charged with the vocabulary of prison and repression, constantly speak of the tragic side of life – but it is a tragedy that is seen through the poet's everyday experience, directly related to the life around him, rather than through the heroic visions and technical pirouettes of the poets of the preceding generation.

It is too early to predict how exactly these new trends will work themselves out in the twenty-first century. In formal terms, contemporary Arabic poetry remains split between free verse and prose poetry, but different commentators appear to have taken very different views of the prospects for its development. Taking an optimistic view, the translator and poet James Kirkup,[31] for example, writes in his preface to a recent anthology of Arabic poetry in translation, that 'the Arabic language remains the passionate pulse of poetic Arabic expression', and that:

> Arab poetry is not something apart from the general public. It is not the toy of a select and diminishing group of academics and professional writers that it appears to be in non-Arab lands. It belongs to everyone, for poetic idiom and imagery are the life-blood of the rich intricacies of music and meaning of the Arabic language, providing the reader and listener with a unique aesthetic pleasure that transcends class and country. These statements remain true of even the most 'modernist' poetry in Arabic.

James Kirkup's view would appear to be supported by the poems included in the anthology itself, representing the work of a wide variety of poets from all parts of the Arab world, including some writing in French or English rather than in Arabic. In his introduction to a recent volume of avant-garde Egyptian poetry in translation, however, another commentator, Mohamed Enani, appears to take a somewhat more guarded view.[32] Referring to the diversity of linguistic registers and poetic structures currently in use, he refers to a 'crisis' in modern Arabic poetry and notes that:

> The crisis persists. Apart from Arabic professors [...] few people write today in the classical variety of Arabic, and their audience is definitely limited [...] In the vernacular, the poem may stand a better chance of getting read, or heard. Poems in MSA are better received, especially if belonging to the kind I have described elsewhere as the 'New Poetry', but the future of this 'kind' is dim, and the poets are not encouraged by any promises of glory – much less of fame and fortune.

Mohamed Enani's comments are of particular interest in the context of the anthology compiled by Mohamed Metwalli, which represents the work of young Egyptian 'rebel' poets writing largely in 'alternative' or 'underground' literary magazines such as *al-Garād and al-Kitāba al-ukhrā*; although Metwalli's collection is confined to Egyptian writers, the style can certainly be paralleled in other parts of the Arab world and can indeed also be observed by anyone browsing on the web. Structurally, Enani notes the increasing prevalence of prose poetry in the work of these younger poets who, 'intent on liberating their minds from the tradition of Arabic [...] attempt a style reflecting the mode of thought which appears to fit a "thoughtless" world. But they cannot escape another tradition, namely that of the New World Order, which seems to be foisted on a whole generation.'[33]

It is too early to tell whether Enani's confidence that some at least of these poets 'hold the promise of a real revival of poetry in Egypt and the Arab world' is justified. What does seem certain is that, in their constant striving for a form of cultural and poetic expression that responds to the realities of contemporary life, the new generation of poets are doing no more, and no less, than following in the footsteps of earlier generations of modern Arabic poets who effected radical changes in the direction of the Arabic poetic tradition. As such, they represent an exciting phenomenon, and one that is certain to attract considerable attention in the years to come.

Notes

1 See further below.
2 See Chapter 1 above, p. 11.
3 See Badawi, *A Critical Introduction*, p. 225.
4 Ibid., p. 224.
5 Also known as a historical novelist. See below, p. 100.
6 Called by Moreh the 'Egyptian school', as opposed to the later 'Iraqi school'. See *EAL*, pp. 236–7, s.v. 'free verse'.

7 For further details, see *EAL*, p. 154, s.v. 'blank verse'.
8 Nāzik al-Malā'ika's *Dīwān*, published in 1970, also contains revised versions of the poem entitled *Ughniya li-l-Insān 1* and 2. See Badawi, *A Critical Introduction*, pp. 28–9.
9 Badawi, *A Critical Introduction*, pp. 223–4.
10 Originally published in 1922, and many times reprinted.
11 First published 1922, in *The Criterion*.
12 Translated into English by Khalil I. Semaan as *Murder in Baghdad*. The English title, as Cachia points out (*Arabic Literature: An Overview*, p. 149), suggests a parallel with T. S. Eliot's *Murder in the Cathedral*.
13 Unless we count poetry related to the Arab–Israeli dispute – for which, see below, pp. 91–3.
14 For whom, see Tibi, B., *Arab Nationalism*, London, 1981.
15 Badawi, *An Anthology of Modern Arabic Verse*, p. xxxvii, rather curiously states that his adoption of this pen name was 'not on account of its implications'.
16 Badawi, *A Critical Introduction*, p. 240.
17 For which, in the classical sense, see above, Chapter 1, p. 11.
18 For this, see Mahmud Darwish, Samih al-Qasim, Adonis, *Victims of a Map*, London, 1984, p. 132.
19 Cobham, C. (tr.), *Adonis: An Introduction to Arab Poetics*, London, 1990.
20 For whom, see the preceding chapter, pp. 61–3.
21 A technical term of Islamic theology, usually translated as 'inimitability'.
22 On this, see Moreh, 'prose poem (*qaṣīdat al-nathr*)', *EAL*, p. 618; also, Jayyusi, *Trends and Movements*, pp. 626ff. For the prose poem generally, see also Moreh, *Modern Arabic Poetry 1839–1970*, pp. 289–311.
23 For whom, see Jayyusi, *Trends and Movements*, pp. 635–40.
24 Ibid., p. 631.
25 Badawi, *A Critical Introduction*, p. 222.
26 Translated into English by I. Muhari as *Memory for Forgetfulness*, Berkeley, 1995. For other English translations of Darwīsh's works, see Altoma, S. J., *Modern Arabic Literature in Translation*, London, 2005 and 'Darwish, Mahmud' in O. Classe (ed.), *An Encyclopedia of Literary Translation into English*, London, 2000, pp. 344–5 .
27 For this, see below, Chapter 10.
28 S. K. Jayyusi, 'Modernist Poetry in Arabic', in *Modern Arabic Literature*, ed. by M. M. Badawi, pp. 173ff.
29 Ibid., p. 174.
30 Kamal Abu-Deeb, 'al-Māghūṭ, Muḥammad', *EAL*, p. 488.
31 Preface to *A Crack in the Wall: New Arab Poetry*, ed. Margaret Obank and Samuel Shimon, London, 2001, p. 9.
32 *Angry Voices: An Anthology of the Off-beat New Egyptian Poets*, tr. M. Enani, compiled by M. Metwalli, Fayetteville, 2003, Introduction, p. xv.
33 Ibid., p. xxvii.

6

Prose literature: early developments

We have already noted in Chapter 2 above the important role played by the rise of the press and growth of a wider reading public during the second half of the nineteenth century in laying the foundations for the development of modern Arabic prose literature. The period covered by the present chapter, roughly 1880–1933, represents a crucial one in the emergence of modern Arabic narrative in the form of the novel and short story as usually understood in the West. Perhaps more than any other chapter, it will be dominated by developments in Egypt – though, as with the early development of the modern Arab theatre, Syrian émigrés also played a crucial, contributory role.

The *Maqāma* Form

As noted in Chapter 2, the short essay and article had, partly for economic reasons, begun to emerge as the dominant prose forms in Egypt and much of the rest of the Arab world during the second half of the nineteenth century. Despite, or perhaps because of, the British occupation of Egypt in 1882, translations into Arabic from European languages at this stage continued to be dominated by French novels and short stories; these were often heavily adapted, and were frequently no more than worthless tales of romantic love. At the same time, however, and despite the influx of new forms of expression from the West, traditional narrative structures were still being used to considerable effect by some writers, albeit in decreasing numbers. Muḥammad al-Muwayliḥī's *Ḥadīth 'Īsā ibn Hishām*, published in serial form between 1898 and 1902 and in book form in 1907, is usually held to be the last major literary work to use the *maqāma* form,[1] though the changing times are already apparent in his use of the form as a vehicle for contemporary social criticism: the book relates the story of a pasha from Muḥammad 'Alī's time who is resurrected to find himself in a new, Europeanised Cairo; by this means, the author is enabled to compare present-day Egypt with that of the past, and to comment on the influence of Europe on Egyptian society. Some idea of the topics covered may be gleaned from the titles of the various chapters, which include, for example, 'The Police', 'The Parquet', 'The

Shari'a Court Lawyer', 'Medicine and Doctors', 'Religious Scholars', and so on.[2] Towards the end of the series of episodes, a group of three characters, an 'Umda,[3] Playboy and Merchant make an appearance, reappearing for several episodes, during which they visit a Restaurant, a Tavern, a Dance Hall, a Theatre, and even the Giza Pyramids – of whose history the Merchant gives a rather curious account. Later editions of the work included a sort of appendix, entitled *al-Riḥla al-thāniya* ('the second journey'), in which the author describes the visit that he made to the Great Paris Exhibition of 1900, following a visit to England in the same year to cover the Khedive's state visit.

In general terms, this account clearly stands in a direct line of descent from al-Ṭahṭāwī's work *Takhlīṣ al-ibrīz ilā talkhīṣ Bārīz*;[4] more specifically, it appears to reflect an end-of-the-century fascination with Exhibitions and other events of this nature, for, as Timothy Mitchell notes in his book *Colonising Egypt*, 'of the eight works published in Cairo during the last years of the nineteenth century describing the countries and ideas of Europe, five were accounts of a trip to an Orientalist congress or a world exhibition'.[5] Much of al-Muwayliḥī's account of the Paris visit, indeed, is devoted to the Exhibition (for which a French Orientalist serves as a guide), in particular to the Egyptian exhibit, where the author describes the shame of seeing first a group of belly dancers, followed by a tableau depicting a traditional school, with a schoolmaster drumming Qur'anic verses into the pupils while beating them with palm leaves, as visitors to the Exhibition jeer at the state of education in Egypt.[6]

Although, in some respects, *Ḥadīth 'Īsā ibn Hishām* clearly stands at the end of an era, in other ways it marks the beginning of a new period in the development of Arabic prose literature: indeed, it has sometimes been identified as the 'beginning of the Egyptian novel'.[7] Indeed, although the relationship between the culture of Islam and that of the West had been a concern of Egyptian writers since al-Ṭahṭāwī's, or even al-Jabartī's time,[8] al-Muwayliḥī's treatment of the theme was by far the most imaginative to date. The deliberate neo-classicism of the work is apparent from the name of al-Muwayliḥī's narrator, 'Īsā ibn Hishām, the same name used by Badī' al-Zamān al-Hamadhānī in his pioneering classical *maqāmāt*.[9] Stylistically, however, as in many other ways, the work is something of a mixture, for although the author uses *saj'* for the opening of each chapter of his work, he soon lapses into a simpler, more direct style of narrative, including – in many chapters – a copious use of dialogue. Significantly, however, he almost never resorts to the use of colloquialism, and as a work of stylistic excellence, the work belongs squarely in the classical tradition.

For all its fascination, the use of the *maqāma* form in an extended work of this sort at this date may be regarded as something of an oddity, for in the meantime attempts at genuine, original novel writing had already begun to be made. Mention has already been made above of al-Shidyāq's *al-Sāq 'alā al-Sāq*, described by Boutros al-Hallaq as 'the first real attempt at fiction in modern Arabic literature',[10] but this work, certainly ahead of its time, had no direct successor. More immediately relevant from the point of view of later developments were the writings of Fransīs Marrāsh (1836–73), Buṭrus al-Bustānī (1819–83) and in particular his son Salīm al-Bustānī (1846–84), whose translations and adaptations, mostly from French fiction, helped to lay the groundwork for the development of the short story and historical novel; the contribution of this family to the 'literary revival' in general terms has already been discussed above in Chapter 2.

The historical novel

As will be apparent from the discussion above, al-Muwayliḥī's *Ḥadīth 'Īsā ibn Hishām*, despite the endless fascination of its contents, was arguably an anachronism when viewed against the background of other contemporary developments. More significant for the future development of the Arabic novel than any other of the early attempts at fictional writing, however, was the series of some twenty-two historical novels produced by the Lebanese writer Jurjī [Jirjī] Zaydān (1861–1914). Originally intending to qualify as a doctor, Zaydān followed a path taken by many Syrian and Lebanese intellectuals in the second half of the nineteenth century by emigrating to Egypt, where he developed an interest in history and literature, founding in 1892 the journal *al-Hilāl* (still in existence), which played an important, indeed crucial, role in the dissemination of scientific, historical and cultural material for over a century.

As a non-Muslim Arab, writing extensively about Islamic history, both in fictional and non-fictional form, Zaydān's career is itself of considerable interest. His novels, however, (*riwāyāt ta'rīkhiyya*) are the work of an educator rather than a *litterateur*, and they strike the modern critic, both stylistically and thematically, as at times almost unbearably pedestrian.[11] Each is based on a period or incident in Islamic history, but the historical narrative is seldom convincingly integrated with the other elements in the works, which almost invariably also involve a hero and heroine in love. It is perhaps largely for this reason that, although they have continued to be popular with Arab readers and have been many times reprinted, they have received comparatively little critical attention from Western critics.[12] As a proponent of a new, more direct, prose style, however, Zaydān's importance cannot be underestimated, and he undoubtedly played a major part in opening new horizons, both literary and historical, to a rapidly expanding readership. Arguably, indeed, the novels are in need of reassessment, for they exemplify not a few of the innate tensions and contradictions that characterised contemporary intellectual activity and debate – in particular, the situation of literature, caught between 'education' and 'entertainment'.

The historical trend in novelistic activity initiated in Egypt by Zaydān was continued by a number of other writers in succeeding years and though none of them (thankfully, perhaps!) was as prolific as Zaydān, their work is not without interest, both from a literary and, often, a historical point of view. The increasing interest in prose writing of this sort can be demonstrated by the fact that even the neo-classical poet Aḥmad Shawqī made an excursion into the field, publishing a short novel (or 'novelette', as Matti Moosa terms it)[13] in 1897 entitled *'Adhrā' al-Hind aw Tamaddun al-Farā'ina*. This was followed by two further works in the same genre, each treating some episode of ancient history, from Egypt or elsewhere, but the results, which relied heavily on the supernatural or fantastic, were unconvincing, and they are best regarded as another isolated tour de force.

More significant from the point of view of the development of the historical novel as such were the efforts of Muḥammad Farīd Abū Ḥadīd (1893–1967), whose novel *Ibnat al-Mulūk* appeared in 1926. Set during the period of Muḥammad 'Alī's struggles with the Mamluks in 1804–7, the work successfully conveys a sense of political intrigue, which forms an effective backdrop to the events of the story. The author's narrative technique represents a significant advance on that of Zaydān, for although he preserves Zaydān's basic formula of a tale of romance in a historical setting, he is more successful in integrating the historical and romantic elements (though it may be doubted whether the heroine's expertise in artificial respiration is historically accurate!). Like many authors of the time and later, Abū Ḥadīd combined his literary interests with a career in public service, including a post in the Egyptian National Library, Dār al-Kutub; he went on to produce some half-dozen more historical novels of increasing maturity and realism, the most successful of them being probably *al-Wi'ā' al-marmarī* (1951), which revolves around the life of Sayf ibn Dhī Yazan, the popular Yemeni hero from the time of the Abyssian invasion in the early sixth century AD. The strand of development of the historical novel represented by Abū Ḥadīd's work was continued in Egypt by later authors including 'Alī Jārim (1881–1949), 'Alī Aḥmad Bākathīr (1910–69), 'Abd al-Ḥamīd Jūda al-Saḥḥār (1913–) and some early works of Najīb Maḥfūẓ (1911–), some of which will be discussed in the following chapter.[14]

Another author who made a significant contribution to the development of the historical novel was the Lebanese Ya'qūb Ṣarrūf (1852–1927), another member (like Zaydān himself) of the wave of educated Syrian Christians who emigrated to Egypt during the last decades of the nineteenth century. Best known as the co-founder of the journal *al-Muqtaṭaf*, which played an important role in disseminating modern scientific ideas in the Arab world, Ṣarrūf also published three novels, *Fatāt Miṣr* (1905), *Fatāt al-Fayyūm* (1908) and *Amīr Lubnān* (1907); the last of these, which depicts the massacre of the Christians by the Muslims and Druze in 1860, is of particular interest, revolving as it does around an episode in the history of mid-nineteenth-century Lebanon that itself contributed indirectly to the evolution of modern Arabic literature, through the ensuing exodus of intellectuals from the country.

This period also saw the emergence of a number of women novelists. A use of the novel form to reflect on social relationships may be seen in the works of the female Lebanese writer Labība Hāshim, whose novel *Qalb al-rajul* (1904) depicts a romance between a Lebanese Christian and a Druze woman. Another female novelist active around this time was the Lebanese Zaynab Fawwāz (c. 1850–1914), better known as a pioneering non-fiction writer on women's rights, who like so many of her educated compatriots spent much of her life in Egypt. Fawwāz published two novels, *Ḥusn al-ʿawākib aw Ghādat al-Zāhira* (1899) and *al-Malik Kurush awwal malik al-Fārs* (1905), the first and better known of which, set in Lebanon among the Druze community, revolves around the competition between two princes for the hand of their cousin; in addition to her fictional work, Fawwāz also compiled a biographical dictionary of women entitled *al-Durr al-manthūr fī ṭabaqāt rabbāt al-khudūr* (1894).

As will already have become apparent, a feature common to much novelistic writing of this period is the use of exotic or foreign settings and characters, particularly in stories revolving (as many did) around an often improbably romantic tale. One motivation for the use of such devices appears to have been the need to escape the criticism of more conservative elements of society, who looked with disfavour on the portrayal of potentially immoral behaviour in a contemporary context. This is not to say, however, that contemporary representation was entirely absent from novelistic activity during this period. An interesting example of the novelistic form used to portray a recent incident of political importance is provided by Maḥmūd Ṭāhir Ḥaqqī's[15] *ʿAdhrāʾ Dinshawāy* (1906, republished 1964), the plot of which revolves around the notorious incident of the same year, in which a British officer hunting pigeons in the village of Dinshawāy was killed during a skirmish with the villagers, a number of whom were subsequently hanged after a show trial. Although the author claimed in his introduction that the work was fictitious, it is in fact based closely on the actual characters involved, the realistic effect being further enhanced by the use of colloquial Arabic for the peasant dialogue. The overall significance of the work in the development of the modern Arabic novel appears to have aroused some controversy, however: as Matti Moosa points out,[16] Yaḥyā Ḥaqqī's statement that *ʿAdhrāʾ Dinshawāy* was 'the first Egyptian novel about the *fellahin*, their lives and problems depicted in their own colloquial language' was not strictly correct, as the work had to some extent been anticipated by Maḥmūd Khayrāt's *al-Fatā al-rīfī* (1902) and *al-Fatāh al-rīfiyya* (1905). What is, however, certain is that the work marked a significant stage on the progress of Egyptian narrative towards the first full-length novel to combine a local, contemporary setting with a plot developed on Western lines – Muḥammad Ḥusayn Haykal's *Zaynab*, written in Paris in 1910–11 and first published in 1913.

Haykal's *Zaynab*

Haykal's novel deserves our attention, because it has been almost universally recognised – and extensively discussed – not merely as an important milestone, but indeed as a focal turning point, in the development of the Egyptian and Arabic novel.[17] The author, a member of a wealthy landowning family, had been sent to France to study for a doctorate in law, and the work carries more than a hint of nostalgia for his native country; it is a particularly interesting comment on the status of literary activity at the time that the work originally appeared under a pseudonym – *Miṣrī fallāḥ* ('a village Egyptian') – as the author did not wish his novelistic activities to stand in the way of his projected legal career.[18] The essential plot of the work, which can be summarised in a few sentences, revolves around two main *personae*: a peasant-girl Zaynab, and the more educated Ḥāmid, a student in Cairo who returns to visit his family in the countryside during the vacations. In what would seem almost a parody of a romantic novel, were it not for the work's 'milestone' status, Zaynab falls in love with a fellow-peasant, Ibrāhīm, but is married off to Ḥasan when Ibrāhīm cannot afford the bride price; while for his part, Ḥāmid, who has enjoyed a brief flirtation with Zaynab, is for a second time frustrated in love with his cousin ʿAzīza, whom he had always expected to marry. In a classically romantic ending to the plot, obviously inspired by Western models, Zaynab dies of tuberculosis, asking to be buried with Ibrāhīm's handkerchief, while for his part Ḥāmid first escapes to the city, then disappears without trace, leaving behind a long letter explaining his actions to his parents and putting forward his views on society and its problems.

It is clear that in writing *Zaynab* the author was, to some extent at least, creating a self-portrait in the character of Ḥāmid. Indeed, this tendency of early novelists to invest their heroes, either explicitly or implicitly, with autobiographical qualities, is a feature that we shall notice in many authors of this and the next generation. Moreover, although it is beyond dispute that *Zaynab* represents a major advance in Arabic novelistic technique, it has to be said that its faults are equally obvious. Neither the characterisation nor the plot itself is impressive, the stories of Zaynab and Ḥāmid developing to a large extent in isolation from each other. Most obviously, however, the novel is marred by overlong descriptive passages – passages that seem to have been inserted almost without regard for their function within the narrative, and which to a large extent probably simply reflect the author's own feelings of nostalgia for Egypt during his stay in Paris. In this connection, the novel's subtitle, *manāẓir wa-akhlāq rīfiyya* ('country scenes and manners'), is undoubtedly of some significance.

Whatever our view on the overall artistic merit of *Zaynab*, however, there is no doubt that it not only marked a significant landmark in the development of the novel as an Arabic literary form but is also of considerable interest in its own right. The author's endorsement of the use of colloquial Arabic for peasant dialogue while retaining formal Arabic for the narrative sections of his work, though not original, provided a model that was widely imitated by succeeding writers. More generally, and despite its idealised, at times even sentimental, attempts at the portrayal of village life, Haykal's attempt to integrate an element of social criticism into a Western-style plot provided a model for future development – albeit a model ahead of its time, for with the exception of the writings of Jubrān Khalīl Jubrān, which belong to a rather different stream of development, it was several years before another novel of comparable interest or importance appeared, either in Egypt or elsewhere in the Arab world. Nor did Haykal himself make any attempt to repeat the formula he had employed in Zaynab; the author went on to enjoy a distinguished career in public service, serving twice as Minister of Education, and producing a number of works on the Islamic heritage, beginning with *Ḥayāt Muḥammad* (1935), but his only subsequent novel, *Hākadhā khuliqat* (1955), attracted little attention and is of no significance for an account of the modern Arabic novel.

Although romances and other works of popular fiction continued to be translated and composed in Egypt during the 1920s, few original works of great interest or significance appeared during this period. The next Egyptian writer to produce a work of major significance in the development of what for the moment we may call the 'non-historical' novel was Ibrāhīm 'Abd al-Qādir al-Māzinī (1890–1949),[19] who in 1931 published *Ibrāhīm al-kātib*. The autobiographical basis for this work is again immediately suggested by its title, though vigorously denied by the author at the time; the work had in fact been started by al-Māzinī in the mid-1920s, then lost and reconstructed. The increasing attention being given to novel writing at this time is evidenced by the institution of a novel-writing competition, which was won by al-Māzinī's work; interest in the novel form had probably in turn been boosted by the republication of Haykal's *Zaynab* in 1929. In the meantime, autobiographical writing had been stimulated by the appearance in 1926–7[20] of the first volume of the blind author Ṭāhā Ḥusayn's (1889–1973) *al-Ayyām*, an account of his early childhood in an Upper Egyptian village that was itself heavily fictionalised. The work offered the reader, and other novelists, not only a psychological insight into Egyptian country life but also a prose style which, if slightly idiosyncratic, was of exemplary clarity; the first work of modern Arabic literature to become widely known outside the Middle East, it has since been translated into several languages. The impact of the work can only have been increased by the fact that the author was, at almost exactly the same time, engaged in a major controversy over a work of literary criticism, *Fī al-shi'r al-jāhilī*, in which he questioned the authenticity of much pre-Islamic poetry (a view no longer widely accepted). In the field of imaginative literature, the author himself went on to produce a number of novels, beginning with *Adīb* (1935), another work in which the autobiographical element is prominent, and including also *Du'ā' al-Karawān* (1942?) and *Shajarat al-bu's* (1944) – though his importance, recognised by the accolade 'Dean of Arabic Literature', lies rather in his contribution to the intellectual and educational development of twentieth-century Egypt than in his fictional works *per se*.

At all events, Ibrāhīm al-Māzinī's *Ibrāhīm al-kātib* represents an important development not only in novel-writing as such, but also in the evolution of a theme that was to resurface in much writing through the next decade (not least, in the novels of Tawfīq al-Ḥakīm) – the plight of the contemporary Egyptian, or Arab, intellectual, caught between tradition and modernity, or, to put it in a slightly different way, between East and West. In the case of *Ibrāhīm al-kātib*, the dilemma is played out through the narrator's relations with three women – a Syrian nurse, Marie, who nurses him through an illness; his cousin Shūshū; and the more westernised Laylā, with whom he has a passionate affair but who leaves him after she discovers that she is pregnant. Like the earlier *Zaynab*, the novel suffers both from structural faults and from inconsistent characterisation, as well as an excessively egotistic outlook – to the extent that it has been described by one critic as a novel of self-praise (*fakhr*).[21] It clearly represents an advance on its predecessors in terms of its vivid and amusing portraits, however, particularly of the minor characters, who provide welcome relief from the writer's generally egotistic and self-centred outlook. Interestingly, al-Māzinī generally rejected Haykal's adoption of colloquial Arabic for dialogue, preferring instead to use a form of straightforward standard Arabic that nonetheless attempted to preserve the vitality of everyday speech; this strategy was later also to be used by the Nobel Prize-winning novelist Najīb Maḥfūẓ. Most notoriously, however, the work was criticised by al-Māzinī's contemporaries for plagiarism. In a preface attached to the work, the author had taken issue with his predecessor Haykal, who had maintained that the slow development of the novel in Egypt was due to lack of training in the finer emotions. Al-Māzinī argued that it was incorrect to assume that the Egyptian novel had to be based on Western models and values, but the work belied his own argument, for it was soon noticed that he had himself inserted into his work some pages from a work by the Russian writer Artsybashev, and this, combined with other instances of 'borrowing' in his works, caused his reputation to suffer.

Al-Māzinī went on to write a successor to *Ibrāhīm al-kātib* entitled *Ibrāhīm al-thānī* (1943), the title of which itself is perhaps enough to suggest the rather unoriginal nature of the work, in which an older and more melancholy Ibrāhīm, now married, 'enjoys' relationships with two younger women, ʿĀ'ida and Mīmī. More cerebral than the earlier work, *Ibrāhīm al-thānī* is largely lacking in the wit and humour of *Ibrāhīm al-kātib*, and the work is of little significance for the development of the Arabic novel. Instead, al-Māzinī's talents as a prose writer found more successful expression in a number of shorter works, including *Thalāthat rijāl wa-mra'a* (1943), *Mīdū wa-shurakā'uhu* (1943) and *ʿAwd ʿalā badʾ* (1943), in which the talent for humour evident in parts of *Ibrāhīm al-kātib* makes a welcome reappearance.

If the account of the Arabic novel thus far has given the impression that, after the initial phases, it was an entirely Egyptian affair, the impression is probably not an entirely inaccurate one.[22] A recent study by Hamdi Sakkut[23] suggests that, despite the important contributions to the Arabic literary revival (*nahḍa*) made by writers in Syria and Lebanon in the nineteenth century, no further novel of value was produced in Lebanon until the publication of Tawfīq Yūsuf ʿAwwād's *al-Raghīf* in 1939 and none in Syria until the publication of Shakīb al-Jābirī's *Naham* in 1937; in Iraq, the first novel worthy of the name, Dhū al-Nūn Ayyūb's *al-Duktūr Ibrāhīm*, appeared in 1939. In other parts of the Arab world, development was even slower: in Palestine, for example, the first novel of literary merit arguably did not appear until 1963, when Ghassān Kanafānī's *Rijāl fī al-shams* was published; while in Tunis, despite the publication of forward-looking works such as ʿAlī al-Duʿājī's *Jawla bayna ḥānāt al-baḥr al-mutawassiṭ* as early as 1935, novel-writing did not develop on a large scale until the late 1950s and may be regarded as essentially a post-colonial phenomenon.

Despite this, the development of the Arabic novel in the period under discussion was not entirely confined to Egypt. In New York, the Arab Mahjar[24] writer, poet and artist Jubrān Khalīl Jubrān (1883–1931), produced a number of works of 'prose poetry' (*shiʿr manthūr*) from 1903 on, in which he attempted to bridge the gap between poetry and prose, using techniques that married the influence of French Romantic poetry with that of Arabic translations of the Bible.[25] These experiments, however –which also show the influence of Fransīs Marrāsh – had little or nothing in common, either stylistically or thematically, with the contemporary development of the 'mainstream' Arabic novel that was taking place in Egypt and Greater Syria, and it was only at a considerably later date that the two streams of development can be said to have merged in any meaningful way.

A definitive evaluation of Jubrān's contribution to the development of the Arabic novel is hampered by a number of factors, not least the fact that many of his best known works (most notably *The Prophet*, a work that appears to have acquired cult status in some circles in the West, and has been claimed as 'the most widely read book of the twentieth century'[26]) were originally written in

English, then translated into Arabic. Be that as it may, Jubrān's early works in Arabic, which include *'Arā'is al-Murūj* (1906), *al-Arwāḥ al-Mutamarrida* (1908) and *al-Ajniḥa al-mutakassira* (1912), clearly deserve a prominent position in any account of the development of Arabic prose fiction, both for their distinctive style and for their thematic material, which is characterised by a radical anti-clericalism that recalls that of Fāris al-Shidyāq[27] in certain passages of *al-Sāq 'alā al-Sāq*. Jubrān's writing in these works (most of which are best classified as collections of stories) is both idiosyncratic and, at times at least, egocentric: *al-Arwāḥ al-mutamarrida*, for example, includes a character called 'Khalīl the Heretic', which immediately suggests identification with the author himself.

Jubrān's work links a rather conventional Romantic idea of a return to nature with a quirky mysticism that attempts to unite East and West. His appeal to his admirers has been well characterised by Pierre Cachia as that of 'lush imagery and glossy diction',[28] and, as this formulation may suggest, his work unfortunately often lapses into sentimentality. This, combined with its often irritating didacticism and the unorthodox nature of many of his ideas, undoubtedly limited its appeal to his contemporaries, particularly mainstream Muslim intellectuals. His attempt to mould the rhythm of Arabic in a new way, however, mirroring patterns of thought through the use of devices such as parallelism and repetition, represented an important early experiment in bridging the gap between poetry and prose; this technique was further developed by a number of other writers, most notably his fellow Mahjar writer Amīn al-Rīḥānī (1876–1940), already mentioned in a previous chapter, who, despite some differences of attitude, shared several features in common with Jubrān. More down to earth than Jubrān, al-Rīḥānī also wrote both in Arabic and in English, and like Jubrān's, his work is tinged with an anti-clerical tone; his Arabic works, influenced by the poetry of, among others, Walt Whitman, were published in the four-volume *Rīḥāniyyāt* (Beirut, 1910–23), though he is probably better known in the English-speaking world for a series of books derived from his travels in the Arab world, including *Ibn Saud of Arabia* (1928) and *Arabian Peak and Desert* (1931).

The short story

The development of the short story during this period was inevitably closely bound up with the development of the novel, and indeed was inseparable from it. As already noted, however, in terms of its production and distribution, the Arabic short story has always enjoyed (and continues to enjoy) a major advantage over the novel, in that it lends itself to publication in newspapers and magazines designed for a general readership as well as those specialising in literary publications. Although many early novels were also published in this way in serial form, the attractions for the author of publishing a work of fiction as a complete unit are self-evident. In an area of the world where literacy rates remained low until comparatively recently, few, if any writers, have been able to make a living from literary production alone, but the combination of journalism with creative writing has been, and continues to be, an extremely common one. The rise of the short story has been inextricably bound up with the expansion of the reading public, the rise in literacy and the development of a modern press on the lines of Western models.

Although the early development and history of the modern Arabic short story, like that of the novel, was an uneven one, certain key figures and dates may serve as landmarks. A key role was played by the members of the Lebanese Bustānī family, particularly Buṭrus al-Bustānī (1819–83) and, more especially his son Salīm al-Bustānī (1846–84), already discussed in Chapter 2 above. As with other genres inspired by Western literary forms, the composition of original short stories followed a period in which first translations, then adaptations, were the norm – indeed, the dividing line between adaptation and original composition during this period is by no means always a clear one. Most translations were from either French or English, though Russian short stories also enjoyed a vogue in some quarters. Salīm al-Bustānī's short stories, like those of some other Levantine writers, were mainly published in *al-Jinān*, a fortnightly magazine founded in 1870 by Salīm's father, Buṭrus, which Salīm himself edited from 1883 to its demise in 1886, and where he also published his novels.

Despite the importance of Salīm al-Bustānī as a pioneer in the field of Arabic fiction, critical opinion has not usually been very complimentary towards him from a literary point of view and his stories (many of which revolve around themes of love and marriage) are now of mainly academic interest. Their main significance in the eyes of many critics today is that they illustrate a writer grappling with the problems of transposing Western techniques and plots to a different social and cultural setting.[29] More interesting than the work of al-Bustānī in a number of respects, however, is the work of the Egyptian ʿAbd Allāh al-Nadīm (1843/4–96), whose literary activities in both poetry and prose were combined (like those of his near-contemporary, the poet al-Bārūdī)[30] with radical political activity; like al-Bārūdi, al-Nadīm became caught up in the ʿUrābī rebellion of 1881–2, and though spared the long exile of al-Bārūdī, was forced to spend several years in hiding. An intriguing figure whose activities included not only teaching, versifying and journalism, but also employment at various times as telegraph clerk and school headmaster, al-Nadīm emerged as the leading orator and journalist of the ʿUrabists. His main contribution to the development of modern Arabic prose, however, came through the satirical magazines that he founded himself, *al-Tankīt wa al-Tabkīt* (June–October 1881), *al-Ṭāʾif* (November 1881–September 1882), and *al-Ustādh* (1892–3). The interest of the pieces that al-Nadīm published in these three magazines is twofold: on the one hand, the subject matter, which is often overtly political in nature, clearly demonstrates the close relationship between the social and political changes in contemporary Egypt and the emergence of new literary forms at the end of the nineteenth century; equally as important, however, is al-Nadīm's style of language, deliberately geared to the new emerging reading public and avoiding the use of the complex constructions that had been a hallmark of traditional Arabic prose style. At one point, al-Nadīm even experimented with the use of colloquial Arabic, but he later abandoned it, opting instead for a straightforward style that nonetheless adhered to the rules laid down by the classical grammarians; as such, his publications played an important part in the evolution of Modern Standard Arabic (MSA) as used today throughout the Arab world. A similarly open-minded attitude characterised his admission to his publications of poems composed by readers in the traditional *zajal* form (colloquial poetry, usually in strophic form), thus harnessing popular poetry to the nationalist cause.[31]

The turn of the century saw writers in a number of countries continuing to publish original short stories, in addition to translations and adaptations of Western originals, usually in newspapers or magazines. An analysis by Sabry Hafez[32] suggests that these writers can be divided into two main groups: one attempted to build on al-Nadīm's work by rejuvenating the *maqāma* form[33] while the second employed a hybrid form sometimes known as the 'narrative essay'. Meanwhile, a third, less significant, group of writers in Iraq was employing a variation on the latter termed *al-ru'ya* ('visionary dream').

Contributions of particular significance were made during this period by writers such as Jubrān Khalīl Jubrān, already discussed above, and the Egyptian Muṣṭafā Luṭfī al-Manfalūṭī (1877?–1924). A comparison of these two authors' works is of considerable interest, for despite the glaring differences in religion, upbringing and outlook, their work shares certain features in common, most notably a Romantic tendency to sentimentality; indeed, al-Manfalūṭī's work has sometimes been regarded as paving the way, at least in part, for the Romantic poetry of the 1920s and 1930s.

The extent of the gap between the Bohemian experiences of Jubrān and the more conventional path followed by al-Manfalūṭī may be gauged by a synopsis of al-Manfalūṭī's life. Born, as his name suggests, in Manfalūṭ in Upper Egypt, al-Manfalūṭī received a traditional education at the al-Azhar University in Cairo and enjoyed a conventional career in the Egyptian civil service, serving in the Ministry of Education, Department of Justice and at the Royal Court. An admirer of the religious reformer Muḥammad 'Abduh, his first publications were in the form of poetry. Despite the apparently conventional nature of his career, however, a latent rebellious streak in his nature had already become apparent when in 1897 he was briefly imprisoned for publishing verse insulting to the

Khedive ʿAbbās II. Although he went on to publish more poetry, however, it is not for his verse that he is remembered so much as for his prose essays, articles and short stories, originally published in *al-Mu'ayyad* and other periodicals, and subsequently republished in a number of collections, of which the most famous were *al-Naẓarāt* (3 vols, 1910, 1912 and 1920), and *al-ʿAbarāt* (1915).

It is easy for a Western critic to underestimate al-Manfalūṭī's contribution to modern literature in Arabic, as much of his writing, with its mood of sentimental romanticism and often moralistic tone, is little to contemporary taste, and unlike Jubrān, his lifestyle had nothing of the exotic about it. Nonetheless, he was widely admired and read by his contemporaries, not least because of his lucid prose style, which stands at a crossroads between the complexities of traditional Arabic prose and the simpler modern prose style that has since become the norm. Not the least point of interest is that the author who, unlike many of his contemporaries, had not studied in the West and knew no Western languages, was able to publish Arabic versions of several French literary works, including Bernadin de Saint-Pierre's *Paul et Virginie* (1923); although it is clear that, for such an enterprise, al-Manfalūṭī must have had some sort of collaborator, the phenomenon is a graphic illustration of the difference between contemporary notions of authorship and the more relaxed standards of the Arab world in the early twentieth century, in which notions of plagiarism were only just beginning to gain currency.

Although the essays and stories of al-Manfalūṭī seem for a short time to have reflected the mood of the moment among at least a proportion of his contemporaries, they strike most modern readers as belonging to an earlier age. In the meantime, other writers had been coming to prominence who were to play a part in reorienting the course of the modern Arabic short story, among them the Egyptian Muṣṭafā ʿAbd al-Rāziq (1885–1947), one of the founders of the literary periodical *al-Sufūr* (1915–24) and brother of ʿAlī ʿAbd al-Rāziq (1888–1966), whose book *al-Islām wa-uṣūl al-ḥukm* (1925) became a *cause célèbre* for its argument that the caliphate was not an integral part of Islam. Among other writers of significance at this time were the Syro-Lebanese brothers ʿĪsā (d.1922) and Shiḥāta (d. 1961) ʿUbayd, who like many of their fellow-countrymen, had emigrated to Egypt from the Levant and appeared to throw themselves with enthusiasm into the spirit of their adopted homeland, calling for a new Egyptian literature that would depict the social and national life of Egypt in a more realistic fashion.

Despite the importance and interest of the ʿUbayd brothers' publications, however, the key role in the maturation of the Arabic short story was played not by immigrants from Syria but by the Egyptian brothers Muḥammad (1892–1921) and Maḥmūd (1894–1973) Taymūr, and by other writers of broadly similar outlook, including Aḥmad Khayrī al-Saʿīd, Ḥusayn Fawzī, Maḥmūd

Ṭāhir Lāshīn (1894–1954) and Yaḥyā Ḥaqqī (1905–92).[34] The names of many of these authors, including Maḥmūd Taymūr and Maḥmūd Ṭāhir Lāshīn, are linked with a literary movement known as the 'Modern School' (*al-madrasa al-ḥadītha*), a group of writers whose literary weekly *al-Fajr*, founded in 1925, played a key role in helping to widen the potential reading public for the short story, and indeed in developing a new literary sensibility appropriate for the period. Known originally as 'Madrasat al-ādāb al-jadīda', the group first met in November 1918 in the Lipton teahouse in Cairo, and had close associations with the Egyptian nationalist movement of 1919; their influence grew considerably with the foundation in 1925 of *al-Fajr*, which to a large extent took over from the literary weekly *al-Sufūr* (1915–24) as the mouthpiece for 'progressive' writers of the day. At first inspired mainly by French literature, some members of the group later developed an interest in Russian writers such as Chekhov and Turgenev, but for practical reasons the group split up at the end of 1926 and *al-Fajr* itself – whose financial basis was as fragile as that of most of its counterparts – folded shortly afterwards.

In the process of developing a specifically Egyptian literature, the Taymūr brothers occupy a particularly prominent position, as members of a distinguished literary family that had already made a considerable contribution to Egyptian cultural life. Their father, Aḥmad al-Taymūr (1871–1930), was a member of a prominent Turco-Circassian family that had migrated to Egypt at the beginning of the nineteenth century, and the family provides perhaps one of the closest Egyptian parallels to the Lebanese families such as the Bustānīs and the Yāzijīs influential in the nineteenth-century *nahḍa*. Aḥmad's elder sister, 'Ā'isha 'Iṣmat al-Taymūriyya (1840–1902), was a noted poetess and early feminist who also composed prose works on girls' education and gender relations,[35] and Aḥmad himself, in addition to compiling a study of Cairene proverbs that is still consulted today, built up a collection of several thousand volumes of books and manuscripts which he subsequently donated to the Egyptian National Library. For his part, Muḥammad Taymūr, Aḥmad's second son, studied law in Paris and Lyon between 1911 and 1914, though, like Tawfīq al-Ḥakīm a little later,[36] his residence in France appears to have been primarily an occasion for developing an acquaintance with the literature of Europe rather than a period of serious academic study. Muḥammad read widely in the works of realistic writers such as Zola and De Maupassant and frequented the French theatre; on his return to Egypt, he composed a number of plays which played an important part in shaping the course of Egyptian drama,[37] and in 1917 began publishing short stories in the style of De Maupassant under the name *Mā tarāhu al-'uyūn*. Like the 'Ubayd bothers, his view of the course that Egyptian literature should take was influenced by contemporary developments, but although he played an important role in helping to shape the emerging genre of the short story, his influence was cut short by his early death, and it was left to others to bring the Egyptian short story to full maturity.

Despite the short-lived nature of the enterprise, the authors of the 'Modern School' (in which the role of the Taymūr brothers was a crucial one) occupy a pivotal position in the development of the modern Arabic short story, playing a key role both in widening the potential readership for the genre and in developing a new literary sensibility appropriate for the period. On an individual level, the three most significant names are those of Maḥmūd Taymūr, Yaḥyā Ḥaqqī and Maḥmūd Ṭāhir Lāshīn. Greatly influenced by the efforts of his brother, whose works he edited after his early death, Maḥmūd Taymūr published his first volumes of collected short stories, *al-Shaykh Jum'a wa-qiṣaṣ ukhrā* and *'Amm Mitwallī wa-qiṣaṣ ukhrā* in 1925; he went on to become one of the most prolific writers in modern Arabic literature, with over twenty volumes of short stories to his name, in addition to novels, collections of essays, and plays, amply justifying the sobriquet by which he is often known – the 'Egyptian Maupassant'. Despite the conscious attempt to anchor his stories in the lives of 'ordinary' Egyptians, however, Maḥmūd's themes and characterisation remained somewhat limited, and it was to Lāshīn's stories (particularly his 'Ḥadīth al-qarya', published in 1929), rather than Taymūr's, that the credit must be given for moving the Egyptian – and indeed, the Arabic – short story into a new, more mature, phase of development. The importance of this story, which has been extensively analysed (and translated) by Sabry Hafez,[38] lies not only in the assurance with which Lāshīn manipulates the narrative form, which incorporates a 'story within a story', but also in its perfect mirroring of the social and political dilemmas facing contemporary Egypt, caught in an unresolved conflict between traditional and modern values. Discouraged by the reception given to his work, Lāshīn unfortunately published comparatively little else,[39] and indeed abandoned writing at the end of the 1930s, but his short stories provided the starting-point for a new, realistic mode of narrative that provided a counterweight to the growing number of lightweight, 'sentimental' works in the genre. This technique was brought to further fruition in the short stories of Yaḥyā Ḥaqqī,[40] much of whose work derives from a two-year period spent as an administrative assistant in the Upper Egyptian town of Manfalūṭ; the conflict between the mentality of the villager and that of the city-educated intellectual that lies at the heart of Lāshīn's 'Ḥadīth al-qarya' is a constant theme in Yaḥyā Ḥaqqī's work – as indeed, at the heart of several major works produced in the succeeding period, including Tawfīq al-Ḥakīm's *Yawmiyyāt Nā'ib fī al-Aryāf* (1937).[41] Yaḥyā Ḥaqqī's best known work, the novella *Qindīl Umm Hāshim* (1946),[42] provides a variation on this theme, recounting as it does the apparently successful struggle of a Western-educated eye doctor to reconcile the values of Western science with the traditional spiritual values of his native Cairo on his return from study abroad, and is justly regarded as a 'classic' work on the conflict between East and West in modern Arab culture.

With the exception of the Mahjar writers of North, and to a lesser extent, South America, few if any other countries of the Arabic-speaking world can match the energy and vitality of the Egyptian short story during this period. Although, by the nature of things, short pieces of imaginative prose writing were appearing almost everywhere, no other country appears by this time yet to have established a tradition of short-story writing capable of forming the basis for productive future development. Despite this, a few individual writers of some significance were beginning to publish elsewhere, whose efforts significantly affected the course of modern fiction in the wider Middle East. Among the most important of these individual writers was the Palestinian Khalīl Baydās (1875–1949),[43] who for a number of years edited the literary magazine *al-Nafā'is al-'aṣriyya*, and whose short stories were collected in the volume *Masārih al-adhhān* (1924). Although Baydās arguably played a significant part in disseminating an appreciation of modern Russian literature throughout the Arabic-speaking Middle East, however, his own imaginative writing failed to live up to the insights of his critical writing, and he founded no enduring tradition of narrative fiction in his home country; significantly, his 1924 collection of short stories was published not in Palestine but in Cairo.

Conclusion

Such, in outline, was the state of development of Arabic fiction at the beginning of the 1930s. In the more advanced countries of the Arabic-speaking world, most obviously Egypt and the Mahjar, the novel and short story as understood in the Western sense had by now almost entirely supplanted indigenous narrative forms such as the *maqāma* as the 'normal' medium of 'high' literary imaginative prose expression. A number of distinct trends can by this time be observed in the novel and short story forms: a historical trend; a romantic trend, and a more realistic trend, exemplified in the approach of writers such as Lāshīn and the Taymūr brothers. In the following chapter, we shall see how the new literary genres, which still rested on a rather precarious basis, both in literary terms and in terms of their readership, were carried forward to maturity by a new generation of writers, and how the novel form began to be progressively adopted on a wider basis throughout the Arab world.

Notes

1 For which, see above, p. 10. For this work, including an English translation, see Roger Allen, *A Period of Time* (Reading, 1992).
2 The translations, and those following, are those used by Roger Allen, in the volume

cited above.

3 Village headman, a position of considerable influence during this period.

4 For which, see above, pp. 27–8.

5 Timothy Mitchell, *Colonising Egypt*, Berkeley, 1988, p. 180.

6 Al-Muwaylihī, *Ḥadīth*, p. 325.

7 Roger Allen, *The Arabic Novel*, Syracuse, 1982, p. 29.

8 See above, pp. 25–6.

9 For whom, see above, p. 10.

10 Boutros al-Hallaq, in 'Love and the birth of modern Arabic literature', in *Love and Sexuality in Modern Arabic Literature*, ed. Roger Allen, Hilary Kilpatrick and Ed de Moor, London, 1995, pp. 16–23.

11 For a fuller discussion, see Paul Starkey, 'Egyptian History in the Modern Egyptian Novel', in *The Historiography of Islamic Egypt (c. 950-1800)*, ed. Hugh Kennedy, Leiden, 2001, pp. 251–62.

12 Thomas Philipp's *Gurgi Zaidan: His Life and Thought*, Beirut, 1979, for example, devotes less than two out of 250 pages to the historical novels.

13 Moosa, *The Origins of Modern Arabic Fiction*, p. 222.

14 For a fuller discussion of these authors, see Hamdi Sakkut, *The Egyptian Novel and its Main Trends from 1913 to 1952*, Cairo, 1971.

15 The uncle of the more famous Yaḥyā Ḥaqqī, for whom see below, pp. 111–12.

16 Moosa, *The Origins of Modern Arabic Fiction*, p. 258.

17 English translation, as *Zainab*, by J. M. Grinsted, London, 1989; for discussions, see, for example, Allen, *The Arabic Novel*, pp. 31–37; Elad, *The Village Novel*; Kilpatrick, *The Modern Egyptian Novel*, pp. 20–6, etc.

18 See Sakkut, *The Egyptian Novel*, p. 12. There are several parallels to Haykal's dilemma, the most obvious being perhaps that of Tawfīq al-Hākīm, whose early plays were written using the name 'Ḥusayn Tawfīq' (see below, p. 178).

19 Al-Māzinī also made a considerable contribution to Egyptian literary life as a poet and critic, most notably as a member of the so-called 'Dīwān Group', for which see above, pp. 65–7.

20 Like many extended works during this period, the work was first published in serial form, in *al-Hilāl*; it was published in book form in 1929. The author subsequently published two further volumes of memoirs.

21 See Hilary Kilpatrick, 'The Egyptian novel from *Zaynab* to 1980' in Badawi (ed.), *Modern Arabic Literature*, pp. 223ff. The use of the term *fakhr* echoes the pre-Islamic poetic theme.

22 For an interesting discussion, see Hilary Kilpatrick, 'The Arabic novel – a single tradition?', *JAL* IV (1974), pp. 93–107.

23 Hamdi Sakkut, *al-Riwāya al-'Arabiyya: bibliyūjrāfiyā wa-madkhal naqdī (1865–1995)/ The Arabic Novel: bibliography and critical introduction (1865–1995)*, Cairo, 2000.

24 'Mahjar' in this context is a term referring to the Arab émigré communities of North and South America. Their contribution to the development of Arabic poetry being generally more significant than to prose, they have been discussed in Chapters 3 and 4 above.

25 On this, see above, pp. 62–3, and S. Moreh, *Modern Arabic Poetry 1839–1970*, Leiden: Brill, 1976, pp. 89–311.

26 See, for example, the dust-jacket of Suheil Bushrui and Joe Jenkins, *Kahlil Gibran:*

Man and Poet, Oxford, 1998.

27 For whom, see Chapter 2 above, pp. 33–4.

28 Cachia, *Arabic Literature: An Overview*, p. 157.

29 For a useful study, see Moosa, *The Origins of Modern Arabic Fiction*, Chapter 7.

30 For whom, see above, Chapter 3, pp. 43–4.

31 On this, see Marilyn Booth, 'Poetry in the Vernacular', in Badawi (ed.), *Modern Arabic Literature*, pp. 463ff.

32 Sabry Hafez, 'The Modern Arabic Short Story', in Badawi (ed.), *Modern Arabic Literature*, p.274. His analysis draws on Shukrī 'Ayyād, *al-Qiṣṣa al-Qaṣīra fī* Miṣr, Cairo, 1968.

33 For which, see above, p. 10

34 See Sabry Hafez, 'The modern Arabic short story', in Badawi (ed.), *Modern Arabic Literature*, pp. 270ff., and Sabry Hafez, *The Genesis of Arabic Literary Discourse*, London, 1993, pp. 215ff.

35 On this, see Margot Badran and Miriam Cooke (eds), *Opening the Gates: A Century of Arab Feminist Writing*, Bloomington and Indianapolis, 1990.

36 For whom, see below, pp. 115–17, 178–86.

37 Discussed below, Chapter 9, pp. 173–4.

38 See references in footnote 34 above.

39 Lāshīn published three collections of short stories: *Sukhriyyat al-Nāy* (1927), *Yuḥkā 'annā* (1930) and *al-Niqāb al-ṭā'ir* (1940). His only novel, *Ḥawwā' bilā Ādam* (1934) is discussed below, p. 117.

40 For whom, see Miriam Cooke, *The Anatomy of an Egyptian Intellectual*, Washington, DC, 1984.

41 Discussed below, p. 116.

42 English translation as *The Saint's Lamp and Other Stories* by M. Badawi, Leiden, 1973.

43 For a discussion of Baydās, see Hafez, *The Genesis of Arabic Literary Discourse*, pp. 152–6.

7

Prose literature: the period of maturity

This chapter continues the account begun in the previous chapter, describing the development of the novel and short story from the 1930s to around 1967, when a major change occurred in the prevailing mood of the Arab world that is reflected in much Arabic fiction. Like all such divisions, the cut-off point between what I have called the 'period of development' and the 'period of maturity' is a slightly arbitrary one – probably even more arbitrary than in the case of modern Arabic poetry, which falls fairly easily into three distinct styles, if not distinct periods. What is clear, however, is that from time to time individual works or authors appear that mark a shift in contemporary attitudes or usher in a new phase of development. Muḥammad Ḥusayn Haykal's *Zaynab*, discussed in the previous chapter, has been almost universally acknowledged as one such work, and though less agreement might perhaps be found among the critics for a corresponding work from the early 1930s, there can be little doubt that a major advance in Egyptian and Arabic novelistic technique occurred during that period. As this advance, to my mind, is well exemplified by the publication of the two parts of Tawfīq al-Ḥakīm's major novel *ʿAwdat al-Rūḥ* in 1933, it is with this work that I shall begin.

Although Tawfīq al-Ḥakīm's continuing reputation undoubtedly owes more to his plays than to his novels, his novels, beginning with *ʿAwdat al-Rūḥ* itself, in fact seem to me to hold a position of an almost equivalent importance for the development of modern Arabic literature generally. Begun in French during his period of study in Paris from 1925 to 1928,[1] *ʿAwdat al-Rūḥ* was closely modelled on the author's experiences in Cairo during the First World War and as such, continues an autobiographical trend prominent during the early development of modern Arabic fiction, as already noted in the previous chapter. Essentially, the work depicts the life and often frustrated loves of a middle-class Egyptian family of the period, culminating in the 1919 Egyptian popular revolt led by Saʿd Zaghlūl that for al-Ḥakīm represented the 'Return of the Spirit' of the work's title. Structurally, the work suffers from numerous faults, most notably the tendency to rambling digression that mars many of al-Ḥakīm's works: long sections in the second part are devoted to a debate about the nature of the

Egyptian *fallāḥ*, whom al-Ḥakīm regarded as directly descended from the builders of the pyramids, and the depiction of the 1919 revolt in the novel's final pages is imperfectly integrated with the rest of the work. The ending has, however, ensured the novel's reputation as a 'nationalist' work, being admired by, among others, the Egyptian president 'Abd al-Nāṣir (Abdel Nasser). Epitomising the new spirit of Egyptian patriotism, the work continues to strike a chord in the hearts of Egyptians to this day for this reason,[2] but the work may also be read on several other levels: as a picture of life in contemporary Egypt; as a novel of adolescent love; as an example of the 'town' versus 'country' theme that had already begun to make an appearance in Arabic literature; or as a contribution to the expression of the 'pharaonic' interpretation of Egypt's role in the world that had been given added impetus by the discovery of Tutankhamun's tomb in 1922.

Tawfīq al-Ḥakīm's *'Awdat al-Rūḥ* was followed by three further novels,[3] in all of which the autobiographical element plays a significant part. The first of these, *Yawmiyyāt Nā'ib fī al-Aryāf*, published in 1937, is also the most successful, not least because the author has almost entirely succeeded in avoiding his tendency to rambling 'philosophical' digression that mars the artistic unity of much of his work. The novel derives from the author's experiences as an attorney in the Egyptian Delta and presents a damning picture of conditions in the countryside and the legal system based on the Napoleonic Code. There is an unbridgeable gulf between the assumptions and mentality of the city-bred narrator, charged with applying that code, and the peasants to whom it is to be applied – a gulf that recalls the 'town vs country' divide in Lāshīn's seminal short story 'Fī al-qarya' discussed in the previous chapter.[4]

Yawmiyyāt Nā'ib fī al-Aryāf's particular combination of hard-hitting social criticism and assured literary technique has seldom been surpassed in modern Arabic literature. Unfortunately, any prospect that it might quickly lead to a vigorous tradition of social criticism was quickly belied by al-Ḥakīm's next novel, *'Uṣfūr min al-Sharq* (1938), which although published later than *Yawmiyyāt Nā'ib fī al-Aryāf*, derives from an earlier period of the author's life. The work explores the conflict between East and West – a theme foreshadowed as long ago as 1834–5 in al-Ṭahṭāwī's *Takhlīṣ al-ibrīz ilā talkhīṣ Bārīz* – through the experiences of Muḥsin, an Egyptian student in Paris who is clearly modelled on al-Ḥakīm himself. The interplay is worked out on two levels: on a practical level, through Muḥsin's ill-fated love affair with the French girl, Suzy, and on a dialectical level, through his discussions with the Russian émigré Ivan. The precise interpretation of the implications of these discussions has been the subject of considerable debate, but whatever one's interpretation might be, the work is of considerable interest, despite its artistic flaws, as an example of the 'East vs West' antithesis that has formed a *topos* of modern Arabic literature through much of its development. *Al-Ribāṭ al-Muqaddas* (1945) continued the sequence of novels partly based on his own life, painting a picture of an 'ivory tower' intellectual, but the novel is marred by a tortured introspection that borders on self-indulgence, and it is perhaps something of a relief to find that, with the exception of *Ḥimār al-Ḥakīm*, the author abandoned the novel form to devote his main artistic energies to the theatre.

To this stage in the development of the Egyptian novel belong also the efforts of Maḥmūd Ṭāhir Lāshīn, already mentioned in the previous chapter, whose one novel, *Ḥawwā' bilā Ādam* (1934), revolves around themes of class conflict and the emancipated woman's search for new forms of relationships with men. Ḥawwā's failure to resolve the conflict in her personal life between traditional culture and the more progressive ideas that were beginning to infiltrate the Arab world, not only leads eventually to her suicide but also appears to mirror the author's own pessimistic evaluation of the prevailing mood: after *Ḥawwā' bilā Ādam* he appears to have almost abandoned his literary activity and, with the exception of a collection of short stories entitled *al-Niqāb al-ṭā'ir* (1940), published nothing else before his death in 1954. Another distinguished literary figure who experimented with the novel form but whose talents clearly lay elsewhere was 'Abbās Maḥmūd al-'Aqqād (1889–1964), one of the most eminent Egyptian men of letters of the first half of the twentieth century, whose one novel, *Sāra* (1938), again revolves around an unsatisfactory love-affair.[5] Flawed by an excess of analysis and abstraction, the novel is from a literary point of view today of mostly historical interest, but its publication is nonetheless significant both as an indication of the extent to which the novel form had engaged the attention of the leading *udabā'* of the day; and as confirming the predominantly autobiographical trend in novel writing at the time.

By the end of the 1930s and the beginning of the 1940s, the novel in Egypt was both beginning to claim for itself a new status (reflected in the institution of a new series of novel-writing competitions in 1941) and to be marked by a number of new directions. The leading writers of the older generation such as Tawfīq al-Ḥakīm, Ṭāhā Ḥusayn, al-'Aqqād and al-Māzinī had all been born within a few years of each other at the end of the nineteenth century and, despite some differences of outlook and temperament, seemed to share a number of common attitudes, formed to some extent no doubt by the experiences of their youth during the period between the 'Urābī revolt of 1881–2 and the Zaghlūl rebellion of 1919. Less homogeneous than the generation preceding it, the next generation of writers took its cue from the corruption of Egyptian politics in the inter-war period rather than the optimism of the 1919 revolution and was beginning to produce works characterised by a new realism. Paradoxically, this trend was accompanied by a new enthusiasm for historical subjects, set either in the pharaonic or in the pre-Islamic or early Islamic historical period.

Among the writers who may be mentioned in this context are ʿĀdil Kāmil (1916–) and Lūwīs ʿAwaḍ (1915–90). A lawyer by training, ʿĀdil Kāmil's two novels exemplify the two trends just mentioned. His first novel, *Malik al-shuʿāʿ*, based on the life of Pharaoh Akhnaton, won first prize in the novel-writing competition organised by the Fu'ād I Academy in 1942. His second novel, *Millīm al-akbar*, by contrast, attempts to explore the class structure of contemporary Egyptian society through the lives of two young men from different social backgrounds, but the result is unconvincing and it is perhaps not surprising that the work failed to win a prize in the 1944 competition; the author, apparently disillusioned like Lāshīn by his lack of success, effectively abandoned his literary interests to devote himself again to the law.[6] For his part, Lūwīs ʿAwaḍ, ʿĀdil Kāmil's near contemporary and, like Kāmil, from a Christian background, produced only one full-length novel, *al-ʿAnqā' aw ta'rīkh Ḥasan Miftāḥ*: written in 1946–7 partly in Cairo, partly in Paris, this truly 'revolutionary' novel, which explores class structures and political activism through the eyes of the Marxist Ḥasan Miftāḥ, has been described as a 'landmark in modern Arabic literature' and 'one of the most violent expressions of revolt to have come out of Egypt';[7] for obvious reasons, it could not be published in Egypt until after the 1952 Free Officers' revolt, but it clearly deserves to be more widely known, being one of the few contemporary literary representations of the volatile mood of the country in the period between the Second World War and the assumption of power by the Free Officers in 1952. Although he wrote no more full-length novels, the author, Lūwīs ʿAwaḍ's contribution to Egyptian literary life, which extended over a period of more than half a century, was by any standard a major one, including not only a groundbreaking volume of avant-garde free verse, *Plutoland wa-qaṣā'id ukhrā* (1947), but also an autobiographical work written in Egyptian dialect (*Mudhakkirāt ṭālib baʿtha* (1965), in addition to a large number of often iconoclastic critical works, and translations of works by Shakespeare, T. S. Eliot and others.

The 'popular reader' and the romantic novel

At this point, it may be as well to inject a note of caution. If the above account suggests that this period was an exciting one in terms of experimental literary production, that is not in itself untrue; the average reader, however, whether in Egypt or indeed elsewhere, has at most of the periods under discussion been far more likely to have been reading, if not translations, then probably short stories or novels of a 'popular' or 'romantic' kind. These sorts of novels and short stories, which for possibly dubious though obvious reasons have usually received scant critical attention from the critics, have clear counterparts in a Western context, on some levels at least, and to a large extent represent a continuation of the tradition of translations and adaptations of popular European works that had started in the nineteenth century.

A fascinating example of the interaction of these two literary strands, as well as of the twists and turns taken by the Egyptian literary heritage more generally, is provided by the works of Iḥsān ʿAbd al-Qaddūs (1919–90), the son of Fāṭima al-Yūsuf, known as Rūz al-Yūsuf (born c. 1895), who had originally worked as an actress with ʿAzīz ʿĪd and Jūrj Abyaḍ,[8] before abandoning the stage to found in 1925 the political and satirical magazine, *Rūz al-Yūsuf*. This periodical, which in addition to less serious fare, published contributions from such illustrious authors as al-Māzinī, al-ʿAqqād and Maḥmūd Taymūr, was subsequently taken over by her son Iḥsān in 1945, nationalised in 1960 and continues to be published to this day. For his part, after taking over control of the periodical, Iḥsān began to devote increasing attention to the output of 'popular' or 'romantic' novels and short stories, of which he produced several dozen volumes. Among his professed social and literary purposes was a desire to break existing taboos on what could be discussed in Arabic literature, and some of his writing appears explicitly designed to provoke discussion on matters such as the rights of women in contemporary Egyptian society. His writing often lapsed into sentimentality, but that did not prevent his works from attaining an enormous popularity: a poll conducted in 1954 by the American University in Cairo found him to be the 'most popular living writer in Arabic',[9] and his works have continued to retain a considerable popularity among readers, not only in Egypt but elsewhere in the Arab world, as well as providing much readily adaptable material for the Egyptian film industry. Other writers whose work may be placed in a similar category to those of Iḥsān ʿAbd al-Quddūs include Muḥammad ʿAbd al-Ḥalīm ʿAbd Allāh (1913–70),[10] whose works combine a romantic interest with social commentary, and the prolific Yūsuf al-Sibāʿī (1917–78), who held a number of important state offices, including that of Minister of Culture, while at the same time producing some twenty collections of short stories and sixteen novels, as well as essays and several plays.[11] Although, with a few exceptions, writers such as these have seldom received much critical attention in the standard accounts of modern Arabic literature, their works continue to form a large part of the standard reading fare of the average Arab reader, and it is arguable that they deserve a fuller study.

The novel outside Egypt

Although Egyptian writers continued to dominate the production of Arabic fiction, the period towards the end of the 1930s also saw a significant increase in interest in the novel form in other parts of the Arab world, including in particular Lebanon, Syria and Iraq. Despite the pivotal role played in the nineteenth-century *nahḍa* by Syria and Lebanon, literary activity in these two countries appears to have suffered something of an eclipse during the first decades of the twentieth century. The reasons for this decline are not entirely clear, though the emigration of a significant number of the most eminent intellectuals to Egypt and the Americas was undoubtedly one factor. Be that as it may, it is not until 1939 that we find a Lebanese novel of a comparable quality and interest to the productions of the 1930s in Egypt just described. The early 1930s had, however, already begun to witness the revival of intellectual and literary activity, most particularly in Beirut, and a circle known as the 'Group of Ten' ('al-'Uṣba al-'Ashara') had begun to inject new life into the city's flagging cultural scene, inspired by the example of the Mahjar poets and others. Closely associated with this group, Tawfīq Yūsuf 'Awwād was already known for two published collections of short stories, *al-Ṣabī al-a'raj* (1937) and *Qamīṣ al-ṣūf* (1937), when his novel *al-Raghīf* (1939) appeared, clearly marking him out as an author of considerable talent. Clearly inspired by contemporary Arab nationalism, the work is set at the time of the Arab revolt of 1916 against the Turks, but, as with some Egyptian historical novels already discussed, the historical setting can hardly disguise its relevance to 'Awwād's own time, and it is perhaps this relevance as much as the work's literary merit that accounted for its popularity. Unfortunately, 'Awwād, who also served part of his life as a diplomat, appears to have lacked the dogged devotion to the novel form shown by, for example, Najīb Maḥfūẓ, and it was not until 1972 that his success in capturing the mood of the moment was repeated, in *Ṭawāḥīn Bayrūt*, a graphic depiction of the fragmented state of Beiruti society in the period between the June 1967 Arab–Israeli War and the outbreak of the Lebanese Civil War in 1975.[12]

Among the other writers coming to prominence in the 1930s and 1940s in Lebanon, many associated either with 'al-'Uṣba al-'Ashara' or with the slightly later Cénacle Libanais (1946–66), were the novelist and short-story writer Khalīl Taqī al-Dīn (1906–87), the poet Sa'īd 'Aql (1912–),[13] and the critic and imaginative writer Mārūn 'Abbūd (1886–1962), whose prodigious output of some fifty books made him one of the most influential figures in Lebanese intellectual and cultural life of his day; of particular importance is his study of Lebanese colloquial poetry (*zajal*), entitled *al-Shi'r al-'āmmī* (1968). To the same intellectual environment, which saw Beirut assume the role of cultural (as well as financial) capital of the Middle East in the period following the Second World War, belongs Suhayl Idrīs, often mentioned in connection with the 'committed' literary periodical *al-Ādāb* – only one of the numerous periodicals and publishing houses to be founded in Beirut during this period. In addition to his role as a publisher, Suhayl Idrīs also made a significant contribution to the novel and short story, in particular through his well-known novel *al-Ḥayy al-Lātīnī* (1954), a work that stands in a direct line of descent from comparable works by Ṭāhā

Ḥusayn, Tawfīq al-Ḥakīm and others[14] on the theme of the cultural conflicts experienced by the 'Arab student in Europe'. Two further novels followed, *al-Khandaq al-ghamīq* (1958) and *Aṣābi'unā allatī taḥtariq* (1962), both – like *al-Ḥayy al-Lātīnī* – partly autobiographical in nature – although neither managed to achieve the justified popularity of the earlier work.

A similar pattern of development that we have observed in Egypt – from early translation, imitation and experimentation, through the historical novel, to mature Western-style novel – may also be observed in Syria, where the pioneering works of Fransīs Marrāsh (1836–73), whose poetic prose style influenced Jubrān Khalīl Jubrān, were followed by the historical novels of Ma'rūf Aḥmad al-Arnā'ūṭ (1892–1948), published between 1929 and 1942: the four novels were subsequently collected together and republished under the revealing title of *al-Malḥama al-kubrā*. Of greater interest for the development of the novel form generally, however, were the efforts of Shakīb al-Jābirī (1912–), generally regarded as the founder of the modern Syrian novel, whose first novel *Naham* (1937), set in Germany, is, like several other works discussed in this section, again highly dependent on the author's experiences while living abroad as a young man. The author's three subsequent novels, *Qadar yalhū* (1939), *Qaws quzaḥ* (1946) and the later *Wadā'an yā Afamiya* (1960) continued this general theme, each being concerned with different aspects of the tensions between 'East' and 'West' on both a personal and a more nationalistic level, though none appears to have achieved the status of *Naham* as a landmark in the development of modern Syrian fiction.

In Iraq also, the end of the 1930s saw major strides in the establishment of a novelistic tradition, with the publication of Dhū al-Nūn Ayyūb's (1908–88) *al-Duktūr Ibrāhīm*, which paints a vivid portrait of an opportunistic young Iraqi who returns home after a period of education in Britain. The purpose of the author, like that of Yaḥyā Ḥaqqī in *Qindīl Umm Hāshim*, was clearly to demonstrate, or at least to suggest, the effects of exposure to Western 'civilisation', though the work almost entirely lacks the subtlety of Ḥaqqī's novella, discussed above. The author subsequently went on to produce a further novel, *al-Yad wa-al-arḍ wa-al-mā'* (1948), describing the conflict between peasants and landowners, though most of his literary output took the form of short stories rather than full-length novels, many originally published in the Mosul journal *al-Majalla*, which he himself edited from 1938 to 1944.

In North Africa, the same period also witnessed the emergence of the Tunisian writer Maḥmūd al-Mas'adī (1911–), whose extended work *al-Sudd* – sometimes classified as a play – constitutes a unique, if slightly idiosyncratic, contribution to the field.[15] The period also saw the emergence of a number of other North African writers, including 'Alī al-Du'ājī (1909–49), sometimes known as the 'father of the Tunisian short story', whose *Jawla bayna ḥānāt al-*

baḥr al-mutawassiṭ (1935) broke new ground with its straightforward but lively and entertaining style (though its title places it squarely in a well-established tradition); the 1930s also saw the growth of literary activity with the publication of the literary periodical *al-'Ālam al-adabī* and the rise of a literary grouping that met in the Taḥt al-Sūr ('Under the Rampart') café – 'Alī al-Du'ājī indeed being closely associated with both activities. Despite these developments, however, and their equivalents in Morocco and Algeria, it remains generally true that the development of élite literature in Arabic in the Maghrib – with the conspicuous exception of the Tunisian poet al-Shābbī[16] – continued to lag behind that of the eastern Arab world for most of the first half of the twentieth century, largely (though not entirely) because of the dominance of French culture and the French language. As already noted, in general, it was not until the moves towards independence from the French in the 1950s, when writing in Arabic began to assume a greater importance, that the countries of the Maghrib began to make their own distinctive contribution to the development of Arabic literature generally.

Najīb Maḥfūẓ

As noted above, 'Ādil Kāmil began his short novelistic career with a historical novel, before turning to a subject of more direct contemporary relevance. The same pattern is exemplified in the career of 'Abd al-Ḥamīd al-Saḥḥār (1913–), whose Pharaonic *Aḥmus* (1943) was followed by two novels, *Fī Qāfilat al-Zamān* (1947) and *al-Shāri' al-Jadīd* (1952), both describing the lives of Egyptian families through a number of generations.[17] More significantly, perhaps, it is exemplified in the early career of Najīb Maḥfūẓ (1911–), one of the most prolific of Egyptian authors and almost certainly the best known writer of Arabic fiction on an international level, following the award to him of the Nobel Prize for Literature in 1988. Born in an old quarter of Cairo, Maḥfūẓ studied philosophy at Cairo University but abandoned his programme of postgraduate study in the subject as his interest in literature began to grow, partly under the influence of Salāma Mūsā. His first literary output consisted of short stories, which he continued to write all his life, but his lasting reputation depends mainly on his novels, of which he has produced over thirty. His career is also a graphic representation of the much repeated statement that few if any writers in the modern Arab world have been able to earn a living from writing alone: in 1939 he joined the Egyptian civil service and from then until his retirement in the early 1970s he divided his energies between creative writing and the Egyptian bureaucracy, serving for a time in the Ministry of Waqfs and from 1954 in the Ministry of Culture, working in particular in the field of cinema, where he adapted for film works of the writers Iḥsān 'Abd al-Qaddūs and Yūsuf al-Sibā'ī, among others.[18]

Maḥfūẓ's output is of importance not only in its own right, but also because, like Tawfīq al-Ḥakīm's output in the field of drama, his works serve as a sort of barometer of changing tastes and priorities in the field generally.

Najīb Maḥfūẓ's prodigious output in terms of full-length novels is indeed a tribute to his meticulous personal organisation of his working time. His first novel, *'Abath al-Aqdār* (1939), a historical novel that owes much to Abū Ḥadīd's work *Ibnat al-Mamlūk*,[19] is probably of little value in itself except as a promise of things to come; two further novels set in ancient Egypt, however, *Rādūbīs* (1943) and *Kifāḥ Ṭība* (1944), the latter of which in particular attracted considerable critical attention, confirmed that Egypt had produced a budding novelist of extraordinary talent. Although he had originally planned an extended series of historical novels, he soon, however, like Ādil Kāmil and 'Abd al-Ḥamīd al-Saḥḥār, redirected his attention to contemporary Egypt, and a series of works followed, set in various quarters of Cairo, which explore the search for new values in the changing society of contemporary Egypt. Peopled with the colourful inhabitants of the Cairo backstreets, these novels include *al-Qāhira al-Jadīda* (1945), *Khān al-Khalīlī* (1946), *Zuqāq al-Midaqq* (1947), *al-Sarāb* (1948) and *Bidāya wa-Nihāya* (1949). This series of novels culminated in the monumental trilogy (*Thulāthiyya*),[20] which won the Egyptian State Prize for Literature in 1957 and on which Maḥfūẓ's international reputation was initially largely based. The work, originally written before the 1952 revolution but not published until 1956–7, lovingly chronicles the life of three generations of a lower-middle-class Egyptian family and the transition from a traditional to a more modern way of life in the period between the two world wars. As in previous novels, a prominent theme is the search for meaning and moral certainty, but a hint of the turbulent period on which Egypt was about to embark is provided at the end of the last section of the novel, when the two brothers Aḥmad and 'Abd al-Mun'im go their separate ways, one to the left wing of the Wafd party, the other to the Muslim Brothers.

Following the 1952 revolution, Maḥfūẓ suffered a crisis, partly personal though partly no doubt engendered by the revolution itself, that prevented him from writing for a period of some five years. His next major work, *Awlād Ḥāratinā*, initially serialised in the *al-Ahrām* newspaper in 1959, had accordingly been eagerly awaited. Far from being a continuation of the realistic style of the trilogy, the work heralded a radical shift in the direction of Maḥfūẓ's writing, which both mirrored certain contemporary concerns and foreshadowed those of the next generation of writers. The work, which is also Maḥfūẓ's most controversial, is essentially an extended allegory, in which the author utilises the stories of the Fall of Man and the figures of Moses, Jesus and Muḥammad to explore themes relating to the search for social justice, the existence of God, and the role of religion in the modern world.[21] The work led to protests from religious conservatives, who made a somewhat simplistic equation between the figures of al-Jabalāwī and God, and the work was banned in Egypt, being published in book form only in Beirut in 1967; debate on the controversial nature of the work was revived in 1988, when Maḥfūẓ publicly supported the author Salman Rushdie following the publication of *The Satanic Verses*, and again in the early 1990s, when the author was attacked and injured in the street by an Islamic fundamentalist.

If the conservative reaction to *Awlād Ḥāratinā* provided Maḥfūẓ with a salutary reminder of the limits of freedom of speech in contemporary Egypt, the work itself could not be judged a success in purely literary terms, and it is not therefore particularly surprising to find that it had no direct successor. Instead, Maḥfūẓ, whose disillusionment with the Free Officers' regime had already been apparent for some while, embarked on a series of novels, beginning with *al-Liṣṣ wa-al-Kilāb* (1961) and culminating in *Mīrāmār* (1967), which may be seen as an increasingly pointed series of protests at the direction the new regime was taking the country. Common to these novels is a distinctive combination of often veiled social criticism with elements of wider metaphysical and existential concerns, providing a counterpart in literary form to Tawfīq al-Ḥakīm's account of his loss of faith in the regime published as *ʿAwdat al-Waʿy* in 1974. The most interesting of this sequence of novels are, in my view, the first (*al-Liṣṣ wa-al-Kilāb*, 1961), the last (*Mīrāmār*, 1967) and *Tharthara fawq al-Nīl* (1966).[22] The first, *al-Liṣṣ wa-al-Kilāb*, is essentially a story of emotional and intellectual betrayal, revolving as it does around the outlawed Saʿīd, a thief newly released from prison, and his search to make sense of his life through revenge; betrayed both by his wife and by his former closest friend, his sole link with human values is provided by a kind-hearted prostitute, but the novel ends in a volley of gunfire, as Saʿīd is shot dead in a graveyard by the police. In *Tharthara fawq al-Nīl*, the profound sense of alienation already evident in *al-Liṣṣ wa-al-Kilāb* is further heightened and transposed to a different social group: set on a houseboat on the Nile, a setting clearly designed to restrict the work's spatial dimension while allowing an apparently endless scope for intense discussion, the novel revolves around a group of Cairo intellectuals who meet on the boat for drugs and sex. The overwhelming mood suggested by the novel is that of powerlessness, of an inability to influence events, and it is tempting, as several critics have done, to regard the novel as almost a prophecy of the 1967 disaster – but however appealing that interpretation may be on one level, the work also has a deeper relevance to the situation of mankind as a whole. Indeed, it is arguably the ability to combine universal relevance with local appeal that marks certain works of Maḥfūẓ off from those of his contemporaries, justifying the award of the Nobel Prize for Literature in 1988.

The last of Maḥfūẓ's novels belonging to this group, *Mīrāmār* (1967), is of importance not only for its continuation of the author's criticism of the course of revolutionary Egypt but also for its structural aspects. In terms of content, the novel represents an extraordinarily frank attack on the Arab Socialist Union as represented in particular by the opportunistic Sirḥān al-Buḥayrī; while in structural terms the novel uses an experimental technique, describing a single set of events through the eyes of four characters – a device already well-known in European fiction, but previously rare in writing in Arabic, though already employed by Fatḥī Ghānim in his novel *al-Rajul alladhī faqada ẓillahu* (1962).[23]

The above account of Maḥfūẓ's early and middle career, condensed as it is, should serve to convey at least some sense of the evolution of his work up to 1967. Unlike those of many other writers, Maḥfūẓ's novels appear to move through a number of fairly discrete phases: from his beginnings as a writer of historical novels, his work moves through a phase of social realism, culminating in the *Trilogy*, to be followed by a series of works in which religious, philosophical and metaphysical concerns are intertwined with an expression of disappointment, if not disgust, with the course of post-revolutionary Egyptian society.

Significantly, perhaps, Maḥfūẓ, who, as earlier noted, had stopped writing altogether for several years after the 1952 revolution, again appears to have undergone a period of self-imposed silence after the Six-Day War of 1967 and produced no further novels until the publication of *al-Marāyā* (1972), a series of vignettes of Egyptian characters arranged, rather curiously, in alphabetical order (he had, however, continued to produce short stories). He subsequently went on to produce a number of further novels, including, for example, works such as *Malḥamat al-Ḥarāfīsh* (1976) and *Riḥlat al-Faṭṭūma* (1982); but although a number of these works are of interest as mirroring some of the structural and thematic concerns of the younger generation (not least, in his return to the 'classical' Arabic heritage as a source of inspiration), much of his writing of this later period conveys a sense of a slightly 'tired' writer who had lost his capacity to surprise.

Social realism

In the meantime, however, a new generation of writers had begun to make their own distinctive mark on Egyptian prose in the wake of the 1952 Revolution, with an output marked by a distinctive realism and by a new slogan, 'commitment' (*iltizām*) – a slogan that had probably first been used about 1950 as a translation of Jean-Paul Sartre's *engagement* and which rapidly spread into most corners of the Arab world. Thrust into prominence by the Lebanese novelist and short-story writer Suhayl Idrīs, the first issue of whose periodical *al-Ādāb* appeared in January 1953, the precise implications of the term, which embraced both literary theory and Arab nationalism in a variety of combinations depending on the writer concerned, were hotly debated in a series of articles in *al-Ādāb* and elsewhere; in these debates, a 'generation gap' quickly became apparent – writers of the older generation such as Ṭāhā Ḥusayn and 'Abbās Maḥmūd al-'Aqqād generally adopting a position of 'art for art's sake' against the 'committed' writers and critics of the younger generation.

The attractiveness of the Sartrean concept of 'commitment' to Arab writers of this period has been generally, and almost certainly correctly, attributed to the political situation in which Egypt, and the Arab world generally, found itself at the end of the Second World War. The disastrous Palestinian War of 1948 leading to the foundation of the State of Israel had cast a shadow over Arab cultural life, but this had to some extent been alleviated by the new spirit of optimism and hope for the future that had followed the Egyptian Free Officers' Revolt of 1952. The new mood is almost certainly best epitomised in the Egyptian novelist 'Abd al-Raḥmān al-Sharqāwī's (1920–87) *al-Arḍ* (1954), described by Robin Ostle – on what evidence, I do not know – as 'arguably the most widely known piece of modern Arabic fiction both inside and outside the Near and Middle East'.[24] (The work is in fact probably better known to most Arabs through Yūsuf Shāhīn's popular film version than through the book itself.) Set in the early 1930s during the dictatorship of Ismā'īl Ṣidqī, the novel depicts a series of conflicts between the downtrodden inhabitants of a Delta village and the authorities: one conflict involves an attempt to deprive the villagers of the water needed for irrigation, while another involves a local land-owner's scheme to build a new road across the villagers' land. In the course of the novel, the author gives us a picture of a number of village 'types' – schoolteacher, smallholder, *'umda*, imam, etc. – the realism of the description being considerably enhanced by the use of vigorous colloquial Egyptian dialect for the dialogue. The novel is also of interest from a structural point of view, falling into three distinct sections, of which the first and third are narrated by a schoolboy returning from Cairo to the countryside for his summer holidays; by contrast, the central section reverts to a more conventional third-person narrative. In addition, the work is also of interest for its use of historical analogy – for which parallels can be found in both earlier and later works[25] – to comment on contemporary political and social developments; for although al-Sharqāwī was ostensibly writing of events during the 1930s, he was also at the same time almost certainly expressing an unspoken fear about the course of developments under the Free Officers' regime. As already noted, this device has often represented an obvious but often effective technique for evading the attentions of the censor, not only in Egypt but also elsewhere in the Arab world.

Unfortunately, although al-Sharqāwī went on to write three further novels (*Qulūb khāliya*, 1957; *al-Shawāri' al-khalfiyya*, 1958, and *al-Fallāḥ*, 1967), he was never able to repeat the success of *al-Arḍ* in capturing the brief period of optimism following the Free Officers' Revolt of 1952; at times, indeed, the later novels seem to degenerate into mere propaganda. The most interesting of the three is undoubtedly *al-Fallāḥ*, set – unlike its predecessors – after the revolution, by which time, the optimism of *al-Arḍ* appears to have vanished for good;[26] as we shall in the following chapter, in this respect, the evolution of al-Sharqāwī's attitudes mirrors that of an entire generation of writers.

The trend towards 'realism' and 'commitment' during this period was not confined to the novel, nor was it confined to Egypt: in one way or another, its effects extended to prose, poetry and theatre throughout the Arab world. Replacing 'romanticism' as the catchword of the moment, it was for much of the 1950s and 1960s an idea that no writer could ignore; despite their reservations, even writers of the older generation such as Tawfīq al-Ḥakīm, Yaḥyā Ḥaqqī and Maḥmūd Taymūr felt compelled to reflect the new 'spirit of the age' in their works. In the meantime, however, a new generation of writers was coming to the fore, both in Egypt and elsewhere, who did not share the assumptions of the previous generation and whose work reflects contemporary reality in a more direct way. Outstanding among Egyptian writers of this generation was the dramatist and short-story writer Yūsuf Idrīs (1927–91), originally trained as a doctor, whose first volume of short stories, *Arkhaṣ Layālī* (1954), was an immediate success – distinguished by the author's keen eye for the foibles of human behaviour across a wide social spectrum; for his evident concern for the subjects of his stories; and, equally importantly in the context of the ongoing debate about the merits of the use of colloquial Arabic in written discourse, for what appears to be a unique, and uniquely lively, blend of 'classical' and colloquial Egyptian Arabic. *Arkhaṣ Layālī* was quickly followed by a further four collections of short stories, in addition to a number of plays[27] and two novels, *Qiṣṣat Ḥubb* (1956) and *al-Ḥaram* (1959),[28] and the author quickly, and rightly, established a reputation as one of the leading writers of the Arab world.

Among other writers in Egypt who achieved prominence at around this time may be mentioned the woman writer Laṭīfa al-Zayyāt (1923–96), whose novel *al-Bāb al-maftūḥ* (1960), echoes to some degree the optimism of al-Sharqāwī's *al-Arḍ*: focusing on the issue of women's liberation, it skilfully intertwines the story of a girl coming to maturity with the quest for national independence. Al-Zayyāt has subsequently published a number of short stories, many also concerned with feminist issues, as well as a second novel, *Ṣāḥib al-bayt* (1994) and the partly autobiographical *Ḥamlat taftīsh: Awrāq shakhṣiyya* (1992).

Another novelist of the same generation whose work shows evidence of a 'committed' approach to literary values is Fatḥī Ghānim (1924–99), who for a time edited the periodical *Rūz al-Yūsuf* mentioned above. His first novel, *al-Jabal* (1959), set in Upper Egypt, deals with another facet of the clash between tradition and modernity, this time in the context of the resettlement of the villagers of Gurna; and although the novel is, from a literary point of view, not entirely successful,[29] it is of interest both for its general subject matter and for the author's use of the local dialect in the novel's dialogue. More successful and already well known to English-speaking readers through Desmond Stewart's translation,[30] is the same author's 'quartet', *al-Rajul alladhī faqada ẓillahu* (1961), covering the period 1922–56, an important contribution to the evolution of narrative technique in modern Arabic prose fiction, whose multi-narrator perspective was subsequently used by Najīb Maḥfūẓ in his novel *Mīrāmār* (1967). Fatḥī Ghānim subsequently went on to publish a number of further novels, including *Qalīl min al-ḥubb wa-kathīr min al-ʿunf* (1985), whose concern with the 'open-door' policies of contemporary Egypt echoes that of some of the so-called 'generation of the sixties';[31] but it is probably not unfair to say that by this stage, his work had been somewhat eclipsed by that of younger writers. The Upper Egyptian setting of Fatḥī Ghānim's *al-Jabal*, however, also reappears in many of the writings of Yaḥyā al-Ṭāhir ʿAbd Allāh (1938–81), who was himself a native of the area; ʿAbd Allāh began writing in 1961 and published five volumes of short stories and three novels during his lifetime[32] – the impact of his writing, which owes something to the popular oral tradition, being considerably enhanced by his habit of reciting his works in the cafés of Cairo.

Despite its dominance by Najīb Maḥfūẓ, the period under discussion was also the period in which other parts of the Arab world, most of which had hitherto lagged behind Egypt in terms of fictional writing, began to account for a greater proportion of the published output of Arabic novels and short stories. In particular, it was at this point that Arabic fictional writing in North Africa (Tunisia, Algeria, Morocco) began to achieve a standard and assume an importance comparable to that of the Mashriq, as the countries of North Africa threw off the yoke of French domination, and the Arabic language began to assume a greater importance relative to French in the cultural life of the area. Meanwhile, in the eastern part of the Arab world, Lebanon, Syria and Iraq – all of which had seen the publication of important contributions to the development of the Arabic novel before the Second World War – saw a continuation of this tradition, while the same period also saw the emergence for the first time of a new generation of Palestinian writers writing in the context of the aftermath of the 1948 War and the establishment of the state of Israel.

Space forbids more than a brief account of some of the main developments and most significant writers during this period. In Syria and Lebanon, two novelists in particular stand out as having made a significant contribution to the development of prose fiction during this period: the Syro-Lebanese Ḥalīm Barakāt (1936–),[33] and the Syrian Ḥannā Mīnā (1924–). Although the work of these two men is in some respects very different, reflecting their different backgrounds and careers, both exemplify more general trends in the development of the Arabic novel and short story during the 1950s and 1960s. Born in Syria but brought up in Lebanon, Ḥalīm Barakāt has made important contributions to the field of Middle Eastern studies as a sociologist and political scientist that go beyond the area of imaginative literature, but his novels and short stories reflect his attitudes in his non-fictional works in their Arab nationalist orientation and their concern with contemporary issues, in particular that of the Palestinians. Of the half dozen or so novels that he has published so far, two in particular stand out: *Sittat Ayyām* (1961) and *ʿAwdat al-ṭāʾir ilā al-baḥr* (1969), both concerned with conflicts related to the Palestinian question.

Despite its 'prophetic' title, Ḥalīm Barakāt's *Sittat Ayyām* does not refer to the Six-Day War of 1967, but deals rather with the fighting of 1948, in particular the efforts of the inhabitants of Dayr al-Baḥr to resist the Israeli siege of their town. The novel cannot be entirely accounted a success from a literary point of view, for despite the author's bold attempt to 'get inside' the mentality of the villagers he is portraying, he is unable to resist the temptation to inject lengthy comments of his own. The second novel to be mentioned, *ʿAwdat al-ṭāʾir ilā al-baḥr*,[34] which revolves around the events of the 1967 War itself, has deservedly received greater critical acclaim; structurally adventurous, the book conveys a vivid picture of the drama of these few days, which for the Arabs not only led to a convincing military defeat but also, for many, finally exposed the hypocrisy of the Arab governments concerned, as their manipulation of the news media collapsed. To quote Roger Allen again, 'Barakāt's work stands out as one of the most effective commentaries on the 1967 débâcle and its implications, and ... it will remain a monument of Arabic fiction written during this century.'[35]

In contrast to that of the intellectual Barakāt, Ḥannā Mīnā's background was a genuinely working-class one. Born in Latakia, on the Syrian coast – an environment that explains the prominence of the sea in many of his works – Ḥannā Mīnā found employment in several capacities during his early life: in addition to journalism, a profession that has commonly accompanied creative writing in the modern Arab world, he worked for a period as a stevedore and a barber, and was imprisoned for a time for his political activities. The early works of Ḥannā Mīnā, who may be regarded as one of Syria's leading novelists (perhaps, indeed, the greatest of them all), fall squarely into the category of 'social realism', being marked by the same attitude of 'commitment' that marks the works of the Egyptian ʿAbd al-Raḥmān al-Sharqāwī. A prolific writer, his first novel, *al-Maṣābīḥ al-zurq* (1954), takes as its main theme the struggle against French imperialism during the Second World War, but is marred (like many 'committed' works of this period) by a failure to integrate the writer's political message into the narrative satisfactorily. The author's technique, however, shows an increasing maturity with the progress of time: his second novel, *al-Shirāʿ wa-al-ʿāṣifa* (1966), often discussed by critics against the background of

Hemingway's *The Old Man and the Sea*, continues the theme of struggle of the first work, with an increased emphasis on class conflict; later works, which show a further development and maturity of technique, include an autobiographical novel, *Baqāyā Ṣuwar* (1974).[36]

The same period that saw the first publications of Ḥalīm Barakāt and Ḥannā Mīnā also witnessed the beginnings of a phenomenon apparently unique to Lebanon in the modern Arab world – the emergence of a group of women writers whose works were not only written from a distinctively 'feminine' perspective, but who also have some claim to be considered a distinct 'sub-group' within the national literary culture of the time. Dominated as their writings are by the Lebanese Civil War of 1975–90, a fuller account of the 'Beirut Decentrists', as Miriam Cooke has termed them, must await the following chapter; for now, it suffices to note that among the women writers coming to prominence during this period were Imilī (Emily) Naṣr Allāh, whose first novel, *Ṭuyūr Aylūl* (1962), a work of partly autobiographical inspiration, explores the fate of women seeking to tread an independent path in the modern world, and Colette Khūrī and Laylā Ba'labakkī, both of whose works earned them notoriety (and in Ba'labakkī's case, even arrest) for breaking the bounds of what was apparently acceptable for a writer – in particular, a woman writer – to publish at the time. Colette Khūrī's novel *Ayyām ma'ahu* (1958?), is an account of a love affair between a young woman and an older man, commonly supposed to be the Syrian poet Nizār Qabbānī,[37] a theme which also finds echoes in Ba'labakkī's novel *al-Āliha al-mamsūkha* (1960); better known among Laylā Ba'labakkī's works, however, are her first novel, *Anā aḥyā* (1958), which revolves around the place of women in the family, and in particular her short story 'Safīnat ḥanān ilā al-qamar' (1964), for which she was arrested for offences against public morality.[38]

In Iraq, also, a number of significant prose writers were emerging during this period, the most prominent among them being Ghā'ib Ṭu'ma Farmān (1927–90), Ismā'īl Fahd Ismā'īl and Fu'ād al-Takarlī. The career of Ghā'ib Ṭu'ma Farmān well illustrates the precarious lives that many Arab intellectuals, not least Iraqis, and not least leftists, have perforce for political reasons been obliged to lead in the period following the Second World War: born in Baghdad, Farmān taught in Lebanon and Egypt before returning to Baghdad after the 1958 revolution, but for much of his professional life he worked as a translator in Moscow. His first publications were short stories (*Ḥasīd al-raḥā*, 1954; *Mawlūd ākhar*, 1960); these he followed, however, with some eight full-length novels, published between 1966 and 1989, of which the best known is perhaps *Khamsat aṣwāt* (1967), which analyses the state of Iraqi society in the lead up to the 1958 revolution as seen by five different characters drawn from the Baghdad bourgeoisie. The novel is interesting not only from the point of view of its technique, but also for its conclusion, which depicts Sa'īd, one of the principal characters, taking leave of his father as he departs for abroad – a situation that would find a resonance not only with the particular author of the novel but indeed with many Arab intellectuals of this time.

To the same period belong the early works of Fu'ād al-Takarlī,[39] whose novella *al-Wajh al-ākhar* (1960)[40] presents a vivid picture of the miserable life of a debt-ridden minor official; much of the author's concern, as elsewhere in his work, is here with the complexities and psychology of male-female relationships in traditional Iraqi society.[41] An accomplished and painstakingly careful author, who has published relatively little by comparison with many of his contemporaries, al-Takarlī's work deserves to be better known, not only in the West but also in other parts of the Arab world – one factor militating against this being the frequent use that he makes, like Ghā'ib Ṭu'ma Farmān, of Iraqi colloquial in the dialogues of many of his works.

The preoccupation with the Palestinian question evident in the works of Ḥalīm Barakāt was during this period also beginning to be reflected in the emergence of a generation of writers from Palestine itself, for whom the Palestinian problem was, in its most literal sense, their own problem. The most prominent and talented of this new group of Palestinian writers was undoubtedly Ghassān Kanafānī (1936–72), whose career combined that of imaginative writer with that of political activist, paying the ultimate price when he was assassinated in a car bomb explosion, almost certainly planted by Israeli agents, in 1972. Born in Acre, Kanafānī had direct experience of the displacement of the Palestinians, being expelled in 1948 with his family first to Lebanon, then to Syria, where he studied Arabic literature at the University of Damascus; he then worked as a journalist in Kuwait before returning in 1960 to Beirut, where he continued his journalistic activities, in addition to serving as official spokesman for the Popular Front for the Liberation of Palestine (PFLP) and editor of its official journal *al-Hadaf*.

Not surprisingly, Kanafānī's personal experiences are directly reflected in his works, which include novels, short story collections, plays and literary criticism. His personal experience of the family's uprooting from its home is directly expressed in his writing, being poignantly conveyed most obviously, perhaps, in the short story 'Arḍ al-burtuqāl al-ḥazīn', which describes the progress of his family from their home in Acre across the border to Lebanon following the establishment of the State of Israel in 1948. What marks Kanafānī out from many other Palestinian authors of his generation is, however, his humanism; despite his intense involvement in Palestinian politics, he always maintained that he was novelist first, politician second, and many critics have remarked on his sympathetic portrayals of Israeli Jews on an individual basis. The elderly Jewish refugees, for example in *'Ā'id ilā Ḥayfā* (1969), receive a sympathetic portrayal and show little of the propagandist stereotyping of many other Palestinian works of that period.

Both Kanafānī's style and outlook appear to have undergone an almost continuous process of evolution during his career, his fiction mirroring the shift in his political beliefs towards a stricter Marxist orientation, while remaining technically adventurous and innovative to the end. The most successful of his seven novels (of which three remained unfinished at his death), however, are undoubtedly the first, *Rijāl fī al-shams* (1963),[42] and *Mā tabaqqā lakum* (1966).[43] The first of these – a graphic story of 'people smuggling', culminating in the death by suffocation of a group of Palestinians in a tanker on the Kuwait–Iraq border – remains one of the most powerful expressions in the whole of modern literature of the hapless fate of the Palestinian people, not only oppressed by the Israelis but exploited by their fellow Arabs; the second, *Mā tabaqqā lakum*, displays an increasing interest in narrative technique, alternating as the author does between first- and third-person narrative as he subtly documents the intersecting destinies of the five 'heroes' of his novel: Ḥāmid, Maryam, Zakariyyā, Time and the Desert.[44] Despite the author's obvious technical mastery, Kanafānī's later works, in particular the short-story cycle named after Umm Sa'd (1969),[45] sometimes appear flat and lacking in inspiration compared with his earlier fiction; overall, however, in its combination of artistic sophistication with commitment to the Palestinian cause, Kanafānī's tragically abbreviated writing career represents one of the most successful attempts to deal with the Palestinian issue in a way that elevates it to universal significance.

A somewhat different expression of the Palestinian experience of exile may be seen in the life and works of Jabrā Ibrāhīm Jabrā (1920–94). Born in Bethlehem, Jabrā studied first in Jerusalem, before embarking on further study in Cambridge, England and in the United States. His subsequent career included academic appointments in Jerusalem and Baghdad, and for a time he was employed by the Iraqi Ministry of Culture and Information. A prolific and versatile artist, who expressed himself through painting and art criticism as well as through writing, Jabrā's written publications include not only novels and short stories, but also essays, two volumes of autobiography, and three volumes of verse, much of it in the form of prose poetry. Like Kanafānī's, Jabrā's writing is shot through with the personal experience of exile, but unlike Kanafānī's, his most memorable characters are intellectuals, usually drawn from the middle classes, and typically alienated from the society in which they live: in this respect, his works provide a link between the publications of the 'classic' generation of modern Arab writers, and those of the generation (to be discussed in the following chapter) that came to prominence after the Arab defeat in the 1967 war with Israel.

Jabrā's prose works include not only novels and short stories in Arabic but also a work of fiction written in English, *Hunters in a Narrow* Street (1960) and a novel *'Ālam bi-lā kharā'iṭ* (1982), co-authored with the Saudi novelist

'Abd al-Raḥmān Munīf;[46] literary outlook aside, the two novelists had a considerable amount of experience in common, not least the experience of exile, and employment in posts connected with the oil industry. Jabrā's best known work, however, is probably the novel *al-Safīna*,[47] which is set on a Greek cruise ship in the Mediterranean. It involves a complex cast of characters, intellectuals for the most part, whose relationships, with all their hopes and frustrations, are worked out during the course of a week-long cruise from Beirut to Athens, through the Corinth Canal, then through the Straits of Messina to Naples. Jabrā's narrative technique is both complex and assured, involving as it does the use of temporal flashbacks and multiple narrators (possibly owing something to Maḥfūẓ's *Mīrāmār*), combined with a copious use of symbolism, and multiple references to works of Western literature that reflect the author's own omnivorous intellectual tastes. The plot of the novel has been described by one commentator as having 'a soap opera-like quality',[48] but although this description may have some validity in terms of the complex shifts in relationships between partners, it is patently misleading in terms of the work's intellectual tone and stylistic register, which often reaches the level of prose poetry. An added poignancy is given to the work by the lengthy account of the battle for Jerusalem in 1948 and by the description of the Jerusalem house that clearly represents Jabrā's own family home in his lost city.

Of Jabrā's later works, mention may be made in particular of *al-Baḥth 'an Walīd Mas'ūd* (1978), in which the author continues his experimentation with the formal aspects of narrative structure in a way that recalls the technique used by one of the Egyptian pioneers of the 'generation of the sixties', Ṣun' Allāh Ibrāhīm (1937–), to be discussed in the following chapter. Like Ṣun' Allāh Ibrāhīm's *Najmat Aghusṭus*, *al-Baḥth 'an Walīd Mas'ūd* revolves around a section of concentrated text that forms a focus for the work as a whole. In the case of *al-Baḥth 'an Walīd Mas'ūd*, the text consists of a taped message left behind by Walīd Mas'ūd in an abandoned car found near the Iraqi–Syrian border; the tape is an almost 'Joycean' stream-of-consciousness narrative that serves as a focus for his friends who gather to mourn his death – each of his friends in turn mirroring some aspect of the vanished man.

Arabic fictional writing in North Africa

Little has been said so far about Morocco, Algeria or Tunisia, in all of which countries fictional writing had remained conspicuously undeveloped by comparison with the central Arab world until at least the 1950s. In Tunisia, the most developed of the Maghrib states in literary terms, the 1930s had witnessed the establishment of a number of literary periodicals such as *al-'Ālam al-adabī*; but despite the efforts of writers such as 'Alī al-Du'ājī and the slightly idiosyncratic

Maḥmūd al-Mas'adī, it was not until the 1950s that the Tunisian novel can be said to have come of age, in the hands of the novelist and short-story writer al-Bashīr Khurayyif (1917–83).[49] Khurayyif's career is itself an interesting one, for he had begun publishing as long ago as the 1930s, but opposition to his use of Tunisian dialect in the dialogue of his stories discouraged him, and it was not until the late 1950s that he began to come to prominence, with his novel *Iflās aw ḥubbuk darbānī* (1958–9), on the conflict between tradition and modernity. This work was followed by the historical novel *Barq al-layl* (1961), set in the period of Hafsid domination of Tunisia in the first half of the sixteenth century, and which clearly invites the reader to draw an analogy between the Spanish invasion of 1535 and the French occupation of Tunisia in more modern times; the technique recalls that of Najīb Maḥfūẓ's early work *Kifāḥ Ṭība*, or that of the later writer Jamāl al-Ghīṭānī in *al-Zaynī Barakāt*.[50] Khurayyif's best-known work, *al-Dijla fī 'arājīnihā* (1969), set in the Nefta oasis of southern Tunisia where the author was born, revolves around the lives and loves of an extended Tunisian family between around 1910 and 1930, which the author depicts with sympathy but without idealisation; divided into sections entitled *'arjūns*, the branches of the family are mirrored by the branches of the date-palm itself. Although the appeal of this work has been limited by the author's generous use of Tunisian colloquial, the novel has been widely acknowledged as one of the triumphs of modern Arabic realism.

In Algeria, despite a surge of literary activity in the years following the end of the First World War, the growth of a tradition of imaginative prose literature in Arabic was hampered by the increasingly oppressive hold of the French, and the French language, on the cultural life of the country, and by the increasingly bloody struggle for independence from the colonial power. Much prose literature in Arabic was dominated by themes related to the War of Liberation, and it was not until considerably after independence from France had finally been achieved in 1962 that a number of novelists of international stature, including most notably Abdelhamid Benhedouga, Rachid Boujedra and al-Ṭāhir Waṭṭār began to emerge. In Morocco, though the political and military struggle for independence was less intense than in Algeria, the linguistic interplay between Arabic and French (not to mention Berber) has remained a more complex one.[51] Despite this, the development of Arabic prose literature in Morocco seems to have undergone a roughly similar process of evolution as in Algeria, with the first prose fiction appearing hesitantly in the 1920s; these hesitant first steps began to come to fruition in the 1940s and 1950s, although the fictional techniques employed during this phase remained rather limited, and much Moroccan writing in Arabic retained a somewhat didactic tone. It is not entirely for linguistic reasons that Francophone Moroccan writers of this period such as Driss Chraïbi (1926–) are better known in the West than are their counterparts writing in Arabic. By the 1960s, however, a number of Arabic writers were beginning to emerge who could claim to hold their own against practitioners of their art further east in the Arab world: these included ʿAbd Allāh al-ʿArawī (1933–),[52] better known for his intellectual and historical studies and fiction; Mubārak Rabīʿ (1935–); and ʿAbd al-Karīm Ghallāb (1917–). Of these, the last named is perhaps the most significant, providing a graphic illustration of the extent to which the struggle for independence dominated the output of many fiction writers in the Maghreb during this period: *Sabʿat abwāb* (1965) recounts the tales of prisoners who have been tortured for their nationalist activities, while *Dafannā al-māḍī* (1966) reflects the social contradictions and tensions under the French occupation through its portrayal of the different members of a family in Fez.

Conclusion

It is clear that in our account of Arabic fiction between Tawfīq al-Ḥakīm's *ʿAwdat al-Rūḥ*, with which this chapter opened, and publications such as *al-Baḥth ʿan Walīd Masʿūd*, we have covered a good deal of ground not only in terms of thematic content and of narrative technique but also in terms of the geographical spread of Western-style fictional writing. Early developments, as already noted, were largely confined to Egypt and Greater Syria, with the Mahjar writers (in particular, Jubrān Khalīl Jubrān) acting as a bridge between contemporary Western fiction and early practitioners of the art in the Middle East itself, contributing their own distinctive strand to the development of modern Arabic prose as well as to Arabic poetry. Following the death of Jubrān in 1931, however, Mahjar writing began to lose its vibrancy, at least in North America; Jubrān's close colleague Mīkhā'īl Nuʿayma, for example, returned to his native Lebanon in 1932, and no writers of comparable stature appear to have emerged in the Americas during the following generation. Although, as we have seen, Egyptian authors remained central to developments during this period, from the late 1930s competent novelists and short story writers increasingly began to emerge in other parts of the Eastern Arab world, to be joined rather later by writers in Arabic of the Maghrib countries.

Central to the rapid and substantive development of the Arabic novel during this period was, of course, the Nobel prize-winning Najīb Maḥfūẓ, whose output dominated prose writing in Arabic during the 1950s and 1960s and whose works provide almost a barometer of changing tastes for much of this period. By the time of the mid-1960s, however, it was clear that the optimistic outlook of immediate post-revolutionary Egypt was no longer in tune with the times, and that the invitation to literary and political 'commitment' that had resonated through much, if not most, of the Arab world, during the 1950s had outlived its usefulness as a rallying cry for 'progressive' writers. The new mood of pessimism that is often dated from the Arab defeat in the Six-Day War of 1967 but which in fact had begun to be apparent considerably before that will be discussed in the following chapter; ironically, as we shall see, far from hindering the development of creative writing, the new mood has led to an explosion of experimentation in which the influence of classical, medieval Arabic models can often be felt no less than that of avant-garde Western narrative.

Notes

1 For a fuller account of Tawfīq al-Ḥakīm's life, see Chapter 10 below, pp. 178–86.
2 For a more detailed discussion, see Starkey, *From the Ivory Tower*, pp. 84–92.
3 Al-Ḥakīm also published a fifth novel, *Ḥimār al-Ḥakīm* (1940), but this is inferior artistically and of no significance in the present context.
4 See Starkey, *From the Ivory Tower*, 140–53. The novel has been translated into English by Abba Eban as *The Maze of Justice* (London, 1947; new edn, with foreword by P. H. Newby, London, 1989).
5 Translated by M. M. Badawi as *Sara*, Cairo, 1978.
6 For a discussion of *Millīm al-akbar*, see Kilpatrick, *The Modern Egyptian Novel*, pp. 60–5.
7 Kilpatrick, ibid., pp. 65–71.
8 For whom, see below, Chapter 9, p. 169.
9 See Trevor LeGassick, introduction to Ihsan 'Abd al-Quddus, *I Am Free and Other Stories*, Cairo, 1978.
10 For a discussion of whom, in particular his novel *Shams al-Kharīf*, see Sakkut, *The Egyptian Novel and Its Main Trends*, pp. 41–5.
11 On al-Sibāʿī, see Gail Ramsay, *The Novels of an Egyptian Romanticist: Yūsuf al-Sibāʿī*, Edsbruk, 1996.
12 Translated into English by Leslie McLoughlin as *Death in Beirut*, London, 1976. The date of publication of this work, after the 1967 catastrophe, places it more properly chronologically in the following chapter.
13 Discussed above in Chapter 4, pp. 73–5.
14 And ultimately, therefore, from Rifāʿa Rāfiʿ al-Ṭahṭāwī's *Takhlīṣ al-ibrīz ilā talkhīṣ Bārīz*, for which see above pp. 27–8.
15 For a discussion, see R. C. Ostle, 'Mahmūd al-Masʿadī and Tunisia's "Lost Generation"', *JAL* 8 (1977), pp. 155–66.
16 For whom, see above, p. 71.
17 For al-Saḥḥār, see Sakkut, *The Egyptian Novel*, pp. 112–13. As Sakkut notes, al-Saḥḥār's contribution to Egyptian life was more significant as a publisher than as an author in his own right.
18 For whom, see above, p. 119.
19 For which, see above, p. 100.
20 *Bayn al-Qaṣrayn* (1956), *Qaṣr al-Shawq* (1957) and *al-Sukkariyya* (1957). For details of the extensive secondary literature on Maḥfūẓ, see the bibliography below, in particular El-Enany, *The Pursuit of Meaning*, London, 1993, which includes a useful

'Guide to Further Reading'.

21 Translated into English by P. Stewart as *Children of Gebelawi*, London, 1981.

22 Other novels forming part of this sequence include *al-Summān wa-al-kharīf* (1962), *al-Ṭarīq* (1964) and *al-Shaḥḥādh* (1965).

23 Translated into English by Desmond Stewart as *The Man Who Lost His Shadow*, London, 1980.

24 Introduction to *Egyptian Earth*, tr. Desmond Stewart, London, 1992.

25 See below, for example, p. 144, for a discussion of Jamāl al-Ghītanī's *al-Zaynī Barakāt*.

26 For a discussion, see Kilpatrick, *The Modern Egyptian Novel*, pp. 126–40.

27 For which, see below, p. 188.

28 Yūsuf Idrīs has generally been accounted less successful as a novelist than as a short-story writer and playwright. On Yūsuf Idrīs generally, see Allen, *Critical Perspectives on Yūsuf Idrīs*, Colorado Springs, 1994; D. Cohen-Mor, *Yūsuf Idrīs: Changing Visions*, Potomac, MD, 1992.

29 See Allen, The *Arabic Novel*, pp. 82–4, for a discussion.

30 *The Man Who Lost His Shadow*, London, 1980.

31 For whom, see the following chapter.

32 A collection of short stories entitled *The Mountain of Green Tea* has been translated into English by Denys Johnson-Davies, London, 1991.

33 Ḥalīm Barakāt was born in Syria but raised in Beirut, where he subsequently worked as a university lecturer before moving to the US in 1976.

34 Translated into English by Trevor LeGassick as *Days of Dust*, Wilmette, Illinois, 1974. For a discussion, see Allen, *The Arabic Novel*, pp. 114–20.

35 Ibid., p. 120.

36 English version, as *Fragments of Memory*, tr. L. Kenny and O. Kenny, Austin, 1993.

37 For whom, see above, Chapters 4 and 5, pp. 76–7, 91.

38 The latter has been translated into English by Denys Johnson-Davies as 'Spaceship of tenderness to the moon', in *Modern Arabic Short Stories*, London, 1976, 126–34.

39 Sometimes transliterated as al-Tikirlī.

40 Sometimes described (less accurately, in my view) as a short story collection. See, for example, *EAL*, II, 755, s.v. An expanded edition of the work was later published in 1982.

41 See Wiebke Walther, 'Distant Echoes of Love in the Narrative Work of Fu'ād al-Tikirlī', in Allen, Kilpatrick and de Moor (eds), *Love and Sexuality in Modern Arabic Literature*, pp. 131–9.

42 English translation as *Men in the Sun* by Hilary Kilpatrick, Washington, DC, 1985.

43 English translation as *All That's Left to You* by Mayy Jayyusi and Jeremy Reed, Austin, Texas, 1990.

44 See *al-Āthār al-kāmila*, Beirut, 1972, I, p. 159. For a discussion of the novel, see Allen, *The Arabic Novel*, pp. 108–14.

45 Translated as *Palestine's Children* by Barbara Harlow, Washington, DC, 1985.

46 Discussed in the following chapter, pp. 154–5.

47 English translation, as *The Ship*, by A. Haydar and R. Allen, Washington, DC, 1983; for a discussion of the work, see Allen, *The Arabic Novel*, pp. 138–44.

48 Stefan Meyer, *The Experimental Arabic Novel*, p. 37.

49 For general accounts of Tunisian literature, see J. Fontaine, *La littérature tunisienne*

contemporaine, Paris, 1991; also, S. Pantuček, *Tunesische Literaturgeschichte*, Wiesbaden, 1974.

50 Discussed in the following chapter, pp. 144.

51 On this, see J. Kaye and A. Zoubir, *The Ambiguous Compromise*, London, 1990.

52 Also spelled al-ʿIrwī, French spelling Laroui.

8

The sixties generation and beyond

The previous chapters have described the development of the Arabic novel and short story through overlapping phases in which a number of distinct trends can be identified: a historical novel, a romantic trend, a realistic trend, and a later 'social realistic' approach that mirrored the emerging political realities of the Middle East in the period following the Second World War. As has already been seen, this last-named approach, with its distinctive catchword of 'commitment' (*iltizām*) was a comparatively short-lived phenomenon, for even by the late 1950s, the initial naïve optimism induced by the 1952 Free Officers' Revolution in Egypt was beginning to wear thin. This disillusionment can be seen as one of the two main characteristics evident in the series of novels produced by Najīb Maḥfūẓ between 1961 and 1967, the other being an increasing appetite for experimentation in terms of formal structure; and it is indeed these two very characteristics that provide the main impetus for many of the new generation of novelists.

Although the sense of disillusionment that characterises much Arab prose writing (and poetry) from the end of the 1960s has often been held to spring directly from the Arab defeat in the Six-Day War of 1967, the seeds of that disillusionment in fact date from considerably earlier. Indeed, although it was undoubtedly the Six-Day War that most obviously crystallised Arab feelings of political and cultural impotence during this period, most literary critics give the credit for producing the first work of the new trend to a work that actually first appeared in 1966 – Ṣun' Allāh Ibrāhīm's (1937–) novella *Tilka al-rā'iḥa*. Be that as it may, it was not long before a group of intellectuals, predominantly but not exclusively Egyptian, began to come together, driven by a common sense of purpose, to publish their output in a new literary and cultural magazine, *Gallery 68*, eight issues of which appeared between 1968 and 1971; the magazine was edited by, among others, Edwār al-Kharrāṭ (1926–), himself one of the most innovative writers of his generation. Generally known as the 'generation of the sixties',[1] many of these writers shared a number of characteristics, both of attitude and experience: most were politically 'committed', but usually in a more outspoken way than the more optimistic generation of al-Sharqāwī, and their characteristic mood was one of rejection, disillusion and self-doubt rather than optimism. Many, like Ṣunʿ Allāh Ibrāhīm himself, had been, or still were, avowed Marxists, and many, again like Ibrāhīm, had been imprisoned for their political views. At the same time, their self-doubt was combined, in the case of the best writers at least, with a powerful desire to find a new literary orientation for themselves, redefining the role of the writer in Arab society and allowing them to express the attitudes and feelings of the new generation. In many cases, this process has involved a rediscovery of different aspects of the classical Arabic literary heritage, including popular literature and folklore, which, combined with an acquaintance with Western modernist techniques, has provided a basis for an explosion of richly variegated fictional writing across the Arab world.

The 'father figure' of this group of writers, Edwār al-Kharrāṭ himself, was somewhat older than most of the so-called generation of the sixties, and had published his first collection of short stories, *Ḥīṭān ʿĀliya*, as long ago as 1958, but it was not until the late 1960s that he began to come to prominence as a writer of distinctively modernist Arabic fiction; indeed, he might by some yardsticks almost be labelled a 'late developer', for his first full-length novel, *Rāma wa-al-Tinnīn*,[2] did not appear until 1979. The work, however, which revolves around the relationship between the Copt Mīkhā'īl and the Muslim Rāma, was immediately, and justifiably, acclaimed on its appearance as a landmark in contemporary Arabic writing, and with its subtle interweaving of memory, dream and reality, not to mention the author's subtly erudite use of intertextuality, it was almost at once compared with the work of Proust. The relationship between Mīkhā'īl and Rāma (a daring one in itself, in view of the taboos on relationships between Muslim women and non-Muslim men) ranges between the mystical and the overtly sexual; but the work also presents the reader with a vivid picture of Egyptian life in the post-war period, complete with the full apparatus of a police state and its attendant horrors of torture, imprisonment and exile. Moreover, despite an occasional initial impression of meandering, al-Kharrāṭ's language in *Rāma wa-al-Tinnīn*, like that of both his earlier and his subsequent works, is both rich and precise, revealing a mastery of the Arabic language in all its varied registers that considerably surpasses that of most of his contemporaries, as well as making considerable demands on the reader.

The theme of *Rāma wa-al-Tinnīn* was continued in *al-Zaman al-Ākhar* (1985), in which Mīkhā'īl and Rāma resume their relationship after a chance meeting at a conference, and many images from the work also reappear in al-Kharrāṭ's later novels, including the semi-autobiographical *Turābuhā zaʿfarān* (1985), which relives the memories of Mīkhā'īl as a boy in the Alexandria of the 1930s and 1940s. The city of Alexandria also provides the setting for the slightly older Mīkhā'īl of *Yā Banāt Iskandariyya* (1990). In *Ḥijārat Būbillū* (1992), it is the countryside of the Egyptian Delta that provides the setting for a series of reminiscences from the author's childhood; the change of location, however, does little to affect the prominence of the age-old themes that haunt all of al-Kharrāṭ's fictional work – in particular, that of woman as a life-force with neither beginning nor end.[3]

Despite some points of affinity between al-Kharrāṭ's work and that of other authors emerging during the 1960s, al-Kharrāṭ remains a unique voice in modern Egyptian, indeed in modern Arabic, literature. Other authors of the so-called 'sixties generation' have each evolved their own preferred styles and modes of expression, usually involving a directness – even bluntness – quite alien to the subtle intellectuality of al-Kharrāṭ. As an early example of the so-called *adab al-sujūn* ('prison literature'), for example, Ṣun' Allāh Ibrāhīm's partly autobiographically based *Tilka al-Rā'iḥa* conveys a sense of alienation that at times is almost overpowering: the narrator, who has been released from prison on parole, leads a humdrum existence, restlessly moving from place to place in Cairo, recording the minutiae of his daily routines and joyless sexual encounters in a language stripped of all but the barest essentials, his movements monitored in the meantime by the prison authorities. Both the technique and the mood immediately suggest European influences, or at least, parallels, a hint of one of them being provided by a reference to Camus in the text itself.[4] In sum, the rootlessness and meaninglessness of life as reflected in much post-Second World War European fiction appears here transposed, with a remarkable sureness and consistency of technique, to the oppressive, post-revolutionary regime of contemporary Nasserist Cairo.

Ṣun' Allāh Ibrāhīm's *Tilka al-rā'iḥa* immediately gained a controversial reputation on its publication not only for the heated reaction that it provoked in the censor's office, but also for the controversy it aroused among the Egyptian literary establishment – the author Yaḥyā Ḥaqqī, for example, remarking that he found one scene 'absolutely disgusting'.[5] Banned in Egypt, the work reappeared two years later in an edition from which all passages containing political criticism or sexually explicit material had been removed; and despite the appearance of Johnson-Davies's English translation of the full text in 1971, the complete text was not published in Arabic, by a Moroccan publishing house, until 1986. The publishing history of this work is of interest not merely in itself but also as an illustration of the sorts of pressures frequently faced on an almost daily basis by Arab writers not only in Egypt but throughout much of the Middle East, where formal and informal political and religious censorship, in various combinations, make publication a considerably more hazardous activity than in most Western societies.[6]

Undeterred by the reception of *Tilka al-rā'iḥa*, Ṣun' Allāh Ibrāhīm has in the forty or so years following, produced a varied series of novels that, while not all equally accomplished from a literary point of view, have continued to attract considerable interest in Egyptian intellectual circles and beyond. *Najmat aghusṭus* (1974), a work based partly at least on a journey made to Upper Egypt by the author in the summer of 1965 with Kamāl al-Qalash and Ra'ūf Mus'ad, is a satirical account of the building of the Aswan High Dam that is also of interest for its formal construction – the first and third of the three parts into which it is divided being written in a matter-of-fact, first-person, narrative style, while the second (the shortest) consists of a single sentence extending over several pages, in which dream and reality are interwoven. His most successful novel, however, is almost certainly *al-Lajna* (1981), which represents one of the most powerful attacks on dictatorship in the modern Arab world: the narrator receives an order from an unnamed 'Committee' to write an account of the most eminent contemporary Arab personality, but before he can record his conclusions, he is condemned to 'eat himself'.[7] As in the author's previous works, irony here plays a large part, the narrator's desperate situation being constantly juxtaposed with the Committee's assurances that he is free.

In his subsequent novels, Ṣun' Allāh Ibrāhīm appears to have eschewed the small-scale format of the novella that he had so successfully used in *Tilka al-Rā'iḥa* and *al-Lajna*, preferring a larger canvas on which to paint his distinctive vision of the modern world. *Bayrūt Bayrūt* (1984), which derives its inspiration from the Lebanese civil war of 1975–90, sees the narrator flying to Beirut to find a publisher for his latest book – a concern that forms a sort of counterpoint to the second literary enterprise on which he is engaged, the writing of a commentary on the Lebanese civil war itself. The novel is of interest as one of the few examples of an Egyptian novel set in another part of the Arab world – a characteristic which it shares with the later and more complex *Warda* (2002), the subject of which revolves around the war of liberation in Dhofar at the end of the 1960s and early 1970s, and whose location shifts back and forth between Cairo, Beirut, Muscat and the towns and desert of the southern Arabian Peninsula. In contrast to these works, narrated wholly or largely in the first person, stand *Dhāt* (1992) and *Sharaf* (1997), satirical critiques of Egyptian society in which the author uses irony and sarcasm to often devastating effect: the enigmatically entitled *Dhāt*[8] represents an attack on the commercialisation of Egyptian life that followed the introduction of President Sadat's 'open-door' economic policy in the 1970s, while the later *Sharaf* uses a Cairo prison as a symbol for Egyptian society generally, providing an ideal setting for the author to bring together the themes of corruption, hypocrisy and sexual frustration conspicuous in his earlier novels, with a new emphasis on religious fanaticism that reflects a shift in Egyptian society itself. Both novels further illustrate the author's taste for structural experimentation, with their deliberate patterning of narrative modes:[9] *Dhāt*'s nineteen chapters (written largely in third-person, 'omniscient narrator' mode) alternate between chapters chronicling the life of an ordinary Egyptian family in the 1970s and 1980s, and chapters dealing with contemporary Egypt at a national and international level; while the chapters of *Sharaf* for the most part alternate between first-person and third-person narrative.[10] A conspicuous feature of *Dhāt* in particular is the author's frequent use of 'intertextuality' as a means of advancing the narrative, through his frequent use of newspaper clippings and other 'external' documents embedded in the fictional text.

Both Ṣun' Allāh Ibrāhīm's general taste for structural experimentation and some specific features of his technique – not least, his use of 'intertextuality' – have of course been shared by many other members of his generation. Indeed, the increasing use of 'intertextual' references is perhaps one of the most distinctive features of this generation of writers. The novels of Yūsuf al-Qa'īd (1944–), for example, Ibrāhīm's near contemporary, make extensive use of 'intertextuality' of various kinds; at the same time, they show a clear evolution of both technique and theme from *al-Ḥidād* (1969), which revolves around the comparatively conventional theme of family retribution in the Egyptian countryside, through *Akhbār 'Izbat al-Manīsī* (1971),[11] set in the same environment, to the more outspoken *Yaḥduth fī Miṣr al-ān* (1977) and *al-Ḥarb fī barr Miṣr* (1978),[12] both of which deal explicitly or implicitly with contemporary Egyptian politics. In *Yaḥduth fī Misr al-ān*, for example, set against the background of President Nixon's visit to Egypt in 1974, the author adopts an explicitly anti-American tone in an attempt to expose the hypocrisy of the Egyptian government's new-found friendship with the USA. More successful, not least because the social and political criticism is better integrated into the narrative structure, is *al-Ḥarb fī Barr Miṣr*, set at the time of the 1973 War, in which a village headman devises an impersonation in an attempt to avoid his son's being drafted into the army. Unsurprisingly, the author encountered difficulties in publishing both these novels: *Yaḥduth fī Misr* could only be published at the author's own expense, after being rejected by several Egyptian publishing houses, and *al-Ḥarb fī Barr Miṣr* had to be published in Beirut. Al-Qa'īd's most ambitious work to date is the trilogy *Shakāwā al-Miṣrī al-faṣīḥ* (1981–5), in which an impoverished Cairene family move from the City of the Dead,[13] where they have been living, to Maydān al-Taḥrīr, where they attempt to put themselves up for sale; the novel describes these events, set on 19 November 1976, and their aftermath in the context of political developments of the time, ending with President Sadat's return to Egypt from Jerusalem, where he had been attempting to initiate the peace process – an episode that many, probably most, of Egypt's contemporary intellectuals found distasteful. The events provide a peg on which the author hangs a scathing critique of Sadat's policies, both domestic and foreign. Although the work is undoubtedly of interest for its experimental approach to novelistic technique, however, as well as its political commentary, the reader cannot quite escape a feeling that the author has slightly overstretched himself, and it is perhaps significant that although al-Qa'īd has continued to produce a number of further novels, as well as several collections of short stories, he has not again attempted a work on this scale.[14]

Although many of the attitudes of Ṣun' Allāh Ibrāhīm and Yūsuf al-Qa'īd towards contemporary Egyptian society and politics appear to have been widely held among their fellow writers, not all have adopted their strictly 'neo-realist'[15] approach. The works of Jamāl al-Ghīṭānī (1945–), for example, while sharing with both Ṣun' Allāh Ibrāhīm and Yūsuf al-Qa'īd a strong sense of the potential of 'intertextuality' as a narrative technique, also demonstrate a particular awareness of the potential of rediscovered literary traditions of Arab culture as a point of departure for contemporary narrative; although far from unrecognised by writers at an earlier stage in the development of modern Arabic literature, the awareness of this potential gained additional momentum from the search for new forms of expression both in imitation of, and as a reaction to, the various forms of Western 'modernisms'. (As previously noted, a further motivation in some cases has been an attempt to avoid the attentions of the censor, through the use of a historical period as a metaphor for the present.) In his first novel, *al-Zaynī Barakāt* (1971),[16] for example, al-Ghīṭānī makes extensive use of the Egyptian historian Ibn Iyās's (1448–c. 1524) *Badā'i' al-zuhūr fī waqā'i' al-duhūr*, which he both quotes and parodies, in addition to introducing other 'fictional' medieval texts. Al-Ghīṭānī's work itself, one of the most accomplished productions of the Egyptian 'generation of the sixties', is set in sixteenth-century Cairo during the reign of the Mamluk Sultan al-Ghawrī, just before the Ottoman invasion of Egypt in 1517 and takes as its 'hero' al-Zaynī Barakāt ibn Mūsā, a historical figure who served as *muḥtasib* of Cairo from AD 1505, surviving the fall of the Mamluks into the first years of Ottoman rule. His character is a somewhat ambiguous one, but he is clearly both an opportunist and a survivor, and in this, as in his almost puritanical obsession with reform, he is a clear metaphor for Jamāl 'Abd al-Nāṣir [Abdel Nasser], whose survival of the defeat in the Arab–Israeli war of 1967 parallels al-Zaynī's survival of the Mamluk defeat of 1517. Despite the historical setting, this is not a 'historical novel' in the usual sense of the term, however: al-Gḥīṭānī has no compunction about including in his narrative events and personalities that have no historical basis whatever – the result being a superb work of fiction in which the dividing-line between historical fact and the author's imagination is so blurred as to be indistinguishable.

Echoes of al-Ghīṭānī's use of Ibn Iyās's text in *al-Zaynī Barakāt* to construct his own 'hypertext'[17] can be seen in many of his subsequent works. In *Waqā'i' Ḥārat al-Za'farānī* (1976),[18] which like *al-Zaynī Barakāt* deals with themes of power and coercion, this time in the setting of a working-class quarter of Cairo, al-Ghīṭānī makes extensive use of official reports and newspaper extracts[19] to further a narrative that includes a cruel but prophetic caricature of an increasingly desperate President Sadat in the period leading up to his assassination in 1981. In the later work *Khiṭaṭ al-Ghīṭānī* (1980), the author returns us to the medieval historiographical tradition, parodying the traditional *khiṭaṭ* form to create a *khiṭaṭ* of contemporary Egypt. Little imagination is required to equate al-Ghīṭānī's 'al-Ustādh' in his account with President Nasser, and the reference to contemporary developments becomes still more obvious when 'al-Ustādh' disappears to be replaced by 'al-Tanūkhī', under whose authority corruption increases still further, as he is caught up in a war with *al-A'dā'* ('the enemies') – a clear, if indirect, reference to President Sadat's capitulation, as perceived by a majority of the Egyptian intelligentsia, to the Israelis, as most obviously manifested in his visit to Jerusalem in 1977. Al-Ghīṭānī's most ambitious work to date, the trilogy *Kitāb al-Tajalliyāt* (1983–6), uses Ibn 'Arabī's (1165–1240) *al-Futūḥāt al-Makkiyya* as a source text for a work that mingles strands of directly inspired autobiography with mystical, Sufi elements, and political and social criticism of contemporary Egypt. The 'Sufi' strand of thought and inspiration is continued in some subsequent works, most particularly *Shaṭḥ al-madīna* (1991), in which themes of alienation dominate the text.

A somewhat different perspective on contemporary Egyptian life is provided by 'Abd al-Ḥakīm Qāsim (1935–90), whose writing – somewhat marginalised in much recent critical discussion – is grounded in his own peasant upbringing. Although many of Qāsim's attitudes and experience of prison, for example, mirror those of many other writers of his generation, they also reflect his experience as an intellectual of peasant origin trying to make his way in a different economic and social environment. His best known work, *Ayyām al-insān al-sab'a* (1968),[20] which revolves around the annual pilgrimage to the shrine of al-Sayyid al-Badawī in the Egyptian Delta town of Ṭanṭā, can be read on one level as a variation on the 'town vs country' theme, but it also reflects the generation gap and the conflict between tradition and modernity that runs like a constant thread through much modern Arabic literature, and as such stands in a direct line of descent from seminal works such as Maḥmūd Ṭāhir Lāshīn's *Ḥadīth al-Qarya*.[21] Although 'Abd al-Ḥakīm Qāsim went on to produce several further works of interest, none of them quite matches the power and subtlety of *Ayyām al-insān al-sab'a*, whose strength derives from the 'insider's' perspective on the events described, combined with an imaginative use of the 'seven day' device, in which each of the days representing the different stages of planning and completion of the pilgrimage is set in a different year. Among his other works, *Muḥāwala li-l-khurūj*, published in 1980 though apparently written earlier, represents a variation on another well-worn theme – that of a relationship between a Middle Eastern man and a Western woman – though unlike many of its predecessors, the setting is here Cairo rather than the West, allowing the author an opportunity for some pungent social and political criticism of contemporary

Egyptian society. *Qadar al-Ghuraf al-Muqbiḍa* (1982), clearly autobiographically based, documents the progress of its hero from his native Egyptian village via the Egyptian cities of Cairo and Alexandria to Berlin, through a series of descriptions of the rooms he has had to occupy; the descriptions include a vivid description of prison life. His novella *al-Mahdī* (1978) is an original and courageous account of the forced conversion to Islam by Islamic fundamentalists of a poor Copt.[22]

Space forbids a detailed discussion of the many other Egyptian writers of fiction coming to prominence during this period, but mention should be made at least of the novelist and short-story writer Bahā' Ṭāhir (1935–), whose political and social criticism – as in *al-Khāla Ṣafiyya* (1991)[23] – is characterised by a lively sense of humour; and of a number of women writers, including not only Laṭīfa al-Zayyāt, already discussed,[24] but also, among others, Alīfa Rif'at (1930–95), Salwā Bakr (1949–) and Nawāl al-Sa'dāwī (1931–). The careers of many of these writers are of almost as much interest from a sociological as from a literary point of view: Alīfa Rif'at, for example, began writing short stories at an early age, but for a long time published under a pseudonym, and for several years stopped publishing altogether because of her husband's opposition, while Nawāl al-Sa'dāwī, a doctor and psychiatrist by training and probably the best known Egyptian feminist writer of all, has undoubtedly attracted more attention for her courageous stand on women's issues than for the literary merits of her fiction: although al-Sa'dāwī had been publishing fiction since the late 1950s, it was only with her book *al-Mar'a wa-al-jins* (1972) that she achieved widespread recognition as a writer, for a work that led to her dismissal from her post as Egypt's Director-General of Health Education for its frank and outspoken treatment of issues related to women's sexuality. She was imprisoned in 1981, and in 1993, after her name had appeared on an Islamic fundamentalist group's death list, she was forced into self-imposed exile in the United States for some years. A prodigious writer, her work includes not only novels and short stories, but also non-fictional studies on sexuality and gender such as *al-Mar'a wa-al-jins* and *'An al-mar'a* (1988) and a number of autobiographically based works, the best known of which is probably *Mudhakkirātī fi sijn al-nisā'* (1983).[25] Among the most successful of her novels, all of which are related directly or indirectly to her sociological and psychological interests, are *Imra'a 'inda nuqṭat al-ṣifr* (1974) and *Imra'atān fi imra'a* (1975).[26]

As Margot Badran and Miriam Cooke have shown in their wide-ranging anthology, *Opening the Gates*,[27] the rapid growth in literature written by women – not all of which, of course, has necessarily to be regarded as 'feminist' in a polemical sense – can be paralleled in most, if not all, parts of the Middle East and North Africa during the same period. Space precludes a comprehensive account of this body of writing, which has attracted considerable attention not only in the Middle East but also outside it – an attention which, it is tempting to suggest, may at times have owed as much to a somewhat prurient, almost 'Orientalist', interest in the condition of women in the traditionally patriarchal Middle East as to any very sophisticated appreciation of the merits of their literary production. Be that as it may, the most challenging manifestation of this phenomenon is undoubtedly that of the group of women writers who emerged in Lebanon during the Civil War of 1975–90 and who have been extensively studied by Miriam Cooke in her book *War's Other Voices*.[28] Termed by Miriam Cooke, not entirely felicitously, the 'Beirut Decentrists', this group of writers would include, among others, by Cooke's own account, Ghāda al-Sammān, Ḥanān al-Shaykh, Emily Naṣr Allāh, Laylā 'Usayrān, Daisy al-Amīr, Claire Gebeyli and Etel Adnan.[29] Of these, Claire Gebeyli, who writes in French, and Etel Adnan, who writes in French and English, strictly speaking fall outside the scope of this volume; several of the other authors, however, many of whom have combined journalism or teaching with imaginative writing as a means of earning a livelihood, merit some brief individual consideration, for although sharing much in common, they also differ considerably among themselves.

Probably the best known, and certainly the most prolific, of this group of writers writing in Arabic is Ghāda al-Sammān (1942–). A Syrian by birth, Ghāda al-Sammān studied at the American University of Beirut and in London before settling in Beirut in 1969 – by which time, she had already been writing and publishing short stories, essays and poetry for almost a decade. *Bayrūt 75* (1975),[30] widely interpreted as a prophecy of the Civil War itself, was followed by one of her most powerful works, *Kawābīs Bayrūt* (1976), written during the months of October and November 1975 which saw some of the fiercest fighting of the early war years. During this period, she lost her personal library, including some unpublished manuscripts, in the fighting. Despite these setbacks, it was not until 1984 that she finally left Lebanon with her family to settle in Paris, from where she continued to write and publish, dividing her literary activities between Paris and Beirut; among her later works may be mentioned the novels *Laylat al-milyār* (1986), *al-Riwāya al-mustaḥīla* (1997), which chronicles the coming of age of a girl in Damascus, and a collection of ten 'supernatural' short stories, *al-Qamar al-Murabba'* (1994). As may be inferred from the subject of *al-Riwāya al-mustaḥīla*, Ghāda al-Sammān's writing, though heavily marked by the horrors of the Lebanese war, is by no means limited by it; though strongly feminist in orientation, it has been characterised by her awareness and willingness to express herself on all aspects of oppression, be it in the context of the Palestinian problem, the position of women in the Middle East, or social and political repression in the Middle East more generally.

Unlike Ghāda al-Sammān, the Lebanese Ḥanān al-Shaykh (1945–) left Beirut only a few months after the start of the Lebanese Civil War, claiming that it was impossible for her to remain in a place where the only dialogue possible was 'that of the deaf with the deaf'.[31] Her alienation from the culture of her homeland, or at least from that version of it in which she herself had been brought up, had begun, however, a good earlier, when in 1963 she had left Lebanon to study in Cairo at the American College for Girls; since then, she has lived in Beirut, Saudi Arabia, the Gulf, and more recently mainly in London. Although her first novel, *Intiḥār rajul mayyit* (1967), was written and published while she was in Cairo, it was only with the publication of *Ḥikāyat Zahra* (1980), which treated erotic themes in the context of the Civil War itself, that she began to attract serious critical attention; the book was banned in several Arab countries for its frank treatment of sexual topics. She has subsequently gone on to publish two volumes of short stories and a number of experimental dramas, as well as a total of some half-dozen novels. These include *Misk al-ghazāl* (1983), whose themes include the relationship between expatriates and the local Arab community; *Barīd Bayrūt* (1996), on the return to post-war Lebanon; and *Innahā Landan yā 'azīzī* (2001), which revolves around expatriate Arab life in the Western capital. Ḥanān al-Shaykh's lengthy residence in London has ensured that her books have sometimes been translated into English almost as soon as they have appeared, and she has occasionally been 'accused' of writing with an eye on the English-speaking market as much as on the Arabic-speaking one – though why this should be regarded as reprehensible, even if true, has never been clear to me.[32]

Space forbids more than a brief account of the work of the other 'Beirut Decentrists', each of whom has retained their own individual personality and outlook in their writings. Imilī (Emily) Naṣr Allāh (1938–) came to prominence with her partly autobiographical novel *Ṭuyūr Aylūl* (1962), which treats the subject of women's emigration from the villages of Lebanon in search of work and education, and won the author several literary awards. Many of her later works, both novels and short stories, are related to the Civil War itself; the author herself obstinately refused to leave Lebanon, despite – like Ghāda al-Sammān – losing her books and papers, and this attitude of defiance permeates much of her writing, most notably the novel *al-Iqlā' 'aks al-zaman* (1981).[33] A similar insistence on the need to stay in Lebanon is a characteristic of Laylā 'Usayrān (1936–), whose work also exemplifies the close connection between the Palestinian struggle and the Lebanese Civil War already noted in connection with Ghāda al-Sammān; all of her novels, both those predating the Civil War and those written during it,[34] are related to the Palestinian cause, though her works appear to show a progressive loss of idealism, with the realisation that the Palestinian and Lebanese causes may be at odds: such a tension is also apparent in the male Lebanese novelist Rashīd al-Ḍa'īf's *'Azīzī al-Sayyid Kawabata*, discussed below. For her part, Daisy al-Amīr (1935–), a short-story writer rather than a novelist, and Iraqi rather than Lebanese by origin, produced two collections of stories on the Lebanese civil war: *Fī dawwāmat al-ḥubb wa-al-karāhiya* (1979) and *Wuʿūd li-l-bayʿ* (1981), as well as a collection deriving from the Iran–Iraq war of 1980–88: it is notable that this war, responsible for the deaths of more people than any other Middle Eastern conflict in recent times, has inspired almost no literature of significance, at least by comparison with the Israeli–Palestinian conflict.

Perhaps the most significant feature of this group of writers, who are united by shared experience than by any common or religious political outlook, is the challenge that they have made to the assumption that the literature of war belongs to men rather than women. A recurring theme in the literature, implicit or explicit, is the question that haunted most Lebanese who had the means to leave Lebanon during the fifteen or so years of fighting: 'to stay or not to stay?' This question is one that, in different forms, has of course not been confined to Lebanese writers of the Civil War years: it is a dilemma that has been faced by Lebanese intellectuals at intervals since the religious disturbances of the mid-nineteenth century, and it is one that has had to be confronted by intellectuals in different parts of the Arab world until the present day. Negative in their origins, such exoduses have, as we have at several points already seen, often been positive in their effects, not least in the growth of Mahjar literature and its influence on the Romantic movement in poetry; more recently, the effect of such movements can be seen in the growth of London and Paris as centres of Arab and Arabic intellectual activity and literary publishing.

If the Lebanese civil war, as experienced by the 'Beirut Decentrists', has provided perhaps the most obvious example of a 'cluster' of women's literature in the modern Middle East, the war's effects have also been reflected in the work of the leading contemporary male novelists of Lebanon, most notably Ilyās Khūrī (1948–) and Rashīd al-Ḍaʿīf (1945–). The work of these two authors, variously described as 'modernist' or even 'post-modernist', undoubtedly lies at the 'cutting edge' of contemporary Arabic prose fiction; and although not everything they have written is of the first order, the achievement of their fiction at its best is to mirror the spirit and anguish of war-torn Lebanon in a way that elevates it to a conflict of universal rather than merely local significance. Both writers belong to the Maronite community, but both have been identified, at least for part of their writing careers, with the political 'Left'; and for both, 'fragmentation', on both a social and a personal level, is a key element of at least some of their writings. Ilyās Khūrī, who studied history and sociology in Lebanon and France, has also been closely identified with the Palestinian cause, serving as deputy editor of the Palestinian magazine *Shuʾūn Filasṭīniyya* between 1977 and 1979. In addition to the series of experimental novels for which he is best known, he has also published collections of short stories and essays, many of which reflect his overtly leftist political stance: of these, the most notable is perhaps *Zamān al-iḥtilāl* (1985), which includes a number of editorials written for the leftist Beirut daily *al-Safīr* during the Israeli invasion of 1982. His major novels include *al-Jabal al-Ṣaghīr* (1977), *al-Wujūh al-bayḍā'* (1981), *Abwāb al-Madīna* (1981), *Riḥlat Ghāndī al-ṣaghīr* (1989), *Mamlakat al-ghurabā'* (1993), *Majma' al-asrār* (1994) and, most recently, *Yālū* (2002); a prominent characteristic of Ilyās Khūrī's work is its 'self-referential', or 'metafictional' nature, a strategy that attempts to involve the reader as a creative partner in the making of the text, which both marks the author out as a 'post-modernist' in the full sense of the term but which also reflects the fragmentation of the society to which he belongs.

Like that of Ilyās Khūrī, the work of Rashīd al-Ḍa'īf, who combines his creative writing with an academic career as a teacher of language and literature at the Lebanese American University in Beirut, is marked by a constant spirit of experiment and the search for new techniques. His first published volumes were two collections of poetry, *Ḥīn ḥalla al-sayf 'alā al-ṣayf* (1979) and *Lā shay' fawq al-waṣf* (1980), though it is not for his verse but for his half-dozen or more novels, the first of which, *al-Mustabidd*, appeared in 1983, that he has acquired his present reputation. The most powerful of these is undoubtedly *'Azīzī al-Sayyid Kawabata* (1995),[35] a work which clearly belongs to the modern Arabic tradition of 'autobiography as fiction', but which here takes the nominal form of a letter addressed to the Japanese writer Yasunari Kawabata, who committed suicide in 1972 – an event alluded to at several points during the novel itself. The period covered by the work includes not only the war itself – in which the author was himself injured and came close to death – but also the narrator's childhood in the late 1940s and 1950s, and his adolescence and student days during the turbulent period of the 1960s and 1970s prior to the outbreak of the Lebanese Civil War itself in 1975. On one level, it is a 'classic account of an idealistic young man's awakening', moving as it does through successive stages of the author's life and describing, often in allusive terms, his intellectual, sexual and political education.[36] The narrator's account, however, ends in a mood of disillusion with the collapse of the Soviet Union, which he had once envisaged as the ideal embodiment of the Communist Party to which he once belonged. In any event, the work is at least as interesting in terms of its narrative structure, which depends heavily on a use of anachrony that is both sophisticated and complex – the temporal disruption of the narrative mirroring the narrator's confused state of mind, which in turn echoes the chaos and disorder that were the prevailing characteristic of Lebanon during the Civil War. A further puzzle is the precise relationship between the author, the narrator, and the subject of the story, all of whom are called Rashīd, but whom al-Ḍa'īf is anxious, at least intermittently, to distinguish from each other

Few, if any, of al-Ḍaʿīf's subsequent novels, which include *Fusḥa mustahdafa bayna al-Nuʿās wa-al-nawm* (1986),[37] *Tiqniyāt al-Buʾs* (1989), *Nāḥiyat al-barāʾa* (1997),[38] *Learning English* (2001) and *Tisṭifil Meryl Streep* (2001), can match the power and passion of *ʿAzīzī al-Sayyid Kawabata*. Some passages in *Tisṭifil Meryl Streep* are indeed, in my view, open to accusations of 'bad taste'. Of the others, the most interesting is perhaps *Learning English* (another novel with strong autobiographical elements), which reflects the frustrations of the author at his lack of proficiency in English compared with French and may perhaps be counted as a product, albeit an indirect one, of the 'literature of globalisation'; while *Tiqniyāt al-Buʾs* is of interest for its affinities (presumably unintentional) with the work of some of the Egyptian 'generation of the sixties', not least in its concentration on the minutiae of everyday life.

Among Palestinian authors of this period, the works of Ghassān Kanafānī and Jabrā Ibrāhīm Jabrā appear to have had few direct successors, and despite the efforts of a number of competent writers such as Yaḥyā Yakhlaf (1944–) and others, the Palestinian contribution to the 'modernist' trend has in general not been a particularly outstanding one. A significant exception to this general judgement is provided by Imīl Ḥabībī, whose work is of interest not only in its own right, but also in the light of the author's status as an 'Israeli Arab', which has ensured that his writing has been the subject of considerable controversy; the ambiguous relationship of Palestinian Arabs to the Israeli state was nowhere better illustrated than in 1972, when Ḥabībī was awarded the Israeli Prize for Literature – a dilemma that the author neatly resolved by accepting the prize, but donating the money to a Palestinian charity. In this connection, it is worth noting that, like many Arab writers living in Israel, Ḥabībī was fluent in both Arabic and Hebrew; unlike Anṭūn Shammās, however, whose novel *Arabeskot*[39] was written and published in Hebrew as a deliberate choice, Ḥabībī chose to write his imaginative works in Arabic.

Like his Lebanese counterparts Ilyās Khūrī and Rashīd al-Ḍaʿīf, Imīl Ḥabībī (1921–96), was closely associated during his lifetime with the Arab 'left', having indeed been a founder member of the Israeli Communist Party, whom he represented in the Israeli Knesset for a number of years. Ḥabībī, who combined his political and creative literary activities with those as a journalist and broadcaster, came to prominence with a collection of six stories entitled *Sudāsiyyat al-ayyām al-sitta: riwāya min al-arḍ al-muḥtalla* (1968), a work inspired by the reunion of Palestinians from the West Bank and those from Israel following the Israeli occupation of the West Bank after the Six-Day War of 1967. His enduring reputation, however, will undoubtedly continue to depend on his novel *al-Waqāʾiʿ al-gharība fī ikhtifāʾ Saʿīd Abī al-Naḥs al-Mutashāʾil* (1974),[40] which occupies a unique position in the history of modern Arabic literature. Often described as 'picaresque', the work, which portrays the precarious status of

Arabs living as Israeli citizens, is characterised by a lively sense of paradox and irony apparent even in the work's title – *al-mutashā'il* ('pessoptimist') deriving from a combination of *mutashā'im* ('pessimist') and *mutafā'il* ('optimist'). The 'hero' (or more correctly, 'anti-hero') of the work, Sa'īd, at first works as an informer for the Israelis, but rejects this role after being put in prison and beaten by his masters; but he fails to find an alternative role, and at the end of the work is transported to outer space by an extraterrestrial being – an ironic epilogue informing us that the whole narrative was contained in a letter sent from a lunatic asylum by an inmate who has now disappeared. The 'plot' of the work, however, gives little indication either of the nature of its appeal, which depends on a subtle interplay of humour and grim reality, or of the richness and complexity of its structure, which with its rapidly shifting short chapters owes a considerable amount to the traditional Arabic *maqāma* form,[41] but which also draws on Arab history, folk literature and geographical references to underline the Palestinians' loss of their homeland. Irony and symbolism are apparent in the author's choice of names, not only for his 'hero', Sa'īd ('happy'), but also those for his sister, Yu'ād, and wife, Bāqiya – the former denoting 'return' and the latter 'remaining' – these names also being used as titles for the three parts into which the novel is divided.

Though all are of interest, none of Ḥabībī's later works quite matches the subtlety or power of *al-Waqā'i' al-gharība* ..., which has been aptly compared not only with Voltaire's *Candide* but also with Jaroslav Hašek's *The Good Soldier Švejk*.[42] Neither his play *Luka' ibn Luka'* (1980), an attempt to dramatise the Arab–Israeli conflict using a different literary medium, nor his later novel *Ikhtayyi* (1986), a celebration of traditional Palestinian culture, has achieved the status of *al-Waqā'i' al-gharība* ... as a seminal work in the modern Arabic narrative tradition. It is, however, perhaps significant that towards the end of his life Ḥabībī showed an increasing interest in the use of Palestinian folktales, and traditional storytelling techniques, most notably in his *Khurāfiya: Sarāyā, Bint al-Ghūl* (1991), which has been read as an 'attempt to retrieve the past through ... writing'.[43]

Certain aspects of Ḥabībī's technique find echoes in works by several other prominent authors, including the Jordanian Ramaḍān al-Rawāshida's *al-Ḥamrāwī* (1992) and the Syrian Kurdish writer Salīm Barakāt's (1951–) autobiographically based *al-Jundub al-ḥadīdī* (1980).

Salīm Barakāt's work deserves some further discussion at this point, for two reasons. First, as a Syrian-born Kurd, born in Qāmishlī, he had experience of living as an ethnic minority under Arab domination – a situation that, despite the obvious differences, cannot help but recall the plight of the Israeli Arabs. In addition, he appears to be have been arguably undeservedly neglected in many discussions of the field, despite having been described as 'perhaps the master prose stylist writing in Arabic today';[44] for this neglect, the difficulty of his language may itself be partly the reason. Be that as it may, Salīm Barakāt's first major work, *al-Jundub al-ḥadīdī*, continues a long tradition in modern Arabic literature of autobiography-as-fiction – a tradition that, as already noted, began as long ago as 1848 with the publication of Fāris al-Shidyāq's *al-Sāq 'alā al-Sāq* and produced perhaps its best known example in the 1920s in Ṭāhā Ḥusayn's *al-Ayyām*.[45] A second volume of his autobiography, describing his adolescence, was published in 1982 as *Hātihi 'āliyan: hāti al-nafīr 'alā ākhirihi*, and the two volumes were reissued as *al-Sīratān* in 1997. Unlike these two volumes of literary autobiography, *Fuqahā' al-Ẓalām*, Barakāt's next major work, is clearly a novel in the full sense of the word: set in the region in which the author grew up, a small Kurdish village near the Syrian–Turkish border, the work describes the miraculous events that follow the birth of a child to Mulla Binav – events that end with the coming of the time of the mysterious Sages of Darkness. Suffused with mystery, the work, with its many anthropomorphic elements, evokes a strong sense of identification with the land that is at times reminiscent of some of the Sudanese writer al-Ṭayyib Ṣāliḥ's work; its purpose, however, is clearly partly at least political: to express a sense of Kurdish identity that has been all but crushed by Arab nationalism. Since then Barakāt, a prolific author who has published poetry as well as prose, has gone on to produce several new major works, one of which, *Arwāḥ handasiyya* (1987), in his own words, attempts to 'give shape to the ambience of madness that issued from the Lebanese war'[46] – a telling reminder of the extent to which that conflict challenged the consciences of many intellectuals in the region, even outside Lebanon itself.

In Iraq, political conditions during the period in question have not been favourable for the development of contemporary fiction. The Iraqi writer Fu'ād al-Takarlī (1927–), whose name has already been mentioned in the previous chapter for his work *al-Wajh al-ākhar* (1960, enlarged edn, 1982), has not lived in Iraq since 1979, though he has continued to produce several novels of significance. *Al-Raj' al-ba'īd* (1980)[47] is of particular interest in providing a panorama of Iraqi society in the period immediately preceding the fall of 'Abd al-Karīm Qāsim's regime in 1962–3. Focused largely on an old house in the Bāb al-Shaykh area of Baghdad where the author himself grew up, the work employs a polyphonic structure in order to construct a complex picture of Baghdad society through the eyes of the various family members. As in *al-Wajh al-Ākhar* and other writing by al-Takarlī, the reader is conscious of the weight of tradition and of the stultifying effect of social customs.

Little has been said so far about the modern prose literature of the Arabian Peninsula itself, an area that for students of modern Arabic literature has often seemed marginal. Although it is indeed true that Arabia as such has not been at the forefront of any great literary movements, a brief glance at Salma

Khadra Jayyusi's anthology *The Literature of Modern Arabia*[48] will be sufficient to convince even the most sceptical reader that much vigorous and varied writing has been, and is being, undertaken there, both in Saudi Arabia and in the other states of the Peninsula. Short story writing appears to be particularly flourishing. In Kuwait, for example, the short stories of the Kuwaiti writer Muḥammad al-Murr, to name but one writer, have a freshness and vitality that is all their own, while the feminist Laylā al-'Uthmān's novels, short stories and poetry have deservedly acquired a wide reputation, not only for their literary merits but also for the courage that their author has exhibited in the face of censorship and persecution.[49]

Among Saudi writers, two novelists deserve particular attention, for different reasons: 'Abd al-Raḥmān Munīf (1933–2004) and Turkī al-Ḥamad (1953–); of these, 'Abd al-Raḥmān Munīf is deservedly the better known. Born in Jordan of Saudi parentage, Munīf also studied in Baghdad and Cairo and gained a PhD from the University of Belgrade, Yugoslavia, before embarking on a career in the oil industry, working mainly in Syria and Iraq. Of all contemporary Arab writers, he perhaps comes closest to justifying the description 'Arab cosmopolitan', for although born a Saudi national, he was stripped of his Saudi citizenship for his political criticisms of the Saudi regime and spent most of his life abroad

Although he first began publishing fiction in 1973, it was not until the late 1970s that Munīf began to acquire a reputation as a leading Arab novelist, with works such as *al-Nihāyāt* (1978), set in a small village on the edge of the desert, and *Sibāq al-Masāfāt al-ṭawīla: Riḥla ilā al-sharq* (1979), set in Iran in the Mosaddeq period. These twin characteristics, a passion for history and a natural feeling for desert life that forms such a contrast with the urban orientation of most leading Arab novelists, found monumental expression in the astonishing quintet *Mudun al-Milḥ* (1984–9), originally conceived as a trilogy, which charts the changes wrought on a desert community through the discovery of oil. Beginning with the arrival of the Americans in the village of Wadi al-Uyoun, this is clearly first and foremost a 'historical novel' on a grand scale – though this should not blind us to the fact that, although conservative by some standards, Munīf's narrative technique is not without its experimental aspects.[50] On another level, it is clearly designed to challenge not only 'the official Saudi account of the establishment of the Kingdom of Saudi Arabia',[51] but also the Western colonial view of history.

Of Munīf's later works, particular mention may be made of *Sīrat Madīna: 'Ammān fī al-arba'īnāt* (1994), an account of the city in which he himself grew up, and *Arḍ al-Sawād*, which reflects the environment of central Iraq in the nineteenth century. It might be expected that, when placed beside the monumental masterpiece of *Mudun al-Milḥ*, Munīf's other work would fade into insignificance, but it is perhaps an indication of his quality as writer that this is in fact not the case; indeed, both the quality and quantity of his output is truly astonishing, considering that for much of his life, creative writing, as for so many Arab writers, could be little more than a hobby – a distraction, almost, from his main profession.

The second Saudi writer to be mentioned here, Turkī al-Ḥamad, shares with Munīf a reputation for speaking his mind. Though by no means in the same league as Munīf in terms of literary accomplishment, al-Ḥamad's case is an interesting one, illustrating as it does how literary merit and publishing success are by no means always linked. A political analyst and academic by profession, who has taught in the American University of Beirut, al-Ḥamad came to fiction rather late, emerging as a novelist in the late 1990s with a trilogy entitled *Aṭyāf al-aziqqa al-mahjūra*. The first two of the trilogy's three parts, entitled respectively *al-ʿAdāma* and *Shumaysī* (named after quarters in Dammam and Riyadh respectively),[52] describe Hishām's education and coming of age – a coming of age that is marked by alcohol, illicit sex and illegal political activity; from there, the progression to the third part, *al-Karādīb*, a political prison outside Jeddah, seems almost inevitable. The work's style has been variously described as 'turgid', 'feeble' and 'outdated', but the work provoked a storm of protest on publication, quickly being banned not only in Saudi Arabia itself but also in Kuwait and Bahrain; the author received several death threats, and *fatwās* were issued against him, largely on the basis of the third volume, where the imprisoned Hishām muses that God and Satan may be interchangeable. Al-Ḥamad's purpose in writing the work was explicitly provocative: 'Where I live there are three taboos, religion, politics and sex. It is forbidden to speak about these. I wrote this trilogy to get things moving.'[53] Al-Ḥamad's work seems unlikely to survive for long as a literary masterpiece, but the episode serves as yet another reminder, if any were needed, that the sort of freedom of speech that is taken for granted in Western societies simply does not exist in the Middle East.

In North Africa, this period is chiefly notable not only for the vigorous continuation of the tradition of fiction in Arabic that had emerged at a comparatively late date, but also for the appearance for the first time of a Libyan writer of genuinely international stature, Ibrāhīm al-Kawnī (1948–). Although some earlier attempts had been made in Libya at the writing of fiction, and at least one writer, Aḥmad al-Faqīh (1942–) had produced a notable trilogy, entitled *Ḥadā'iq al-Layl*,[54] fiction writing – and indeed, modern literature in general – had been even slower to mature in Libya than in the rest of North Africa. With al-Kawnī, however, we find a writer who is not only able to hold his own with his contemporaries from other countries in the Arab world, we are faced with a substantial body of work that is entirely distinctive, reflecting the particular heritage and outlook of his region in a way that no writer had succeeded previously in doing. Like the writing of Munīf, al-Kawnī's work typically evokes a feeling of kinship with the desert that is foreign to most of the leading writers of Egypt and the Levant; in addition, it is marked by the particular cultural features and mystical outlook of the North African tribes, which he has succeeded in integrating into the form of the modern novel and short story in a remarkable way. Ibrāhīm al-Kawnī's first publications date from 1974, when he published *al-Ṣalāḥ khārij niṭāq al-awqāt al-khamsa*, but his most memorable works did not emerge until the 1990s, with *al-Tibr* (1990) and *Nazīf al-ḥajar* (1990). Since then, he has gone on to publish new material at an astonishing rate, in particular the monumental *al-Majūs* (1991) in two volumes, and is beginning to establish a reputation not only in the Arab world, but also, through translations, in Europe where he has lived for several years.

In the other countries of the Maghrib, the vigour that characterised the rapid growth of Arabic fiction in the late 1950s and early 1960s has continued apace – though in Algeria and Morocco at least, the legacy of what Roger Allen has termed 'the pervasive influence of French culture' has continued to be felt in the dichotomy between Francophone writers and those writing in Arabic. Fictional writing in Tunisia received a boost at the beginning of the 1960s with the increasing popularity of several new literary journals, including *Qiṣaṣ* and *al-Fikr*. It appears to have reached something of a high point from the late 1960s onwards, when ʿIzz al-Dīn al-Madanī (1938–), better known as an innovative playwright and almost universally regarded as the father of the contemporary avant-garde movement in Tunisia,[55] produced an unfinished novel *al-Insān al-ṣifr* (1968–71), which unsurprisingly incurred the displeasure of the religious authorities for its attempt to imitate the style and language of the Qur'ān. Of equal interest, though less well known, is al-Madanī's novel *al-ʿUdwān* (1969),[56] which revolves around a young Tunisian man serving a jail sentence for the rape of a Swedish tourist: while the general theme of relations between an Arab man and a Western woman has been a common one in modern Arabic literature since the nineteenth century, the particular scenario here envisaged, with the Tunisian cast in the role of villain, gives the theme a new, and somewhat unconventional, twist.

Among other Tunisian novelists and short story writers coming to prominence at around the same time, mention may be made of Muṣṭafā al-Fārisī (1931–), whose novel *al-Munʿaraj* (1966) explores some of the ambiguities and tensions among the generation of Tunisians that achieved independence; and Muḥammad Ṣāliḥ al-Jābirī (1940–), whose novel *Yawm min ayyām Zamrā* (1968) revolves around the exploitation of the Tunisians by the Europeans; al-Jābirī's reputation was further confirmed by his *Laylat al-Sanawāt al-ʿAshr* (1982), which explores social themes of exploitation and oppression in the run-up to the political crackdown of 20 January 1978. Unsurprisingly, like the novels of al-Bashīr Khurayyif before them, the works of many fiction writers of this period continue to be preoccupied, in differing ways, with the legacy of the French colonial period. The eponymous heroine of Muḥammad al-'Arūsī al-Maṭwī's *Ḥalīma* (1967), for example, is heavily involved in gunrunning for the Tunisian resistance, and the work, which is rich in 'set piece' demonstrations and ends with the return of the 'supreme, beloved freedom-fighter Bourguiba to his homeland',[57] is marred by what can only be regarded as crude nationalist symbolism;[58] although this style seems to have been widely imitated by other writers, al-Maṭwī's later novel, *al-Tūt al-murr* (1989) shows a less naïve treatment of the theme, fusing the nationalist theme with a romantic love story as Khurayyif had previously done in *Barq al-Layl*.[59] A similar approach is used in 'Abd al-Raḥmān 'Ammār's explcitily named *Ḥubb wa-thawra* (1969). The most ambitious of this type of novel is undoubtedly Muḥammad Mukhtār Jannāt's *Urjuwān*, an extended work in three volumes entitled *Ṭarīq al-rushd* (1970), *al-'Awda* (1970) and *Khuyūṭ al-shakk* (1972) respectively: his technique, in attempting to fuse overtly patriotic themes with the human and romantic interest of ordinary Tunisian families, produces some abrupt changes of narrative direction, however, and in terms of a description of the nationalist movement itself, the series of novels strikes one as rather conventional.

It is striking that so many novels relating to the ultimately successful struggle against the French should have appeared in Tunisia in the years immediately following the 1967 Arab defeat in the Six-Day War with Israel, and it is tempting to suggest that part of the appeal of such historical narratives centred on a 'successful' struggle lay precisely in providing an antidote to unpleasant developments in the 'real' world. Be that as it may, later writers have, as might be expected, been less preoccupied with the legacy of the French colonial era: Muḥammad Riḍā al-Kāfī's *Khayṭ Aryān* (1987), for example, returns us to the well-worn theme of the relationships between the sexes across two cultures – but the French colonial experience itself seems almost irrelevant to the narrative. In this respect, the work may perhaps herald a reintegration of the Tunisian novel within the mainstream Arabic novelistic tradition – an example of the attitudes of a new generation of Tunisian writers who, while still preoccupied with issues of identity in the context of contemporary society, are more open to outside influences and less disposed to view the French/Tunisian struggle as providing the main, or even the sole, focal point for their writing. More recently, the rise of Islamic fundamentalism in the country has become a significant factor in influencing the social development of the country, in which the prospects of a vigorous development for a literature of fiction seem at present extremely difficult to predict.

If the struggle against French colonialism formed a significant theme in the works of many Tunisian writers, it is hardly surprising that the even bloodier struggle to achieve Algerian independence should also be directly reflected in the works of leading writers of this period. Although a large number of collections of short stories in Arabic had been published in the preceding decades, it was not until Algerian independence from France had been finally secured in 1962 that we can begin to speak of any significant Arabic novelistic tradition in the country: indeed, it is doubtful whether any such tradition exists even now, given the continuing problems of publishing and distribution and a lack of a solid indigenous readership, all of which have been compounded by recent political problems associated with Islamic fundamentalism. Be that as it may, a number of talented Algerian authors have achieved some prominence; of these, the most significant are undoubtedly al-Ṭāhir Waṭṭār (1936–), ʿAbd al-Ḥamīd Ben Haddūqa [Benhedouga] (1929–), and Rachid Boudjedra (1941–).

Although the first of these writers to emerge, al-Ṭāhir Waṭṭār, had begun publishing short stories in Tunis as early as 1955, he did not come to prominence as a novelist until the 1970s, with his novels *al-Lāz* (1974), *al-Zilzāl* (1974) and *ʿUrs al-Baghl* (1978), and it is arguably Abdelhamid Benhedouga's first novel, *Rīḥ al-janūb*, published in 1971, rather than Waṭṭār's work, that marks the emergence of the mature Algerian novel written in Arabic. Ben Haddūqa subsequently went on to produce some four further novels and several collections of short stories, the prevailing theme in which can be summarised as the clash between the freedom of the individual and social and political paternalism in modern Algeria; his later works are also characterised by an increasing tendency towards experimentation in terms of narrative technique.

The sense of preoccupation with the state of contemporary Algeria, and the legacy of the struggle against the French, is reinforced by a consideration of Waṭṭār's novels, beginning with *al-Lāz* which, like many Tunisian novels of the same era, is clearly in some sense a 'resistance novel', though distinguished from many others of this category by the human dimension that characterises the work. All Waṭṭār's subsequent works are likewise related, either directly or indirectly, to the evolution of the society to which he belongs, although the craftsmanship is generally sufficiently developed to avoid any sense of cliché. His later novels, which include *al-Ḥawwāt wa-al-qaṣr* (1980) and *Tajriba fī al-ʿishq* (1989), show an increasingly powerful use of symbolism. It is the case of Rachid Boudjedra, however, the most iconoclastic of the Algerian writers, which presents perhaps the most interesting example of the continuing dilemma that has haunted Algerian and Moroccan writers, torn between a 'nationalist' drive to write in Arabic and the obvious attraction of writing in French, with the likelihood of wider sales – particularly in France itself, where some North African writers have achieved a considerable measure of popularity. Rachid Boudjedra's early works, including *La Répudiation* (1969), *L'Insolation* (1970), *Les 1001 années de la nostalgie* (1979) and others[60] were written in French, but in 1982 he announced that he was switching to writing in Arabic, and a series of novels followed, including *al-Tafakkuk* (1982), *al-Marath* (1984), *Layliyyāt imra'a āriqa* (1985), *Ma'rakat al-zuqāq* (1986) and *Fawḍā' al-ashyā'* (1991). The novels, however, were so quickly translated into French that some critics were even led to question whether the author's 'conversion' to writing in Arabic was a genuine one.

In Morocco, mention may be made of a number of distinguished writers who have risen to prominence during the period in question, including the critic and novelist Muḥammad Barrāda (1938–), a prose stylist of the first order; Muḥammad Zafzāf (1942–2001), best known for his short stories; the novelist and short-story writer Muḥammad Shukrī (1935–), and Ben Sālim Ḥimmīsh (1947–). Of these, the last two present an interesting study in contrasts, for unlike the academic Ḥimmīsh, who has combined fiction writing with an academic career, Muḥammad Shukrī remained illiterate until the age of nineteen and at first found some difficulty in gaining acceptance for his work, much of which has its roots in the 'low life' environment in which he himself grew up. In addition to his short stories, collected in *Majnūn al-Ward* (1979) and elsewhere, he is known for two volumes of autobiography, the first of which in fact appeared in an English adaptation before being published in Arabic: *al-Khubz al-ḥāfī* (1979) and *al-Shuttar* (1994).[61] By contrast, Ḥimmīsh's works have tended to be grounded in the historical environment with which he is also concerned as an academic: *Majnūn al-ḥukm* (1989) is set in the period of the tenth-century Fatimid caliph al-Ḥākim bi-amr Allāh, while *al-'Allāma* (1997) is centred on the Arab philosopher and historian Ibn Khaldūn (on whom Ḥimmīsh has also published an academic study);[62] echoes of al-Ghīṭānī's intertextual techniques in *al-Zaynī Barakāt* may be found in Ḥimmīsh's use of medieval Arab historians in these contexts.

Conclusion

The above account is inevitably a condensed one, which can do little more than give an impression of some of main developments that have characterised Arabic fiction since the 'watershed' year of 1967. The choice of authors and works discussed is inevitably also somewhat selective: others will no doubt complain that I should have included X rather than Y; but an attempt to include everything, or everyone, would run the risk of producing something little more than a list of names. My emphasis in the latter part of the account has been on the novel rather the short story, since it seems to me that it is in the field of the novel that the most exciting developments have taken place during the period in question, but this approach has inevitably meant that a number of talented and important short-story writers have been somewhat neglected; of these, the most conspicuous example is perhaps the Syrian Zakariyyā Tāmir, whose surrealist stories represent a unique contribution to the development of the genre. As a general comment, it of course remains true that most Arab novelists also write short stories (though the reverse is not always the case), and that short stories are easier to publish, and are probably wider read, in the Arab world, since the 'literary page' and 'literary supplement' that played such an important part in the earlier stages of modern Arabic literary development continue to play a significant role until this day. An Egyptian critic, Jābir 'Uṣfūr, however, has recently claimed that this is the 'time of the novel';[63] and in the light of the vast array and variety of creative talent evident throughout the Arab world in this field (of which I hope to have given some impression above), I personally would find it hard to disagree with him.

Notes

1 The term has sometimes been restricted to writers who actually published in *Gallery 68*, but this distinction has, in my view, lost its usefulness with the passage of time.
2 Translated into English as *Rama and the Dragon* by Ferial Ghazoul and John Verlenden, Cairo and New York, 2002.
3 English translations respectively as *City of Saffron*, by Frances Liardet (1989), *Girls of Alexandria*, by Frances Liardet (1993) and *Stones of Bobello*, by Paul Starkey (2005).
4 *Tilka al-Rā'iḥa*, p. 36: English translation by Denys Johnson-Davies, *The Smell of It*, London, 1971, p. 17.
5 Introduction to *Tilka al-Rā'iḥa*, Casablanca, 1986 edn, p. 6. On Ḥaqqī, see above, pp. 111–12.
6 On censorship generally, see Marina Stagh, *The Limits of Freedom of Speech*.
7 An order that can be interpreted in one of two ways: either, literally, 'to end one's own life', or perhaps, according to an Egyptian colloquial idiom, 'to brood in solitude'. See El-Said Badawi and Martin Hinds, *A Dictionary of Egyptian Colloquial Arabic*, Cairo, 1986, s.v.
8 'Self' in Arabic, but also containing a reference to the mythical princess Dhāt al-Himma.
9 As indeed does *Najmat Aghusṭus*, see above.
10 English translations of *al-Lajna* and *Dhāt* are available as *The Committee*, tr. St German and Constable, 2002, and *Zaat*, tr. A. Calderbank, 2001.
11 English translation as *News from the Meneisi Farm* by M.-T. F. Abdel-Messih, Cairo, 1987.
12 English translation as *War in the Land of Egypt* by L. Kenny, O. Kenny and C. Tingley, London 1986.
13 On the outskirts of Cairo.
14 On al-Qa'īd generally, see Paul Starkey, 'From the City of the Dead to Liberation Square', *Journal of Arabic Literature* 25 (1993), pp. 2–74.
15 To use Ed de Moor's term: see *EAL*, I, pp. 386–7, s.v. Ibrāhīm, Ṣun' Allāh.
16 English translation as *Zayni* Barakat by Farouk Abdel Wahab, London, 1988.
17 For a detailed study, see S. Mehrez, 'Hypertext as Bricolage', unpublished PhD

dissertation, University of California, Los Angeles, 1985.

18 English translation by Peter O'Daniel as *Incidents in Zafrani Alley*, Cairo, 1986.

19 Cf. Ṣun' Allāh Ibrāhīm's *Dhāt* (for which, see above) for a similar technique.

20 English translation as *The Seven Days of Man*, by Joseph N. Bell, Cairo, 1990. For a useful discussion of 'Abd al-Ḥakīm Qāsim, see H. Kilpatrick, "Abd al-Ḥakīm Qāsim and the search for liberation', *JAL* 26 (1995), pp. 50–66.

21 Discussed above, p. 111.

22 English translation, together with another novella, *Turaf min khabar al-ākhira* ('Good News from the afterlife') by Peter Theroux as *Rites of Assent*, Philadelphia, 1995.

23 English translation as *Aunt Safiyya and the Monastery* by Barbara Romaine, Berkeley, 1996.

24 See above, p. 127.

25 English translation as *Memoirs from the Women's Prison* by Marilyn Booth, Berkeley, 1986. A large number of al-Sa'dāwī's other works have also been translated into English and other European languages, considerably contributing to her international reputation. For translations into English, including several made by her husband, Sherif Hetata, see Altoma, *Modern Arabic Literature in Translation*, p. 96. For a study of al-Sa'dāwī, see Fadwa Malti-Douglas, *Men, Women and God(s): Nawāl El Saadāwī and Arab Feminist Poetics*, Berkeley, 1995.

26 Translated into English as *Woman at Point Zero* by Sherif Hetata, London, 1990, and *Two Women in One* by Osman Nusairi and Jana Gough, London, 1986.

27 Margot Badran and Miriam Cooke (eds), *Opening the Gates: A Century of Arab Feminist Writing*, Bloomington and Indianapolis, 1990.

28 *War's Other Voices: Women Writers on the Lebanese Civil War*, Cambridge, 1987.

29 Miriam Cooke, *War's Other Voices*, p. 5. I have slightly modified Cooke's spelling of one or two names.

30 English translation as *Beirut '75* by Nancy N. Roberts, Fayetteville, 1995. For a complete list of translations of al-Sammān's works, see Altoma, *Modern Arabic Literature in Translation*.

31 Quoted in Cooke, M., *War's Other Voices*, p. 6.

32 English translations of the three novels referred to are available respectively as *The Story of Zahra*, tr. Peter Ford, London, 1986; *Beirut Blues*, tr. Catherine Cobham, London, 1995; and *Only in London*, tr. Catherine Cobham, London, 2003. For other translations, see Altoma, *Modern Arabic Literature in Translation*.

33 English translation as *Flight Against Time* by Issa J. Boullata, Charlottetown, 1987.

34 Respectively *'Aṣāfīr al-fajrī* (1968) and *Khaṭṭ al-af'ā* (1970), and *Qal'at al-Usṭā* (1979) and *Jisr al-ḥajar* (1982).

35 English translation as *Dear Mr Kawabata* by Paul Starkey, London, 1999. For a discussion, see Paul Starkey, 'Crisis and Modernity in Rashid al-Da'if's *Dear Mr Kawabata*: an essay in narrative disorder', in *Crisis and Memory: The Representation of Space in Modern Levantine Narrative*, ed. Ken Seigneurie, Wiesbaden, 2003, pp. 115–32.

36 Margaret Drabble, Foreword to *Dear Mr Kawabata* (cf. above, note 35), pp. vii–ix.

37 English translation as *Passage to Dusk*, by Nirvana Tanoukhi, Austin, Texas, 2001.

38 English translation as *This Side of Innocence*, by Paula Haydar, New York/Northampton, 2001.

39 Tel Aviv, 1986. English translation as *Arabesques* by Vivian Eden, New York, 1989.

40 English translation as *The Secret Life of Saeed, the Ill-Fated Pessoptimist* by Salma Khadra Jayyusi and Trevor LeGassick, London and New York, 1985.
41 For which, see above, p. 10.
42 For a useful discussion, see Stefan G. Meyer, *The Experimental Arabic Novel: Postcolonial Literary Modernism in the Levant*, New York: SUNY Press, 2001, pp. 61–8.
43 Ibid., 100–6, for a discussion of this work, including the significance of the term *khurāfiya*.
44 Ibid., p 90.
45 For which, see above, pp. 103–4.
46 Quoted in Donohue and Tramontini, *Crosshatching in Global Culture*, I, p. 221.
47 English translation by Catherine Cobham as *The Long Way Back*, Cairo: AUC Press, 2002.
48 London, 1988.
49 Aspects of the contemporary literature of some Gulf states have been extensively studied by the Polish academic Barbara Michalak-Pikulska in her books *Modern Poetry and Prose of Oman, 1975–2000*, Kraków, 2002, and *The Contemporary Kuwaiti Short Story in Peace Time and War, 1920–1995*, Kraków, 1998.
50 For a discussion, see Meyer, *The Experimental Arabic Novel*, pp. 72–87.
51 In the words of Muḥammad Siddiq, ibid., p. 76.
52 English translations as *Adama* by Robin Bray, London, 2002, and *Shumaisi* by Paul Starkey, London, 2005, respectively.
53 Radio interview with Mariella Frostrup, quoted on the dust-jacket of the English translation of *Shumaisi*.
54 English version published as *Gardens of the Night*, tr. R. Harris, Amin al-ʿAyonti and Suraya ʿAllam, London, 1991.
55 For his plays, see Chapter 10 below, pp. 194–5.
56 The novel was serialised in *al-ʿAmal* in 1969 and republished in book form in 1989.
57 Al-ʿArūsī al-Maṭwī, Muḥammad, *Ḥalīma*, Tunis, 8th edn, 1980, p. 116.
58 On this and related themes, see Paul Starkey, 'Some Aspects of the French Colonial Legacy in the Tunisian Novel of the 1960s and 1970s', *Oriente Moderno*, XVI (LXXVII), n.s. (1997), pp. 151–61. This volume of *Oriente Moderno*, on the theme of 'The Arabic Literatures of the Maghreb: Tradition Revisited or Response to Cultural Hegemony?' contains a valuable collection of articles on modern North African literature, and is a useful starting point for anyone interested in conducting further research on the subject.
59 For which, see the previous chapter, p. 134.
60 For a full list, see *EAL*, s.v. 'Boudjedra, Rachid'.
61 English translations available respectively as *For Bread Alone*, tr. Paul Bowles, London, 1973; and *Streetwise*, tr. E. Emery, London, 1994.
62 English translations of *Majnūn al-ḥukm* and *al-ʿAllāma* are available respectively as *The Theocrat*, tr. Roger Allen, Cairo, 2005 and *The Polymath*, tr. Roger Allen, Cairo, 2004.
63 Jābir ʿUṣfūr, *Zaman al-Riwāya*, Beirut, 1999.

9

Drama: early experiments

As already suggested elsewhere,[1] the existence of an indigenous dramatic tradition in the Arab world, and the implications that this may have for an account of the development of Arabic drama during the nineteenth and twentieth centuries, has been the subject of considerable controversy in recent years. Although proponents of different viewpoints have on occasion been vociferous in proclaiming their own interpretations, the essential facts are hardly in doubt: for while, on the one hand, it is impossible to deny the existence of numerous dramatic elements in Muslim culture and Arabic literature, it is equally clear that until the mid-nineteenth century the Arab world had not been home to a theatrical tradition of the type found, for example, in the classical civilisations of Greece or Rome, or in Elizabethan England.

To a far greater extent than modern Arabic poetry or prose writing, modern Arabic drama – as M. M. Badawi has suggested –is 'an importation from the West'.[2] However, it is not *solely* an importation from the West, and some understanding of the local historical antecedents is essential, both because without it, it is impossible to understand the way in which the imported forms were received and regarded by the local population, and because echoes of the local tradition can be found in the work of even the most serious dramatists (e.g. Tawfīq al-Ḥakīm)[3] up to the present day. Although most Islamic scholars considered the theatre unworthy of scholarly attention, or indeed, of the status of 'literature' (*adab*) at all, the eastern, Shiʿite, Islamic world had had a tradition of the 'passion play' (*taʿziya*) from at least the eighteenth century, and probably considerably earlier. Still older and more widespread was the phenomenon of the 'shadow-play' (*khayāl al-ẓill*),[4] an importation from the Far East, mainly China and India, which was carried westward by Muslim merchants and reached as far as Muslim Spain.

The earliest accounts of the shadow play date from the eleventh century AD, and the three shadow plays composed by the oculist Ibn Dāniyāl (d. 1310) in particular have excited much scholarly interest.[5] Composed in a blend of classical and colloquial Arabic, and a mixture of verse and rhymed prose that suggests a development from the *maqāma* form,[6] they present a graphic picture of contemporary lower-class Cairo society, and as such represent a valuable source of information both for linguists and for social historians; the final play concludes with a banquet attended by homosexuals and perverts of every persuasion – though all three plays also embrace the concept of moral repentance. Although there was undoubtedly a falling off in their degree of sophistication, shadow play performances in Cairo lasted well into the twentieth century, when the local cinema industry (and later, television) began to constitute a rival attraction.

Beside the shadow play, live performances also existed in medieval Islam. Unlike in classical Greece or Rome, however, these performances, far from forming one of the most prestigious modes of literary expression, were essentially expressions of popular culture. In the fourteenth century, for example, the North African writer Ibn al-Ḥājj (d. 1336) described a performance in which an actor painted his face, stuck on a fur beard, and dressed himself in a red or yellow dress and conical cap, before riding through the streets on a donkey.[7] Later accounts by European travellers in the late eighteenth and nineteenth centuries suggest that these techniques had developed little over the preceding five centuries. In 1780, Carsten Niebuhr witnessed a farce in the courtyard of a Cairo house, and in 1815 G. Belzoni saw two farces, one of them apparently focusing on an Arab couple who deceive a European into believing they are rich.[8] Slightly later, the Orientalist E. W. Lane described performances of farces by itinerant actors known as *muḥabbazūn*, or *Awlād Rābiya* (after the actor Abū Rābiya);[9] these performances, which had their equivalents in most other parts of the Arab world, continued well after the introduction of Western-based theatrical forms in Egypt and Syria towards the middle of the nineteenth century.[10]

As already noted, recent research has uncovered an Arabic play published in Algiers in 1847, entitled *Nazahāt al-mushtāq wa-ghuṣṣat al-ʿushshāq fī madīnat tiryāq fī al-ʿIrāq*;[11] the play is written in a mixture of prose and verse, and based largely on material from the *Thousand and One Nights* and Ibn Ghānim al-Muqaddasī's *Kitāb Kashf al-Asrār ʿan Ḥikam al-Ḥuyūr wa-al-Azhār*.[12] Pending further research, however, it is uncertain whether this work is better regarded as one of the last examples of the traditional Arabic drama or as the forerunner of the new.

Mārūn al-Naqqāsh (1817–55) and his successors

Prior to the discovery of the Algerian play, the honour of composing the first modern Arabic drama had traditionally been held to belong to the Lebanese dramatist Mārūn al-Naqqāsh (1817–55). Born in Sidon, Mārūn al-Naqqāsh moved with his family to Beirut in 1825 and acquired an education that combined commercial skills with an interest in various facets of the arts. In addition to Arabic and Ottoman Turkish, he learned French and Italian, and for a time served as chief clerk in the Beirut customs house; he later became a businessman, travelling not only in Syria, Lebanon and Egypt but also to Italy, where in 1846 he made the acquaintance of Italian theatre and opera. On his return to Lebanon, he wrote and produced three plays in Arabic which have some claim to be regarded as the first true examples of 'modern' Arabic drama, and which certainly set the tone for much of the subsequent early development of modern Arabic theatre, both in their emphasis on musical elements in the drama, and in their combination of local and imported material and techniques. Unfortunately, Mārūn al-Naqqāsh's dramatic career came to a premature end when he fell ill on yet another business trip and died in Tarsus in 1855, but his plays were subsequently collected and published by his brother Niqūlā al-Naqqāsh under the title *Arzat Lubnān* in 1869.

Mārūn al-Naqqāsh's first play, *al-Bakhīl*, was first performed in Mārūn's own house towards the end of 1847 before an audience that included a number of foreign consuls and other dignitaries. An indication of the innovative nature of the event is the fact that the author saw fit to introduce the play with a speech describing the civilising function of the European theatre, as well as explaining his preference for musical theatre, which he thought the audience would find more to their taste. The play itself is remarkable not only for being composed entirely in verse, and for being entirely set to music, but also for the mixture of registers of Arabic that the author saw fit to employ – a blend of classical Arabic and Lebanese colloquial, but also incorporating some Egyptian dialect, as well as an attempt to mimic Turkish speakers with an imperfect knowledge of the language. The extent of al-Naqqāsh's indebtedness to Molière's *L'Avare* when composing this play has been the subject of some controversy: what is certain is that, although the work is in no sense a translation of the French original, it is substantially indebted to it.

By contrast, Mārūn al-Naqqāsh's second play, *Abū al-Ḥasan al-Mughaffal*, is, superficially at least, based on a story from the *Alf Layla wa-Layla* that tells of the man who became caliph for a day (a theme subsequently used also by Tawfīq al-Ḥakīm).[13] Written in a mixture of rhymed prose and classical Arabic verse, and performed before the Ottoman governor in 1850, the play (which some have claimed, rather than *al-Bakhīl*, to be the first 'original' play in Arabic), is considerably more than a simple adaptation of the story from the *Alf Layla* for the stage; for al-Naqqāsh not only uses it to illustrate the theme of fantasy and reality, but also injects a theme of romance and even (so it has been suggested)[14] social criticism. His third play, *al-Salīṭ al-Ḥasūd*, 'probably the most symmetrically structured of al-Naqqāsh's plays',[15] is set in nineteenth-century Beirut and was staged in 1853 in the author's own theatre beside his house. The plot, which revolves around a jealous suitor, with a series of love and marriage intrigues, is again written in a mixture of verse and rhyming prose, and includes the use of a chorus that changes its role through the play. The work has occasioned considerable debate about the sources that al-Naqqāsh used in writing it: Landau's claim that it was 'an adaptation of Molière's *Tartuffe*'[16] seems highly unlikely, although echoes of the French author's *Le Bourgeois Gentilhomme* and *Précieuses Ridicules* can almost certainly be heard.

Mārūn al-Naqqāsh's three plays, together with those of Ya'qūb Ṣannū' in Egypt a little later, set the tone for the development of Arabic drama for at least the following half century. Among their most obvious characteristics are the mixing of musical and dramatic elements; complex plots, in which servants play a crucial part; and an obvious indebtedness to Molière in the general approach to dramatic writing. Mārūn's early death was a blow to the development of the theatre in Syria, but his enthusiasm was passed on to other members of his family, in particular his brother, Niqūlā al-Naqqāsh (1825–94) and nephew, Salīm Khalīl al-Naqqāsh (1850–84). In addition to writing plays of his own, Niqūlā published Mārūn's plays after his death, together with a study on the theatre, in *Arzat Lubnān*; while for his part, Salīm formed a theatrical troupe that, despite criticism, for the first time included actresses. At the behest of the Khedive Ismā'īl, he also took his troupe to Egypt, where, in addition to his uncle's plays, he staged his own adaptations of works by Corneille and Racine, and a version of Verdi's *Aïda* sung largely to popular Arab tunes of the day. His productions did not, however, enjoy much success, and recruited by the religious reformer al-Afghānī as a journalist, he subsequently became caught up in the events of the 'Urābī rebellion and was forced to flee Egypt for a period, though he later returned.

Salīm's work, which continued the pattern of romantic drama established by Mārūn, represented little, if any, advance on his uncle's work in terms of dramatic technique, but in emigrating from Lebanon to Egypt, he set a precedent that was later to be followed by several of his compatriots, among whom may be mentioned Najīb Ḥaddād (1867–99), Yūsuf al-Khayyāṭ (? –1900), Sulaymān al-Qardāḥī, Aḥmad al-Qabbānī (1841–1902), Adīb Isḥāq (1856–84), Jūrj Abyaḍ and Faraḥ Anṭūn. The motive for this move to Egypt was a dual one. On the one hand, the writers and actors concerned were keen to escape persecution by the authorities in Syria, who seem to have been easily swayed by religious opinion: Aḥmad al-Qabbānī, for example, who produced a number of plays in Damascus, some based on the *Thousand and One Nights*, enjoyed the favour of the Governor at first, but his theatre was closed in 1884, after a complaint that his plays were heretical. At the same time, they were no doubt attracted by the prospects enjoyed by the theatre in Egypt which, intermittently at least, enjoyed the Khedive's patronage. Relations with the authorities in Egypt, however, often proved as delicate as those in Syria: the Khedive Ismā'īl's patronage of Yūsuf al-Khayyāṭ, for example, ended abruptly, at least for a time, with a performance of his play *al-Ẓalūm* in 1878, which contained allusions to the Khedive's despotic rule, and al-Khayyāṭ was forced to flee the country for a period. Accounts of the theatre in Egypt during this period also make it clear that it was an economically precarious enterprise.[17] Many of those involved had other jobs, either from choice or necessity, often in journalism, and not infrequently with a political slant. Troupes seem to have 'folded' and been reconstituted with alarming regularity. Al-Khayyāṭ, for example, formed his own troupe in 1876 from the remains of a troupe managed by Salīm al-Naqqāsh and Adīb Isḥāq. In 1882, al-Khayyāṭ's troupe was in turn taken over by Sulayman al-Qardāḥī, and al-Khayyāṭ, with the support of the famous singer and actor Salāma Ḥijāzī, formed a new troupe of his own, but he was unable to compete with al-Qardāḥī and al-Qabbānī's troupes and eventually left the theatre. On occasions, the rivalry seems even to have involved violence: al-Qabbānī's Cairo theatre, for example, was burned down by a mob in 1900, supposedly at the instigation of al-Qabbānī's theatrical rivals. So far as the performances themselves were concerned, they appear to have comprised a mixture of translated, adapted and original plays: adaptations from European classics (mainly French) such as those by Corneille, Racine, Molière, Victor Hugo, as well as Shakespeare. Many performances had a melodramatic flavour, and the use of music continued to form an important feature of many theatrical performances; indeed, many may perhaps better be regarded as 'operettas' than as drama proper. Also of note is the continuation of the tradition foreshadowed by Mārūn al-Naqqāsh himself, of using the Arabic popular folk heritage, in particular the *Alf Layla wa-Layla*, as a source of inspiration. Overwhelmingly, as Cachia notes,[18] the live theatre was at this period in the hands of actor-managers, whose interest in the theatre was mainly in the performances; the result of this is that many works were only printed at a later date, if indeed at all[19] – adding considerably to the difficulty of constructing a reliable history of drama during this period.

The exodus of these writers and actors to Egypt appears effectively to have drained Syria and Lebanon of any theatrical talent worth the name, with the result that theatre as an indigenous live tradition all but disappeared from the Levant until well into the twentieth century. In the meantime, however, Egypt had produced a theatrical pioneer of its own, whose name is often linked with that of Mārūn al-Naqqāsh as one of the two pioneers of the Arabic drama. James Sanua (Ya'qūb Sannū') (1839–1912), an Egyptian Jew who had studied in Italy and taught at the École des Arts et Métiers and at the École polytechnique in Cairo, wrote and produced a number of plays in colloquial Arabic between 1870 and 1872, under the nom de plume Abū Naḍḍāra ('the man with glasses'). Sanua's interest in the drama dated from an early age, when he had attended, and taken part in, open-air performances by European troupes in the Cairo Ezbekiyya Gardens, and his own dramatic productions coincided with the opening of the Cairo Opera House, built to celebrate the opening of the Suez Canal in 1869. His compositions prompted the Khedive to call him the 'Egyptian Molière', partly perhaps from a desire to compare himself with Molière's patron, Louis XIV.[20] Not all his plays are extant, those that do survive being mostly comedies, revolving around the social mores of the contemporary middle and upper classes, the vogue for imitating European customs and so on. His *Molière Miṣr wa-mā Yuqāsīh* may be regarded as his own, probably not entirely reliable, account of the establishment of Arabic drama in Egypt.

Some uncertainty attaches to the reasons for the sudden closure of Sanua's theatre in 1872. The usual assumption has been that it was on account of Sanua's political criticism of the Khedive, but, as Badawi has pointed out, none of the extant plays of this period could be regarded as politically subversive.[21] Whatever the reason, Sanua moved to journalism, launching a series of attacks on the authorities through a number of publications, including *Abū Naḍḍāra Zarqā*, a satirical magazine in colloquial Egyptian, which ran for fifteen issues before it was banned. Exiled to Paris, he continued publishing satirical papers intermittently, in French and Arabic, from 1878 to 1910, attacking the corruption and incompetence of the ruling Egyptian family, while at the same time condemning the British occupation of his country.

The closure of Sanua's theatre brought to an abrupt end a promising line of development of Egyptian drama. Rightly remembered as the founder of politico-satirical theatre in Egypt, Sanua made a distinctive contribution to the genre through his unashamed use of colloquial Egyptian (in marked contrast to Mārūn al-Naqqāsh and others, who had generally used classical Arabic, and were even not averse to the use of *saj'*) and his use of actresses for the first time on the Egyptian stage. He had, however, no direct successor, for by the mid-1870s 'live' theatre in Egypt had effectively passed into Syrian hands. In the meantime, however, despite the theatre-going public's preference for music and melodrama, the ground was being laid for a truly 'Egyptian' theatre of a somewhat different kind, through the efforts of Muḥammad 'Uthmān Jalāl (1829–98), a former student of Rifā'a Rāfi' al-Ṭahṭāwī. Unlike al-Naqqāsh, Sanua and the other early pioneers, Jalāl was neither an actor nor a theatre manager, but a scholar and poet, with a thorough training in the art of translation and a clear sense of what was involved in the translation process. His translations included five plays by Molière, three by Racine and two by Corneille, as well as an original play of his own, *al-Khaddāmīn wa-al-Mukhaddimīn*; in addition to drama, he also translated *Paul et Virginie* and the *Fables* of La Fontaine. His translations largely dispensed with the additions of songs and music that had been a feature of Arabic drama since the time of Mārūn al-Naqqāsh. At the same time, perhaps remarkably, he had no hesitation in using *zajal*, verse in the colloquial Egyptian idiom, for all his dramatic translations, which represent one of the highest achievements of 'Egyptianisation', by which the plays were to be 'stripped of their French costumes and dressed up in Arab robes'. If his plays had less of an immediate impact than might have been expected, this is probably because the Syrian troupes that dominated the theatre during Jalāl's lifetime had little enthusiasm for plays in a 'foreign' colloquial. They quickly gained in popularity after his death, however, and *al-Shaykh Matlūf* in particular, an Egyptianised version of *Tartuffe*, has continued to be a popular favourite with Egyptian audiences since its first performance in Cairo in 1912.

The theatrical foundations laid by Muḥammad 'Uthmān Jalāl were built on by a number of Egyptian and Syrian intellectuals, most notably the secularist Faraḥ Anṭūn (1874–1922), another Lebanese emigrant to Egypt, who translated Nietzsche's *Also sprach Zarathustra* and Rousseau's *Émile*, as well as works by Gorky, Anatole France and Chateaubriand, among others. Like Mārūn al-Naqqāsh and several others of his predecessors, Faraḥ Anṭūn was a firm believer in the civilising function of the theatre, and his theatrical activities included translations of plays and operettas of Alexandre Dumas and other playwrights, as well as an original play, *Miṣr al-jadīda wa-Miṣr al-qadīma*, on the theme of Western influences on contemporary Egyptian society. His writing also demonstrates an acute awareness of the problem of 'diglossia' for the Arab theatre.

By this stage in the development of the Arab drama, we can begin to see, albeit indistinctly, the beginnings of a split between popular taste and the desire to establish a more 'literary' theatrical tradition. An important lead in the attempt to raise the standard of theatrical performance was given by Jūrj Abyaḍ (1880–1959), a Syrian Christian who had settled in Alexandria in 1898 and attracted the attention of the Khedive 'Abbās Ḥilmī, who sent him to Paris where he studied under the actor Sylvain. On his return to Egypt in 1910, Abyaḍ formed his own troupe, which presented mainly tragedies and historical dramas, including Sophocles' *Oedipus Rex* in a translation by Faraḥ Anṭūn. Although financial problems later forced him to make concessions to popular taste, Abyaḍ was largely responsible for introducing the Egyptian public to the idea of a 'classical' theatre, and his performances were attended by, among others, the young Tawfīq al-Ḥakim.[22]

Despite the attempts of Abyaḍ to establish an Egyptian 'classical' theatre, the public continued to favour less serious fare, however. In 1923, Yūsuf Wahbī, a well-to-do Egyptian with Turkish connections who had studied acting in Italy, founded the 'Ramses' company and presented a series of plays, mainly melodramas, some of which he wrote himself. The financial difficulties that had plagued the previous generation of theatre managers continued to rear their heads, however: in 1926 Fāṭima Rushdī left to form her own company, and Wahbī was even forced into partnership with Abyaḍ for a time. In 1933 he took charge of a government-sponsored troupe, and though forbidden to perform exclusively melodramas, it was these, together with historical plays, that made up the main part of his repertoire. Similar entertainment, heavily reliant on music, was provided by a number of others, including the ʿUkāsha brothers, for whose theatre the young Tawfīq al-Ḥakīm wrote six plays during the 1920s. Parallel with these developments, other forms of popular theatre were also emerging, which combined elements from the traditional farce with Western comic techniques that had probably become familiar through the presence of foreign troops during the First World War. Among these were the 'Franco-Arab revue', created by the Syrian-born ʿAzīz ʿĪd, and Najīb al-Rīḥānī's Kish-Kish Bey, a distinctively Egyptian village headman or *ʿumda*, reacting slightly naively, but with fundamental good sense, to world affairs and social developments. Critics scoffed, but his popularity remained immense.

An important development during the last years of the nineteenth and first years of the twentieth century was the institution of tours, not only in the Egyptian provinces, but also abroad, in the Arab world and beyond. Both Aḥmad al-Qabbānī and Sulaymān al-Qardāḥī, for example, returned with their troupes to Syria; al-Qabbānī also played at the Chicago Fair in 1892, and al-Qardāḥī visited the Great Exhibition in Paris. Tours to North Africa were undertaken by al-Qardāḥī in 1908, and by Jūrj Abyaḍ a little later, and after al-Qardāḥī's death in Tunisia in 1909, members of his troupe stayed to form a new company, thus allowing the Tunisians their first opportunity of participating in dramatic performances themselves.

Although by the early years of the twentieth century, the theatre had become part and parcel of the life of European, and Europeanised, society in Cairo and Alexandria,[23] the concept of developing a genuinely 'Arab' or 'Egyptian' theatre had in general not yet engaged the attention of the leading writers of the day. There were, of course, some exceptions to this generalisation: in addition to the contributions of ʿUthmān Jalāl and Faraḥ Anṭūn already discussed, mention may be made in particular of ʿAbd Allāh al-Nadīm (1843/4–96), a prolific writer and poet, as well as a political activist, who also made important contributions to the development of Arabic prose style.[24] As headmaster of an Islamic charitable school founded in 1879, Nadīm wrote two plays in Egyptian colloquial Arabic, *al-ʿArab* and *al-Waṭan wa-ṭāliʿ al-tawfīq*, but for whatever reason he did not pursue his theatrical activities and like many of his colleagues, including Sanua himself, turned back to political journalism. Another writer who seems to have been at least fleetingly attracted to the theatre was Muḥammad Luṭfī Jumʿa (1884–1953). The real process of 'coming of age' of the modern Arabic theatre, however, may be dated to the period of the First World War, when a number of playwrights working in Egypt began to produce work that demonstrated not only a new level of artistic maturity but also an obvious concern with the situation of contemporary Egypt, together with a clear understanding of the problems of creating an 'Egyptian' or 'Arab' drama. Among this generation, the names of most significance are those of Anṭūn Yazbak,[25] Ibrāhīm Ramzī (1884–1949), and Muḥammad Taymur (1892–1921). Though forming an obvious 'group' through their employment of Egyptian colloquial in preference to 'classical' Arabic, both the careers and the work of these three playwrights were very different from each other, and it will therefore be appropriate to discuss them individually at some length.

Of the three playwrights, Ibrāhīm Ramzī[26] was the most prolific, both in the number of plays he produced, and in his other activities. In addition to composing some dozen original plays, he wrote novels and translated works by Shakespeare, Shaw, Sheridan and Ibsen, as well as others on subjects as varied as history, sociology and ethics – all this while working full-time as an Egyptian civil servant. Of all his activities, however, it is those as a dramatist that have proved the most significant, for, as Badawi has argued, he can not only be described as the author of the 'first fully fledged truly Egyptian social comedy' (*Dukhūl al-ḥammām mish zayy khurūguh*, c. 1915), he can also claim, in *Abṭāl Manṣūra* (1915), to have 'produced the first historical drama of literary merit in modern Arabic literature.'[27]

Like that of many other early pioneers of the Arabic theatre, Ramzī's interest in the theatre seems to have been developed, partly at least, during a period of study in the West, though unlike most of his contemporaries, his experience of the West was not of France but of England, where he studied social sciences. His dramatic works include four social comedies; three serious dramas; and six historical plays, all but one of which revolve around Fatimid, Ikhshidid or Mamluk Egypt – the exception being *Ismāʿīl al-Fātiḥ*, which deals with the conquest of Sudan by the Egyptian khedive Ismāʿīl in the nineteenth century.

Of Ramzī's social comedies, the first, *Dukhūl al-ḥammām*, has been analysed in some detail by Mustafa Badawi. Set in the unlikely surroundings of a Cairo public bath in a poor quarter of Būlāq, the plot revolves around the despairing baths' manager, Abū Ḥasan, and his seductive and enterprising wife, Zaynab, who with the help of the bath attendant, Nashāshqī, succeed in exploiting an *ʿumda*'s (village headman's) weakness for the female sex and robbing him of his money. Although this type of situation had been utilised on occasion by previous playwrights, the assurance with which Ibrāhīm Ramzī handles both the dramatic requirements of the plot and the portrayal of the characters was unprecedented, ensuring that the play was a success whenever it was performed. Some idea of the humour and repartee involved may be gleaned from the extract of several pages translated into English by Badawi.[28] The play is also notable for its relevance to contemporary Egyptian society, however, at a time when the inflation brought on by the war had led to an increase in crime and corruption, as well as for its treatment of the theme of the countryman coming to town

– a particular instance of the 'town vs country' motif that frequently reappears in much modern Arabic literature, and of which a number of instances have already been discussed in previous chapters dealing with fiction.[29] Successors to the type of scenario and distinctive brand of Egyptian humour embodied in *Dukhūl al-ḥammām* can be found in the countless plays, films and television soap operas for which Egypt has become renowned and which have been widely exported throughout the Arab world.

In terms both of technique and of thematic treatment, *Dukhūl al-ḥammām* on one level stands a world apart from Ramzī's historical plays, of which *Abṭāl Manṣūra* is probably the best known example. What links them, perhaps – in addition to the sureness of the author's technique – is that neither genre can be taken entirely at its face value: for just as the humour of *Dukhūl al-ḥammām* conceals a serious streak of social criticism, so the historical framework of *Abṭāl Manṣūra* conceals an obvious reference to the plight of contemporary Egypt. This technique of using the past as an analogy for the present has already been encountered several times in our discussion of modern Arabic fiction. In the case of Ramzī's play, which unlike his social comedies is written in classical Arabic, the action revolves around the Sixth Crusade led by Louis IX of France in 1248, and the ultimately successful struggle of the Egyptians to expel the European invaders from Egypt; in the final act, we find that a new Sultan, Tūrānshāh, has been installed, but his autocratic powers are quickly curbed by his generals, who force him to accept that the age of absolute monarchy is over. The relevance of this plot to the situation of contemporary Egypt would be self-evident, even without the author's explicit comments in the introduction to the work, and it is no surprise to find that the work was banned by the British authorities for some three years after its composition until 1918.

The second member of this theatrical trio, Anṭūn Yazbak,[30] was, as a 'Syro-Egyptian', continuing a tradition that had played not merely an important, but indeed, a crucial part in the development of Egyptian theatre in the second half of the nineteenth century. A lawyer by profession, Yazbak worked for a time with Jūrj Abyaḍ, with whom he had studied in Beirut and whose troupe performed his *'Āṣifa fī al-bayt* at the Cairo Opera House in 1924. Known as one of the pioneers of the mature Egyptian melodrama, his best-known work is *al-Dhabā'iḥ* (1925), which revolves around a retired general's relationship with an Egyptian, Amīna, and a European woman, Noreska, whom he marries after divorcing his first wife. Themes involving relationships between Egyptian, or more generally, Arab, men and Western women have, of course, been common in modern Arabic literature, particularly fiction, at most stages of its development,[31] since the different sexual mores of Middle Eastern and European society provide a fertile ground both for imaginative writing and for authorial reflection. At all events, Yazbak's play, which is written in colloquial Arabic, represented a significant advance in the depiction of human relationships on the Egyptian stage at the time of its first production on the stage in 1925. Despite the play's popularity, however, the author for some reason quickly fell into obscurity until 'rediscovered' by the Egyptian critic Muḥammad Mandūr[32] at a considerably later date, and his work has seldom been accorded the recognition that it deserves.

The most important contribution, however, to this stage of the development of Egyptian drama – and indeed, to Arabic drama as a whole – was made by Muḥammad Taymūr (1892–1921), a member of a distinguished literary family, whom we have already encountered as a pioneer of the modern Egyptian short story.[33] Although Taymūr's career was cut tragically short by his premature death, his early career bears a curious resemblance to that of his slightly younger contemporary Tawfīq al-Ḥakīm (1898–1987), who was later to become the Arab world's greatest playwright to date. After studying at the 'Abbās Khedivial School in Cairo, Muḥammad Taymūr travelled in 1911 to France, where for three years he studied law in Paris and Lyon; in practice, however, the majority of his enthusiasm seems to have been devoted to Western literature rather than to law, and in Paris he began to frequent the Odéon Theatre, stimulating an ambition to become an actor or playwright.

On his return to Egypt, Muḥammad Taymūr quickly set about turning his new enthusiasms into practice, producing four comedies in colloquial Egyptian between 1918 and 1921. Deriving his inspiration from a belief that to raise standards it was necessary to 'Egyptianise' the theatre, he attempted to treat social and domestic themes of relevance to the Egyptian public; at the same time, he deliberately strove to avoid the sort of cheap theatrical devices commonly employed in the popular comedies of Najīb al-Rīḥānī and others.

The first of Muḥammad Taymūr's plays, *'Uṣfūr fī al-qafaṣ* (1918), originally written in classical Arabic but later 'translated' into Egyptian colloquial, revolves around a young man from a well-to-do family who marries his Levantine nurse, Marguerite, preferring freedom and poverty to the tyrannical control of his distant but wealthy father; the play ends, however, with a reconciliation between father and son. The play is an obvious example of the universal theme of the conflict between the generations; at the same time, however, it is rich in Egyptian humour, and on one level seems to stand in a direct line of descent from the plays of James Ṣanua.

Unfortunately, in the face of competition from more popular forms of entertainment, *'Uṣfūr fī al-qafaṣ* failed to achieve much success at the box-office. In an attempt to attract a better audience, Taymūr composed a second, more light-hearted comedy, *'Abd al-Sattār Effendi* (1918), based around a middle-class employee of that name, who is dominated by his loud-voiced wife, Nafīsa, and their spoiled, unemployed son, 'Afīfī; the work shares with *Uṣfūr fī al-qafaṣ* a theme related to the conflict between the generations, though in the case of

'Abd al-Sattār Effendi, it is the son rather than the father who tyrannises the other members of the family. In any event, despite the work's obvious merits, most obviously the author's talent for dramatic characterisation, the play again failed to satisfy the public. Discouraged, Muḥammad Taymūr turned away from the theatre to devote most of his energies to the short story and other literary activities, including editing the periodical *al-Sufūr*, and he produced only two more dramas: *al-'Ashara al-ṭayyiba*, a sort of *opéra bouffe* in colloquial Arabic prose and verse, adapted from the French comedy *Barbe-Bleu*, with music by Sayyid Darwīsh; and a final work, *al-Hāwiya*, which he completed shortly before his death in 1921. The first of these two plays, *al-'Ashara al-ṭayyiba*, which portrayed the tyranny of Mamluk rule in Egypt, proved no more successful than the author's previous productions, being heavily criticised for offending the Turkish establishment in Egypt. Ironically, it was only with his fourth play, *al-Hāwiya*, first performed some two months after his death, that the author seems to have achieved a measure of theatrical success. The play, which is generally agreed to be both the best and the most important that the author wrote, portrays a young aristocrat who loses everything – his wife, his fortune and eventually his life – as a result of addiction to cocaine; although the main theme obviously relates to the problems of drug addiction among the Egyptian aristocracy, some aspects of the work have also been read as a support for the emancipation of women – or at least, for their fair treatment.

Despite their limited success in terms of their popular appeal, which was unable to compete with the less intellectually demanding entertainment of Najīb al-Rīḥānī and others, Muḥammad Taymūr's plays are clearly of great significance, both in terms of technique and conception; they carried forward the concept of an 'Egyptian theatre' further than any other writer had so far done, proving that serious, contemporary social problems could be treated on the stage in colloquial Egyptian.

The next phase in the development of the Egyptian theatre was dominated by the figure of Tawfīq al-Ḥakīm, who between 1921 and 1926 produced some six plays in colloquial Arabic for the popular theatre of the 'Ukāsha brothers; an account of these plays, together with al-Ḥakīm's subsequent dramatic works, will be given in the following chapter. By way of background, however, it may be noted that the 1920s in Egypt were a time of considerable uncertainty and contradictory trends for the theatre and dramatic activity. When al-Ḥakīm returned to Egypt in 1928 from his period of study in Paris, for example, he found many of his former theatrical associates bankrupt. At the same time, however, there were signs that the Egyptian government was beginning to sense the value of serious drama: prizes were offered, and scholarships awarded for Egyptians to study drama in Europe – incentives that culminated in 1930 with the establishment of a school of dramatic arts under the directorship of Zakī

Ṭulaymāt. Another factor working in favour of the development of the drama at this time was the increasing interest being shown in, and indeed at times the direct participation in, the theatre by well-educated members of Egyptian society, including a number of leading intellectuals; of these, the most prominent was undoubtedly Ṭāhā Ḥusayn, who had written about, and translated extracts from, classical Greek drama. A further boost to the standing of the genre was provided by the neo-classical poet Aḥmad Shawqī, who had dabbled with the drama as a young man, composing in 1893 a play entitled *'Alī Bey al-Kabīr* (subsequently rewritten and republished in 1932); Shawqī returned to the theatre in 1928, composing during the last few years of his life a comedy (*al-Sitt Hudā*, published posthumously), a prose play (*Amīrat al-Andalus*, 1932) and a total of five poetic dramas, all of which are based on historical or mythical figures; they include *Maṣra' Kilyūbaṭra* (1929), *Majnūn Laylā* (1931), *Qambīz* (1931), *'Alī Bey al-Kabīr* (1932) and *'Antara* (1932). Despite the elegance of their language and conception, however, Shawqī's plays are in general more notable for their poetic than for their dramatic qualities; the author's powers of characterisation are less developed than those of Ramzī, Yazbak or Muḥammad Taymūr, and it is hard to resist the impression of a neo-classical poet trying his hand at drama, rather than that of a dramatist writing in verse. The most interesting of the plays is undoubtedly *al-Sitt Hudā*, which presents us with the interesting and unusual phenomenon of a comedy written in classical Arabic verse set in a working-class quarter of Cairo; the play revolves around a woman who marries a series of nine men, all of whom are interested in her only for her money; only the last outlives her, but only to find that she has made a will leaving all her money to charity or to her friends. Among Shawqī's other plays, *Maṣra' Kilyūbaṭra* shows evidence of the influence of Shakespeare; *Majnūn Laylā* takes its inspiration from the familiar tale of the Umayyad lovers, Qays and Laylā; while *'Antara* is based on the life of the pre-Islamic hero whose romance with 'Abla inspired many popular tales. Although Shawqī's verse dramas made little direct or immediate contribution to the development of the modern Egyptian theatre, his example was nonetheless followed by a number of other authors, of whom 'Azīz Abāẓa (1898–1969), 'Abd al-Raḥmān al-Sharqāwī (1920–87) and Ṣalāḥ 'Abd al-Ṣabūr (1931–81) are the most obvious examples.

There is little to be said about theatrical developments outside Egypt during this period. Political conditions and the associated waves of emigration from Syria and Lebanon from the mid-nineteenth century onwards appear to have drained the urban centres of those two countries of the capacity to develop any lasting theatrical tradition from the seeds sown by Mārūn al-Naqqāsh and others. That is not to say, of course, that interest in the drama had entirely disappeared outside Egypt. In 1917, for example, the Mahjar poet and critic Mīkhā'īl Nu'ayma[34] published a play entitled *al-Ābā' wa-al-banūn* (yet another expression of the conflict between the generations!), which is set in the context of a Christian family living in a Lebanese town at the beginning of the twentieth century.[35] The work, which involves a complex cast of characters, is clearly intended to demonstrate the need for the younger generation to cast off the restrictions of traditional society, not least by allowing young women to choose their own partners in marriage; but despite the promising nature of the subject, the author lacks the talent for characterisation necessary to construct a good play around such a theme, and he fails to solve the problem of which language register to employ, with the result that the dialogue is a curious and unconvincing mixture of classical and colloquial Arabic. Another Lebanese writer to show interest in the drama was Saʿīd Taqī al-Dīn (1904–60), who spent much of his life in the Philippines, and whose best known play, *Lawlā al-muḥāmī* appeared in 1924. In North Africa, as already noted, tours by Egyptian troupes had prompted some local theatrical activity, and both in North Africa and elsewhere, colonial settlers had brought with them a tradition of European theatre and performance that not infrequently led to translations, adaptations or imitations in Arabic. Nowhere else outside Egypt, however, at this period do we find a concentrated and reasoned attempt to establish a national theatrical tradition of the sort that was being attempted by the likes of Muḥammad Taymūr and his colleagues. Through their efforts, although many problems still remained, the groundwork had been laid for drama finally to be admitted into the Arabic literary 'canon' – a status which it was shortly to achieve through the efforts of the most distinguished Arabic playwright to date, the Egyptian Tawfīq al-Ḥakīm.

Notes

1 See *EAL*, s.v. 'theatre and drama, modern'.
2 M. M. Badawi, *Early Arabic Drama*, Cambridge, 1988, p. 7.
3 For whom, see below, pp. 178–86.
4 A number of other Arabic terms were also used, including *khayāl al-izār* and *khayāl al-sitāra*. See Landau, J. M., *Studies in the Arab Theater and Cinema*, Philadelphia, 1958; also S. Moreh, 'The Shadow Play' (*Khayāl al-ẓill*) in the light of Arabic literature', *JAL* 28 (1987), pp. 46–61.
5 *Three Shadow Plays*, ed. Paul Kahle, prepared by Derek Hopwood and Mustafa Badawi, Cambridge, 1992. See also Badawi, *Early Arabic Drama*, pp. 12–24.
6 See above, p. 10.
7 S. Moreh, *EAL*, II, p. 767, s.v. 'theatre and drama, medieval'.
8 J. M. Landau, *Studies in the Arab Theater and Cinema*, Philadelphia, 1958, p. 50.
9 See E. W. Lane, *Manners and Customs of the Modern Egyptians*, London, n.d., pp. 395–6.
10 See Shmuel Moreh, *Live Theater and Dramatic Literature in the Medieval Arab World*, Edinburgh, 1992, especially pp. 152ff.
11 Edited by S. Moreh and P. C. Sadgrove, Oxford, 1996.

12 Paris, 1820. French translation by M. Carcin de Tassy, *Les oiseaux et les fleurs, allégories morales d'Azz-Eddin Elmocaddesi*, Paris, 1821.
13 See below, p. 186.
14 See Moosa, *Early Arabic Fiction*, p. 29.
15 Badawi, *Early Arabic Drama*, p. 50.
16 Landau, *Studies in the Arab Theatre and Cinema*, p. 59.
17 For the nineteenth-century Egyptian theatre generally, see P. Sadgrove, *The Egyptian Theatre in the Nineteenth Century*, Reading, 1996.
18 Cachia, 'The Arab world', in Ostle, *Modern Literature in the Near and Middle East*, p. 37.
19 The fate of Tawfīq al-Ḥakīm's early plays in colloquial Arabic (for which, see Chapter 10 below) is a case in point.
20 See Badawi, *Early Arabic Drama*, p. 32.
21 Ibid., p. 33.
22 For whom, see below, Chapter 10.
23 On this, see Philip Sadgrove, *The Egyptian Theatre in the Nineteenth Century*, Reading, 1996, *passim*.
24 See above, pp. 107–8.
25 I have been unable to discover precise dates for Yazbak's birth or death.
26 For a more detailed account, see Badawi, *Early Arabic Drama*, pp. 74–101. Badawi draws attention on p. 75 to the confusion that has arisen over a play, *al-Mu'tamid ibn 'Abbād*, written in 1893 by another author of the same name.
27 M. M. Badawi, 'Arabic Drama: early developments', in *Modern Arabic Literature*, ed. M. M. Badawi, Cambridge, 1991, pp. 345–7.
28 M.M. Badawi, *Early Arabic Drama*, pp. 80–4.
29 See, for example, above, p. 111.
30 For a fuller account, see Badawi, *Early Arabic Drama*, pp. 120–33.
31 For an obvious example, cf. Tawfīq al-Ḥakīm's *'Uṣfūr min al-Sharq*, discussed above, pp. 116–17.
32 Muḥammad Mandūr, *al-Masraḥ al-Nathrī*, Cairo, 1959, p. 71.
33 Muḥammad Taymūr has been extensively studied by Ed de Moor in *Un Oiseau en cage*, Amsterdam, 1991; see also Badawi, *Early Arabic Drama*, pp. 101–20. For his short stories, see above, pp. 109–11.
34 For whose poetry, see above, pp. 63–4.
35 See Badawi, *Early Arabic Drama*, pp. 134–7.

10

Drama: the period of maturity

This chapter will discuss subsequent developments in Arabic drama from the 1930s to the present. The early part of this period is dominated to an unusual extent by a single figure, whom we have already met as a pioneer of the Arabic novel,[1] Tawfīq al-Ḥakīm (1898–1987).

As already noted, despite the similarities of many aspects of their careers, there is curiously little evidence of any direct link between the advances made by Muḥammad Taymūr and others in the period around the First World War and al-Ḥakīm's own early theatrical production, which were born of a marriage between the Egyptian popular theatre and European theatrical influences – though the combination of serious political and social comment with the use of colloquial Egyptian dialect as a medium for the plays is of course common to both authors.

Born in Alexandria into a middle-class family, al-Ḥakīm appears to have developed a passion for the theatre from an early age, which was reinforced when he moved to Cairo in 1917 to prepare for the school Intermediate Certificate. Attending performances by Jūrj Abyaḍ and other troupes whenever he could, he began improvising plays with friends and soon started writing plays himself; every Thursday afternoon a sketch would be performed in the guest-room of one of the group. So low was the status enjoyed by the Egyptian theatre at this time, however, that al-Ḥakīm was forced to write under the name 'Ḥusayn Tawfīq' to escape the attention of his family.

These activities appear to have formed a direct prelude to the first stage of al-Ḥakīm's theatrical career proper, the first phase of which comprised six plays written for the popular theatre of the 'Ukāsha brothers already mentioned. Of these six plays, two are of particular note for their combination of more serious elements with the elements of comedy and melodrama commonly found in Egyptian drama of the preceding period. The first, *al-Ḍayf al-Thaqīl* (1919?), builds on the nationalistic sentiments expressed in the 1919 Egyptian Revolt and which were subsequently reflected in al-Ḥakīm's seminal novel *'Awdat al-Rūḥ*.[2] In an unmistakable reference to the British occupation of his country, al-Hakīm depicts a guest who continually extends the length of his stay, exploiting the absences of his lawyer host to pass himself off as the owner of the house and collect his clients' fees. The second play, *al-Mar'a al-Jadīda*, takes its title from the work of the Egyptian feminist author Qāsim Amīn,[3] and appears to represent an assault on the unveiling of women. The misogyny implicit in this and other works was later to become one of al-Ḥakīm's hallmarks – though to what extent it reflects a genuine personal feeling, or was simply adopted as a literary hallmark, is a matter of probably irreconcilable debate. Al-Ḥakīm's other four plays from this period followed a more conventional pattern, with music and songs playing a significant part, and in *Aminusa* we find al-Ḥakīm following the common practice described in the last chapter of adapting a Western-language original (in this case, de Musset's *Carmosine*) to local taste by giving the original an Egyptian (in this case, Pharaonic) setting.

Tawfīq al-Ḥakīm's years as a law student in Paris during 1925–28[4] radically changed his view of the possibilities for the development of Egyptian drama. Exposure to the intellectual and avant-garde authors and dramatists such as Shaw, Maeterlinck and Pirandello fired him with the idea of composing a number of 'philosophical' plays, which remain his most distinctive contribution to modern Arabic drama. The first beginnings of this new direction can be seen in some half dozen plays composed during the period 1928–34, while serving in the Egyptian legal service in Alexandria and the Delta – the same period that inspired the novel *Yawmiyyāt Nā'ib fī al-Aryāf*, discussed above in Chapter 7. These plays form a transitional phase between al-Ḥakīm's early productions discussed above and his more mature works. Two of them, *al-Zammār* ('The Piper') and *Ḥayāh Taḥaṭṭamat* ('A Shattered Life') draw on the background of the Egyptian countryside in which al-Ḥakīm was living and working during this period, while a third play, *Raṣāṣa fī al-Qalb* ('A Bullet in the Heart'), revolves around a rather conventional love triangle, depending for its effect largely on a case of mistaken identity. Two other plays, however, *al-Khurūj min al-Janna* ('Exit from Paradise') and *Ba'da al-Mawt* ('After Death') have a more introspective flavour – providing a first glimpse of one of the main themes ('fantasy' vs 'reality') that runs through al-Ḥakīm's later work. *Al-Khurūj min al-Janna* explores the relationship between a writer and his wife, including a Pirandellian twist in the last act with the revelation that the writer has sublimated his experience into a play of the same name; while in *Ba'd al-Mawt* an ageing doctor, convinced that a girl's suicide was due to her frustrated love for him, is apparently rejuvenated and embarks on a life of pleasure, until disillusioned by the news that it was not he, but his namesake, a chauffeur, whom the girl really loved.

Al-Ḥakim: intellectual drama

These plays, interesting though they are, appear to have done little to satisfy al-Ḥakīm's literary ambitions. While in Paris, he had already had the idea of writing a specifically Egyptian tragedy, replacing the Greek idea of man's struggle with fate with what he saw as a more Egyptian concept: man's struggle against time and place. The resultant play, *Ahl al-Kahf* ('The People of the Cave') had been written in Alexandria soon after his return to Egypt, but al-Ḥakīm delayed publication, fearing the ridicule of his colleagues. In this respect, however, al-Ḥakīm's forebodings were probably misplaced, for when the work eventually appeared in 1933 (the same year that also saw the publication of *ʿAwdat al-Ruḥ*),[5] it received an enthusiastic reception, and indeed, when the Egyptian National Theatre was formed shortly afterwards, it opened with al-Ḥakīm's play.

The publication of *Ahl al-Kahf* in 1933 is a decisive date both in al-Ḥakīm's career as a writer and in the history of modern Arabic drama, for the use of a Qur'anic story (that of the sleepers of Ephesus) as the basis for a philosophical play was unprecedented. Although the play provoked widely differing interpretations, al-Ḥakīm clearly intended it to be understood in the context of contemporary Egypt, as the country awoke from centuries of stagnation to face the challenges of the twentieth century and Western civilisation. In this respect, the play lies squarely in the tradition of works exploring the 'East vs West' dilemma beginning with the accounts of al-Jabartī and al-Ṭahṭāwī in the first half of the nineteenth century. What is new is the literary form in which that dilemma is expressed: for despite the Qur'anic story, the play's roots lie not in Islamic Egypt so much as in the tradition of intellectual drama with which al-Ḥakīm had come into contact during his stay in Paris. The play is permeated with the confusion between fantasy and reality that characterises Pirandello in particular: as the sleepers return to their cave to resume their sleep, they are uncertain whether their experience has been real or if they have been dreaming all along; and in an ironic twist, one of the sleepers relates the story of a Christian who had slept for a month, only to have it dismissed as a 'feeble legend'.[6]

Ahl al-Kahf represents the first of a series of 'intellectual' or 'philosophical' plays by the author covering the period from the 1930s to the 1960s. The second, *Shahrazād*, which appeared in 1934,[7] continues the exploration of fantasy vs reality begun in *Ahl al-Kahf*, using characters from the *Thousand and One Nights*. Although al-Ḥakīm here later claimed to have been trying to break down the barriers between popular and serious drama, he in fact makes little direct use of the story of the *Thousand and One Nights*, for when the play begins, the 1001st night has already ended. Instead, drawing on the techniques of Maeterlinck and others, al-Ḥakīm uses the figure of Shahrazād as a symbol of the unknowable, a 'mysterious woman', a figure whose nature is interpreted by the other characters according to their own inclinations but who remains essentially mysterious until the end: for Qamar, the king's vizier, she is an ideal of beauty; for the slave, she is an embodiment of sexual gratification; while for the king himself, she represents pure intellect. Unlike *Ahl al-Kahf*, the play has no obvious relevance to contemporary Egyptian society and it has provoked different interpretations among the critics; one prominent idea, however (picked up in some of al-Ḥakīm's later works) is clearly the futility of the quest for 'truth'. Compared with *Ahl al-Kahf* – which despite its generally subtle writing, is marred by some over-philosophical, undramatic discussion –*Shahrazad* is from a dramatic point of view more assured, al-Ḥakīm's theatrical techniques being here excellently wedded to the subject: three of the four scenes, for example, take place at night, heightening the sense of mystery and uncertainty that pervades the play.

Although al-Ḥakīm's output in various literary forms during the next few years was prolific, it was not until 1942 that he produced another full-length play in the manner of *Ahl al-Kahf* and *Shahrazād*. *Pygmalion* was, as the author's own introduction makes clear, at least partly inspired by Shaw's play of the same name – though in practice, it owes little to Shaw's play directly, as the element of social criticism appears entirely absent. The central theme, however – the relationship of the artist to his work – clearly represents an extension of the fantasy/reality motif of *Ahl al-Kahf* and *Shahrazād*. Tired of his own creation, the sculptor Pygmalion implores the goddess Venus to breath life into his statue, but no sooner has his prayer been answered than he longs for the ivory Galatea again. His dilemma, however, torn between the real and the ideal, between life and art, is incapable of solution and his final act is to smash the ivory statue with a broom, declaring: 'I shall not die before I have made a statue that is a masterpiece of true art. Until now, I have not put my hand on the secret ... the secret of creative perfection. I have wasted my life in a struggle with art, with my talents and with fate.'[8]

The idea of the futility of the search for truth prominent in *Shahrazād* is pursued further in *al-Malik Ūdīb*, published in 1949, an attempt to rework the Oedipus legend (treated not only by Sophocles but also by a number of modern writers in one form or another) to conform with Islamic beliefs, eliminating the idea of 'fate'. Despite the boldness of the concept, in some respects this is among the least satisfactory of al-Ḥakīm's plays, as the problems of interpretation are not satisfactorily resolved and the play closes with the play's basic questions of guilt and responsibility unanswered. However, it remains an important statement of the author's views on the relationship between thought and feeling; for in al-Ḥakīm's play, Oedipus's downfall comes about mainly because of his reliance on his intelligence rather than his heart as a guide to action. When the truth of his relationship with Jocasta emerges, he repents of his curiosity, but (almost incredibly) is still prepared to continue his life with Jocasta as before; only when he learns of her death does he begin to think of his life as worthless.

Like *Shahrazād* and *Pygmalion*, *al-Malik Ūdīb* appears to be an exclusively 'intellectual' play, with little if any direct relevance to contemporary Egyptian society. In other plays, however, al-Ḥakīm's intellectual themes – often tied up with questions of power and government – are clearly intended to relate to the Egypt of the day. *Praxagora*, for example, published in 1939 and loosely based on Aristophanes' *Ecclesiazousae*, reviews various solutions to the 'problem of government', and this play was followed by the somewhat disjointed *Sulaymān al-Ḥakīm* ('Solomon the Wise'), in which the author uses stories from the Qur'ān and the *Thousand and One Nights* to illustrate the incompatibility of wisdom and power. These themes are continued in *Īzīs* ('Isis'), in which al-Ḥakīm derives his inspiration directly from an Ancient Egyptian myth, that of Isis and Osiris. The central problem of the play is whether the end justifies the means; but the author also uses the work to develop, through the characters of Mastat and Tut, a more specific argument about the function of the artist in society and the relative merits of the opposing philosophies of 'art for art's sake' and 'art for life' – a topical debating point of the period, as has already been noted. This play appeared only three years after the Free Officers' Revolt had brought the Egyptian monarchy to an end in 1952, and a strong hint of contemporary relevance is evident in the play's final assertion that judgement in such matters belongs to the people alone. A somewhat similar question forms the theme of *al-Sulṭān al-Ḥā'ir* ('The Perplexed Sultan'), published in 1960, in which al-Ḥakīm turned his attention to a question which, according to the introduction, he regarded as crucial for the world at the time: 'should it seek solutions to its problems through the application of law or of force?' The play is set in Egypt during the Mamluk period, but it is clear from subsequent comments that al-Ḥakīm intended it to serve as a warning to the Egyptian President Nasser, whose democratic ideals had by this stage begun to look a little thin.[9] Taking its cue from the system by which slaves from the bodyguard of the Sultan were granted freedom and brought up to rule the country, the play explores the dilemma posed by the discovery that the Sultan in question has never in fact been freed. His vizier, citing past precedents, urges the Sultan simply to force his subjects to accept his lineage; while the judge, duty bound to uphold the rule of law, insists that the Sultan is a chattel that has reverted to the State on the death of its owner and must now be sold by public auction. A subsidiary theme is introduced in the character of the woman (commonly thought to be a prostitute) in whose name the Sultan is purchased and who apparently represents the civilising influence of art; it is she rather than the vizier or judge who ultimately brings happiness to the Sultan.

Plays of social criticism

Despite the clear, if often indirect, relevance of many of these plays to contemporary Egyptian society, the works discussed above are characterised primarily by a concern with wider intellectual issues. All draw their inspiration, at least in part, from the history and culture of other periods, whether of ancient Egypt, the Qur'ān or the classical heritage. Many are also conspicuously lacking in dramatic qualities – a curious feature, given the origins of Tawfīq al-Ḥakīm's initial interest in the theatre. Not all of al-Hakīm's social criticism is so indirect, however. Unlike many Egyptian writers of his generation, al-Ḥakīm had refused to identify himself with any political party, arguing that a writer must retain his intellectual independence to preserve his moral authority: his articles of the 1930s and 1940s attacked Egyptian politicians of all persuasions, accusing them of having abandoned the spirit of the 1919 Revolt. In this spirit, between 1945 and 1950 he also published in the Egyptian newspaper *Akhbār al-Yawm* a number of plays on social themes (all, with a couple of exceptions, short), about twenty of which were later published in *Masraḥ al-Mujtama'* ('Social Theatre').

The plays of *Masraḥ al-Mujtama'* vary greatly both in quality and interest, but unlike *al-Zammār* and *Ḥayāt Taḥaṭṭamat* from an earlier period of al-Ḥakīm's career, they for the most part reflect the life of Cairo rather than that of the countryside. In his introduction to the collected plays, al-Ḥakīm draws attention to the social chaos that Egypt is suffering as a result of the Second World War: his targets include not only 'the war profiteer, the man of companies and enterprises', but also, again, Egyptian women who, no longer content to cast off their veils, 'have been trying to gain a prominent place in politics and public life'.[10] The movement for the emancipation of women provides the inspiration for *Urīd hādhā al-Rajul* ('I Want This Man'), a fast-moving and light-hearted play in which a young lady, Nā'ila, decides to seek a lawyer's hand as a challenge to the prevailing Islamic system of arranged marriages. A more direct assault on prevailing values, not only the aspirations of Egyptian feminists but also the corruption of politics in contemporary Egypt (a constant theme of the author's essays and articles since the early 1930s), is provided by *al-Nā'iba al-Muḥtarama* ('Honorable Member'), which revolves around a woman Member of Parliament, whose feminine influence a Minister tries to enlist in an attempt to persuade her party to drop her opposition to the government's plans. Tensions develop between the MP and her husband, who resents his inferior status, and the MP resigns. The moral of the play is clear: a woman cannot devote herself both to politics and the family.

Other plays in the collection deal with various facets of bureaucratic corruption and inefficiency. *Miftāḥ al-Najāḥ*, for example, depicts a lone official swimming against the tide of the Egyptian bureaucratic system, while in *Li-Kull Mujtahid Naṣīb* we find a ministry official at a loss to understand why he has not been promoted, in spite of his great efficiency; advised by a colleague that it is precisely his conscientiousness that is holding him back, he resolves to change his ways, and the play ends with an announcement that everyone in his section has been promoted.

The most successful of the plays in *Masraḥ al-Mujtama'*, however, 'Ughniyat al-Mawt', is concerned not with bureaucratic corruption or inefficiency, but with the clash between tradition and modernity in the Egyptian countryside – the same topic that had formed the theme of the author's most accomplished novel, *Yawmiyyāt Nā'ib fi'l-Aryāf*.[11] The play, one of al-Ḥakīm's best constructed, was subsequently turned into a film. The plot centres around the return to his village of a young man, 'Ulwān, whose purpose is in fact to preach a programme of social reform; but his visit is misinterpreted by the other members of his family, who believe that he has come to undertake a revenge killing. When 'Ulwān refuses, he is himself put to death by his family, unable to bear the disgrace of his remaining alive without having done his duty. The different interpretations of 'Ulwān's return allow al-Ḥakīm considerable scope for the construction of fast-moving dialogue between characters talking at cross purposes – an aspect of theatrical technique at which al-Ḥakīm was particularly accomplished.

Post-1952 Egyptian drama: Tawfīq al-Ḥakīm

For much of the period from the 1930s to the 1950s, al-Ḥakīm's dramatic output effectively dominated not merely the Egyptian, but indeed, the Arab, theatrical scene. Following the Free Officers' Revolt of 1952, however, a 'new wave' of Egyptian dramatists began to rise to prominence. Despite this, al-Ḥakīm continued to produce work for the theatre; indeed, although like most Arab writers he continued to produce regular essays and articles for the press, his major works during this period were nearly all plays.

Al-Ḥakīm's reaction to the new regime found early expression in the play *al-Aydī al-Nā'ima* (1954), an essentially optimistic and light-hearted play (if somewhat lacking in dramatic qualities), that contains a strong element of social criticism in its repeated emphasis on work rather than wealth as the basis for social order. *Al-Aydī al-Nā'ima* was followed by other works whose relevance to contemporary Egypt cannot be doubted. In *Īzīs*, for example, he discusses the age-old philosophical question of means and ends against the background of the Ancient Egyptian myth of Isis and Osiris, concluding (in a phrase well suited to the political mood of the moment) that judgement in such matters belongs to the people. The setting of *al-Ṣafqa* (1956), by contrast, is a contemporary one, revolving around the attempt by a group of peasants to secure a land deal in the face of considerable difficulties: the play is also interesting for al-Ḥakīm's attempt (continued in *al-Warta*, 1966) to resolve the dilemma of whether to use colloquial or 'classical' Arabic by employing a simplified 'third language' that can be read either way.

Al-Ḥakīm's theatrical output during this period is indeed remarkable for its variety and innovative approach, which acquired a new impetus from a visit that al-Ḥakīm made to Paris in 1959–60, when he became acquainted with works of the 'Theatre of the Absurd', particularly those of Beckett and Ionesco. The first of his plays to show these new influences, *Yā Ṭāliʿ al-Shajara* (1962), is also, in purely theatrical terms, probably the most successful. The play, the title of which is taken from an Egyptian folksong, centres on the relationship between a man and his second wife, and on the investigation that follows her disappearance. The husband is first arrested, then released when the wife reappears; but her refusal to disclose where she has been during her absence eventually drives him to kill her. The play is characterised by fast-moving dialogue, with a good deal of talking at cross purposes (a technique at which al-Ḥakīm, when not distracted by questions of philosophy was particularly proficient); and there is also use of symbolic elements, as in the character of the dervish and a miraculous, four-fruited tree, nourished on the contradictions of the human body, that seems to represent the tree of knowledge.[12]

Yā Ṭāliʿ al-Shajara is a complex work, defying classification in its complex combination of techniques from the 'Theatre of the Absurd' with elements from the Egyptian folk tradition. Indeed, the extent of al-Ḥakīm's indebtedness to the 'Theatre of the Absurd' is a question that is likely to continue to be much discussed. For although the play, in its expression of the breakdown of communication, undoubtedly owes something to contemporary Western theatre, the work lacks the stark and brutal tone associated with the works of Beckett or Ionesco; the author himself claimed that it was 'Absurd' only on the surface; and some critics have even argued that it can read as a nationalist political statment – Bahādir's two marriages representing the Egyptian revolutions of 1919 and 1952 respectively.[13]

Yā Ṭāliʿ al-Shajara was quickly followed by other experimental plays in which different influences and techniques are apparent. *Al-Ṭaʿām li-Kulli Fam* (1963), for example, uses a domestic situation to reflect the author's concern about the problems of world hunger (though it has to be said that it is hard to take the author's somewhat idealistic proposals for solving the problem very seriously). The play is characterised by a didactic, Brechtian tone; the audience are invited to identify themselves with the main characters in the play, and the actions moves forward in a deliberate linear sequence – in strong contrast to *Yā Ṭāliʿ al-Shajara*, where conventional concepts of time and place no longer apply. The influence of Brecht can probably also be seen in *Majlis al-ʿAdl* (1972), which uses an allegorical technique to comment on the contemporary Middle East situation, when attempts to find a political solution to the Palestinian problem following the Six-Day War had become bogged down in fruitless discussion at the United Nations.

Tawfīq al-Ḥakīm's experimental approach is also apparent in *Riḥlat Ṣayd* (1964), which combines theatrical with cinematic techniques in its use of a screen to represent the images passing through a man's mind, and in *Bank al-Qalaq* (1966) he attempted to fuse the novel and the play in a hybrid form for which he coined the term *masriwāya*. Perhaps the most interesting of these plays, however, is *Hārūn al-Rashīd wa-Hārūn al-Rashīd* (1969),[14] an experiment in improvised theatre using material from the *Thousand and One Nights* and designed to break down the barriers between actors and audience while at the same time satisfying the demands of the censor, who required all material for theatrical performance to be approved in advance. In this, the wheel appeared to have turned full circle – for it was this very tale that had, of course, formed the subject of Mārūn al-Naqqāsh's pioneering play *Abū al-Ḥasan al-Mughaffal*, first performed in Beirut in 1850.[15]

Other Egyptian playwrights

The towering presence of Tawfīq al-Ḥakīm over the Egyptian (and effectively, the Arab) dramatic scene during this period has sometimes threatened to obscure the fact that a number of other dramatists were producing works in Egypt that, while seldom outstanding, are nonetheless not without their interest. 'Alī Aḥmad Bākathīr (1910–69), a Hadramawti, born in Indonesia, but who subsequently made Egypt his home, wrote more than thirty plays, many in verse, on a range of subjects, but with a preference for history, legend and folklore. Among his subjects were two that echoed those of al-Ḥakīm himself: *Ūdīb* (1949) and *Shahrazād* (1953). Although less comfortable with social and political themes, Bākathīr also occasionally ventured into territory of direct relevance to contemporary events: *Mismār Juḥā* (1951), for example, based on the traditional character of Juha, makes allusion to the British occupation of Egypt; but overall his work is of uneven quality and his work appears to have made little lasting impact.

More accomplished as a dramatist, and with some claim to be regarded as a 'successor' to Tawfīq al-Ḥakīm was Fatḥī Raḍwān (1911–88), who combined his literary activities as a playwright and prose writer with a political career. Turning to the drama in 1955, he produced a series of plays on social, philosophical and political issues, somewhat in the manner of Tawfīq al-Ḥakīm's 'philosophical' plays: among the most important are *Akhlāq li-l-bay'* (1957), *Dumū' Iblīs* (1958) and *Shaqqa li-l-ījār* (1959).[16]

The 'New Wave': post-1952 Egyptian drama

Although al-Ḥakīm's drama of the post-1952 period continued to provide a useful, at times even barbed, commentary on contemporary Egyptian life, his near-monopoly of the Egyptian theatrical scene was by this time beginning to give way to a new generation of Egyptian playwrights whose impassioned, even angry, tone contrasted with his more measured tones and who quickly added a distinctively new voice to the development of Egyptian drama. This new mood was heralded by Nuʿmān ʿĀshūr's (1918–87) *al-Nās illi taḥt* (1956), which combines a strong element of popular comedy with an exploration of the class struggle in contemporary Egypt through a group of characters who inhabit a basement. The play was followed the following year by *al-Nās illi fōq* (1957), which represents a powerful condemnation of the old Egyptian aristocracy, by the less well-known *Sīmā Awantā* (1958), in which he viciously satirised the Egyptian cinema industry,[17] and by *ʿĀʾilat al-dughrī* (1962), in which the author uses the break-up of a middle-class Egyptian family to symbolise the disintegration of society in post-revolutionary Egypt. The play provides another vivid illustration of how quickly the optimism engendered by the change of regime had given place to disillusionment.

ʿĀshūr's plays, which attracted audiences of considerable size, are among the first productions of what has sometimes been called the 'new wave' of Egyptian dramatists – a group that also includes, among others, Alfred Faraj, Najīb Surūr, Saʿd al-Dīn Wahba, Maḥmūd Diyāb and Yūsuf Idrīs. Although each of these authors retained his own particular literary stamp, they shared a number of common characteristics. In the first place, like most poets and prose writers of their generation, much of their work is characterised by the attitude of *iltiẓām* ('commitment') that swept the Arab world from the beginning of the 1950s.[18] Some, possibly most, of them had been imprisoned for their political views. Taking their cue from the general nationalistic mood following the 1952 Free Officers' Revolt, many (including even the conservative Tawfīq al-Ḥakīm in *Qālabunā al-masraḥī*, 1967) were consciously attempting to forge a specifically 'Egyptian' drama, and in this, they were aided by the new regime's recognition of the potential of the theatre for political propaganda. Meanwhile, on an artistic level, their work is characterised by an awareness of, and an eagerness to experiment with, dramatic techniques being employed in contemporary Western theatre, including not only the 'committed' theatre of Brecht and Sartre, but also the so-called 'Theatre of the Absurd' of Beckett, Artaud and Ionesco. At the same time, their desire to forge a more 'Egyptian' theatre led many to look back to older indigenous theatrical forms, including the use of the traditional Arab storyteller or *ḥakawātī*. The old dilemma of whether to employ classical or colloquial Arabic in dramatic production was in many cases solved at a stroke through the exclusive use of unadulterated Egyptian *ʿāmmiyya*.

Tempting as it is to see the work of this generation as representing a complete break with the past, it would be a mistake to do so. Both Nu'mān 'Āshūr and Alfred Faraj, among others, acknowledged their debt to Tawfīq al-Ḥakīm, and many of Faraj's plays in particular continue al-Ḥakīm's technique of utilising material from the Arabic literary or historical heritage to comment on issues of contemporary relevance. *Sulaymān al-Ḥalabī* (1964), for example, uses the murder of General Kléber by Sulaymān in 1800 as a peg on which to hang a discussion about freedom and justice; *al-Zīr Sālim* (1967) is a reworking of a medieval Arab romance; while in the comedy *'Alī Janāḥ al-Tabrīzī* (1968), perhaps his most successful play, he continues the dramatic tradition originally started by Mārūn al-Naqqāsh of drawing on the *Thousand and One Nights* to construct a work in which the interplay between fantasy and reality plays a major part.

It is with good reason that the 1950s and 1960s have come to be regarded as one of the most creative periods in Egyptian theatrical history. The new regime's realisation of the potential of the theatre led in 1960 to the establishment of the General Foundation for Theater, Arts and Music, and this was followed by the setting up of several new theatres and theatrical troupes – a development paralleled, as we shall see, in several other countries in the Arab world. At the same time, the regime was making conscious efforts to bridge the gap in other ways between the 'European' theatre and the ordinary Egyptian – for example, by arranging provincial tours of contemporary theatrical productions. Increasingly, theatrical activity was also becoming linked with the new medium of television, which was not only producing drama of its own but also screening adaptations of plays originally written for the theatre.

If Nu'mān 'Āshūr's plays *al-Nās illi Taḥt* and *al-Nās illi Fōq* epitomised the mood of the immediate post-revolutionary period in Egypt, the mood of the 1960s was perhaps best captured by Yūsuf Idrīs in his play *Farāfīr* (1964), which the author apparently composed (like many of his predecessors) with the explicit aim of creating a truly 'Egyptian' drama. In a series of articles in the literary journal *al-Kātib*, Idrīs had argued that it was necessary to break down the barriers between the Western theatre and traditional Arab forms of dramatic entertainment such as the *karagöz* and the *sāmir* – though, despite this theorising, the play almost certainly owes more to Western drama than to traditional Arab forms of entertainment. *Farāfīr*, which revolves around the relationship between 'Farfūr' (a made-up name, symbolising the average Egyptian) and his master, combines a generous dose of Egyptian humour with an obvious social and political commitment, raising fundamental questions about the nature of power and the structure of society. Although Idrīs went on to write several more plays, however, he never surpassed his achievement in *Farāfīr*, and despite his achievements on the stage, it is almost certainly as a short story writer that he is likely to be remembered in the longer term.

Other Egyptian dramatists who made a contribution to the development of the genre during this period and beyond include Mikhā'īl Rūmān, Maḥmūd Diyāb, 'Alī Sālim and Shawqī 'Abd al-Ḥakīm. Some members of this generation (for example, Alfred Faraj) shared the experiences of the 'Gallery 68' generation of novelists and short story writers discussed above,[19] including imprisonment for political activities during the 1960s; periods spent, either from choice or necessity, outside Egypt; and problems of censorship. Many of the devices employed by prose writers to circumvent the attentions of the censor (for example the use of historical analogues as a substitute for direct comment on the present political scene) are also used by these dramatists. Another significant feature of the drama of this generation has been the creative use of folklore and other aspects of the indigenous tradition in order to try to bring the theatre 'closer to the people'. Such an approach is perhaps particularly evident in the drama of Shawqī 'Abd al-Ḥakīm (1936–), whose theatre has sometimes been characterised as *Masraḥ al-fallaḥīn*, and whose works employ devices such as the *hikāya* and chorus in order to produce their effect. 'Abd al-Ḥakīm's best known work is probably *Ḥasan wa-Na'īma*, inspired by a well-known ballad of the same name;[20] among his other plays is *Khūfū* (written during 1964–5), whose roots lie in Ancient Egyptian history.

The most prolific, as well as the most versatile, of this generation of playwrights is probably Alfred Faraj (1929–), already discussed, whose works embrace a wide variety of themes and styles and include plays in both colloquial and classical Arabic. More overtly political are the productions of Mikhā'īl Rūmān (1927–73) and 'Alī Sālim (1936–). Rūmān's controversial and hard-hitting works, which frequently attracted the attentions of the Egyptian censor, depict the struggle of the individual against various sorts of oppression, political, social or psychological; while 'Alī Sālim has not only tackled the issue of censorship head-on (in *al-Bufayh*, 1967?, which shows a playwright pressured by the authorities to change his work), but also, unusually for Egyptian writers, dramatised a situation from the 1967 Arab–Israeli war (in *Ughniya 'alā al-mamarr*). Among the most successful of his full-length plays is *Kūmīdiyā Ūdīb* (1970), in which he follows the *doyen* of Egyptian dramatists, Tawfīq al-Ḥakīm, in adapting the Oedipus legend for his own ends – in this case, to launch a barbed attack on the tyranny of Nasser's regime.[22]

Drama outside Egypt in the twentieth century

As with other genres, theatrical and dramatic development in countries outside Egypt during the twentieth century has been somewhat erratic. Tours by Egyptian troupes to other Arab countries provided an initial stimulus to production in several Arab countries from the first quarter of the century onwards, and the renewed blossoming of drama in Egypt following the 1952 Revolution also had a powerful impact elsewhere in the Middle East. In many countries, however, the first experience of the theatre in the Western sense was provided by the colonisers – in most cases, French or British – a phenomenon that unquestionably helped to shape the attitude of the local population towards the genre. A further factor influencing the development of the theatre during this period has been the politicised nature of much theatrical production.

This feature has worked to the theatre's advantage in certain contexts. The 1950s and 1960s, for example, saw most major Arab states establishing the institutions required to underpin theatrical activity: government troupes, drama schools and the like. Many countries have also established dramatic, or wider ranging artistic festivals, a few of which (Baalbek and Carthage, to name perhaps the two most obvious examples) have acquired a significant international reputation that extends well beyond the Arab world. At the same time, however, this feature has made the theatre vulnerable to the whims of governmental censorship (whether colonial or Arab) in many countries. As a result, as in Egypt itself, the theatre in most Arab countries has led a somewhat precarious existence, with many years (or even longer periods) seeing few or even no works being produced on the stage. A 'history' of the theatre during this period would reveal a series of high and low points, rather than a continuum of development – and the writing of it is made more difficult by the sometimes lengthy gaps between the production of a work on stage and its publication in printed form – the former of which, of course, might either precede or follow the latter.

Despite these caveats, some general features of theatrical development during this period may be noted. The first is that, as the Western genre perhaps furthest removed from the Arab tradition, Arab theatrical development has been very obviously marked by a series of attempts to devise a 'genuine Arab theatre'. This has sometimes involved the use of historical and folkloric elements, including the deliberate revival of medieval forms of popular entertainment such as the *ḥakawātī* or the adaptation of classical literary forms such as the *maqāma*. (As already noted, such recourse to Arab history, of course, may serve a double purpose – history as an analogy for the present enabling the playwright to avoid the attentions of the censor.) It has not infrequently involved the use of music (sometimes even circus elements) as part of the dramatic performance – a feature of much modern Arab drama since its origins in the nineteenth century. Most notably, and in contrast to other written genres, it has very often involved the use of colloquial rather than 'classical', or 'modern standard', Arabic. With some exceptions also, its emphasis has been on the potential of 'theatre as theatre' rather than 'theatre as literature'. Another notable feature of the development of Arab theatre (as in other parts of the world, indeed) during the twentieth century has of course been its progressive involvement with other forms of the modern media, including cinema, radio and, more recently, television; whether this relationship has been beneficial or detrimental to the cause of serious drama is a matter on which there is unlikely to be agreement.

Arab drama in the Mashriq

Against that general background, a consideration of the theatre in individual Arab countries during the twentieth century reveals a somewhat patchy picture, from which it is difficult indeed to draw many general conclusions. Although interesting drama has been produced in countries from Iraq to Morocco, however, it is almost certainly Syria that, after Egypt, has seen some of the most innovative theatre productions in recent years – paradoxically perhaps, since the Syrian Baʿthist regime that has ruled the country since 1970 has for much of this period enjoyed a reputation for authoritarianism that has tended to stifle creativity in other fields. A notable, and slightly curious, feature of much Syrian drama is that, unlike those of many other Arab countries, Syrian playwrights have tended to preserve the tradition of a theatre in close touch with the literary text, often using classical rather than colloquial Arabic.

As already noted, following the emigration of the early Syrian troupes to Egypt in the nineteenth century, the Syrian theatre seems to have entered a period of decline, though a few isolated works of note are recorded by, for example, Maʿrūf al-Arnā'ūṭ, Khalīl al-Yājizī (a play by whom was performed at the Université Jesuite de Beyrouth in 1910) and Muta' Ṣafadī. It was not until the 1960s, however, that the Syrian theatre's revival began in earnest with the plays of Saʿd Allāh Wannūs (1941–97), who had trained in both Cairo and Paris, and whose contribution to the Syrian theatre included work as producer and drama critic as well as a dramatist. Indebted in different ways both to Tawfīq al-Ḥakīm and to Western playwrights as varied as Molière, Brecht and Samuel Beckett, Wannūs's theatre combined an explicit call for 'politicisation' (*tasyīs*) with an unashamed reversion to the medieval *ḥakawātī* and the traditions of the puppet theatre. Although not his first play, his reputation was effectively both made and sealed with his *Ḥaflat samar min ajl al-khāmis min Ḥazīrān* (1968), a hard-hitting reflection on the 1967 defeat of the Arabs in the Six-Day War of 1967 that combined political topicality with an invigorating theatrical technique, involving, *inter alia*, the 'placing' of actors in the audience. Wannūs's subsequent productions, sometimes involving the use of a 'play within a play' technique, confirmed him not only as an imaginative playwright of the first order but also as a true heir of the modern Arab theatrical tradition – his subsequent plays drawing not only on the *Alf Layla wa-Layla* but also looking back to his predecessors in the Syrian theatre such as al-Qabbānī and Mārūn al-Naqqāsh.[23] Among his most significant works are *Mughāmarat ra's al-mamlūk Jābir* (1972),

Sahra ma'a Abī Khalīl al-Qabbānī (1972), *al-Malik huwa al-malik* (1977), and a final play, *Yawm min Zamāninā* (1996), which included attacks on both religious and secular authorities. He died in 1997 after a long illness, his reflections on his life and career having been published in 1996 as *'An al-dhākira wa-al-mawt*.[24]

Although Wannūs is undoubtedly the most outstanding of this generation of Syrian playwrights, he is far from being an isolated figure, and his use of history to comment on the present is echoed in the work of other Syrian dramatists, most of whose plays are, in varying degrees, 'political' in character. Among the most prominent of these dramatists are Wannūs's 'follower', Muṣṭafā al-Ḥallāj, whose productions include the Kafkaesque *al-Darāwīsh yabḥathūn 'an al-ḥaqīqa*, in which a prisoner is arrested for reasons that he is unable to fathom; Walīd Ikhlāṣī (1935–), whose plays often depict the clash between old and new values; Mamdūḥ 'Udwān (1941–); and the poet Muḥammad Māghūṭ, whose work *al-Muharrij* (1983) is a sort of 'black farce', ridiculing contemporary Arab society and featuring a troupe of actors who in turns play Othello, Hārūn al-Rashīd and a character known as 'the Hawk', the founder of Muslim Spain.[25]

The history of the theatre in Iraq in the twentieth century has followed a not dissimilar pattern to that in Syria, though for obvious political reasons its progress has been even less straightforward. Tours by the Egyptians Yūsuf Wahbī and Jūrj Abyaḍ in the early part of the century attracted some interest, and some local, and even national, institutions were established at a comparatively early date, including a 'national theatre company' in 1927. Some interest was also shown by prominent writers and poets such as Jamīl Ṣidqī al-Zahāwī, whose play *Layla wa-Samīr* appeared in 1927. Despite this, however, the development of the theatre in Iraq in the first half of the century appears to have been a halting one. In later years, government support and the opportunities provided by radio (and later television) ensured the survival of some sort of theatrical activity, but political censorship has inhibited the development of an indigenous tradition. Although a number of novelists and other writers, including Fu'ād al-Takarlī and 'Abd al-Raḥmān Majīd al-Rubay'ī have demonstrated some interest in drama, either on stage or on radio, only Yūsuf al-'Ānī (1927–) appears to have achieved a sustained dramatic output comparable with his contemporaries in other parts of the Arab world.

Like that of many of his contemporaries, al-'Ānī's career has combined creative work as actor and dramatist with a number of official posts, including that of Director-General of the Iraqi Cinema and Theatre Authority. His early works consist largely of one-act plays on social themes (the idleness of civil servants, health care issues, etc.), but he later produced a number of longer works, including *al-Miftāḥ* (1967),[26] *al-Kharāba* (1970, on American policy in Vietnam) and *al-Khān* (1976). Socially and politically committed, and with an obviously Brechtian tone, al-'Ānī's plays make use of popular traditions and folklore to reinforce their message, but though effective as spectacle, they lack dramatic qualities.

Perhaps unsurprisingly, in view of the political upheavals of the area, the history of the theatre in Palestine has been even more hesitant than that of many other Arab countries. A few isolated plays appear to have been published in the 1920s and 1930s, and the novelist and political activist Ghassān Kanafānī wrote a play *al-Bāb* (1964) based on the Qur'anic story of 'Ād. More recently, and equally unsurprisingly, the Palestinian–Israeli conflict has tended to dominate productions. Less expected is what appears to be a particular interest in the potentialities of verse drama, not least on the part of the prominent poets Samīḥ al-Qāsim (1939–), and Mu'īn Basīsū (1927–84), who wrote three full-length plays between 1969 and 1971. Of particular interest among these plays are Basīsū's *Thawrat al-Zanj*, which links the Palestinian cause to the Zanj rebellion of the 'Abbasid period,[27] and Samīḥ al-Qāsim's *Qaraqosh* (1970), which features a one-eyed character clearly standing for the Israeli General Moshe Dayan. Unfortunately, none of these plays can be counted particularly successful from a dramatic point of view. The apparent upsurge of interest in the theatre among Palestinians around the beginning of the 1970s was also reflected in the formation of a number of theatre groups, of which the Balalin Company of Jerusalem and the Ḥakawātī Group, founded in 1977, were the most prominent. The Balalin Company quickly folded with the exile of one of its founders, Muṣṭafā Kurd, but the Ḥakawātī Theatre survived longer, enduring years of censorship and harassment from the Israeli authorities in an effort to bring their unashamedly political message, and support for the Palestinian *intifāḍa*, to the stage. From 1977 to 1983, the group had no permanent home, but in 1983 it took over the derelict Nuzha Cinema building in East Jerusalem. Their approach has been a 'collective' one, mingling comment on contemporary events with the traditional Arab culture implied by the group's name, and in addition to local audiences, the group also played abroad, their performances in London being described by one critic as 'theatrically innovative, as well as politically acute'.[28]

Arabic drama in the Maghrib

A not dissimilar pattern of colonial influence and local enthusiasm marks the development of interest in the theatre in the Maghrib countries subject to French domination. The initial seeds were sown for an interest in Western-style theatre mainly by performances in French, and in Tunis the Italian consulate provided some help for a local company as early as 1908. Tours by Egyptian troupes to Tunisia, Algeria and Libya in the early part of the century were also an important factor in stimulating interest in the theatre. The importance of the Egyptian stimulus is evident, for example, in the formation of a troupe called 'al-Jawq al-Tūnisī al-Miṣrī', active in Tunis around 1909, a development almost certainly inspired by Sulaymān al-Qardāḥī, who had recently toured North Africa with an Egyptian troupe. Al-Qardāḥī was followed some ten years later by Jūrj Abyaḍ, who visited Libya, Tunisia and Algeria in 1921. These tours were not always particularly successful: al-Qardāḥī's actors, for example, offended local religious sensibilities during his tour of Tunisia, and Jūrj Abyaḍ's style of production appears to have been little appreciated in Algeria. The fact that theatrical activity and local troupes (including, in Tunis, a Jewish troupe, 'Jawq al-taraqqī al-isrā'īlī) are recorded in all three countries during the early years of the century, however, is an indication that some at least of these outside stimuli found a response among the local population.

Although both Tunisia and Morocco have produced playwrights of some note, the development of an Arabic theatrical tradition in the Maghrib has been no more straightforward than elsewhere. The theatre's potential for awakening undesirable political enthusiasms led to the French banning productions by the Moroccan poet Muḥammad al-Maqrī, for example.[29] In Algeria, French censorship began to act as a powerful impediment to theatrical development from the 1940s, with all plays in the Algerian dialect being banned in 1955 — a direct response to the Algerian nationalists' increasing use of the theatre as a propaganda tool – and although the constraints on theatrical activity in Tunisia appear to have been slightly less oppressive, here too it is only since independence that a local theatrical tradition can be said to have in any sense 'flourished'.

Of the three countries of the Maghrib, it is indeed Tunisia that has produced the most diverse and talented dramatic activity since independence. Following the European and Egyptian-inspired productions of the early twentieth century, there appears to have been something of a hiatus in theatrical development. In 1940, Maḥmud al-Mas'adī (1911–) wrote a unique composition entitled *al-Sudd*,[30] in ostensibly dramatic form, satirising the conflicts between traditional Muslim society and the idealism of social reformers through its two main characters Ghaylan and Maymuna. Mingling narrative passages with blank verse, the play lacks dramatic qualities and, on one level, may be regarded as something of a 'curiosity'; but it has proved an inspiration for later Tunisian writers, not only for its linguistic and intellectual interest, but also for the relevance of its theme to contemporary Tunisia.

A major factor in the development of Tunisian theatre since independence has been the comparative 'decentralisation' of theatrical activity. From the 1960s onwards, municipal theatres were to be found not only in the capital but also in provincial centres such as Sfax and Kairouan. Cultural festivals, some of which have achieved international standing,[31] have also given a boost to theatrical and related activities. Against that background, it is not surprising to find that many writers more usually thought of as novelists, including Muṣṭafā al-Fārisī (1931–) and ʿUmar bin Sālim, have also made forays into the theatrical field. The most accomplished Tunisian playwright, however, and with the exception of al-Masʿadī, the only one to be widely recognised outside his own country, is undoubtedly ʿIzz al-Dīn al-Madanī (1938–).

Although also highly regarded for his modernistic and at times provocative prose,[32] al-Madanī's claim to fame is undoubtedly his series of plays written in the 1970s, in which he utilises the Arab literary and historical heritage to discuss questions of contemporary relevance such as oppression, tyranny and liberation. Four of these plays, *Thawrat Ṣāḥib al-Ḥimār* (1970), *Dīwān al-Zanj* (1972), *Riḥlat al-Ḥallāj* (1973) and *Mawlāy al-Sulṭān Ḥasan al-Ḥafṣī* (1977) were regarded by the author as a 'quartet', united by a common set of themes. In *Dīwān al-Zanj*, for example, al-Madanī takes the ninth-century negro slave revolt against the ʿAbbasid Caliph to comment on the wars of liberation of the twentieth century which often end, he suggests, merely by substituting economic for political domination. The titles of *Riḥlat al-Ḥallāj* and the later *al-Ghufrān* (a title taken from the work of the classical poet al-Maʿarrī) suggest a more literary inspiration. These plays, which share some of the characteristics of the Syrian Saʿd al-Wannūs's drama, are not merely of interest for their thematic material, however, but also for their dramatic technique, as well as the theoretical considerations that lie behind it; for while al-Madanī has, like other dramatists both in Tunisia and elsewhere, used many elements of popular literature in his drama, his search for a 'genuinely Arab drama' has also led him in a distinctive direction through his use of a device he terms 'digression' (*istiṭrād*), which he regards both as a typical feature of classical Arabic literature and as a useful device for the contemporary playwright.[33]

As in Tunisia, theatrical development in Morocco has trod a somewhat precarious path, producing only one dramatist widely known outside Morocco itself, al-Ṭayyib al-Ṣiddiqī (1938–). The first stirrings of theatrical activity in Morocco seem to have taken place following a visit by a Tunisian troupe in 1923 and local troupes were soon formed in imitation, but the example of Muḥammad al-Maqrī was not an encouraging one[34] and it was not until after Moroccan independence in 1956 that conditions became conducive to the development of a dramatic tradition. That it did so at all was almost entirely due to al-Ṭayyib al-Ṣiddiqī, whose name has been described by one critic as 'synonymous with Moroccan theatre'.[35] Following a period of study in France, and working for a time in association with the prodigious Aḥmad al-Ṭayyib al-ʿIlg (1928–), al-Ṣiddiqī founded his own troupe and theatre in Casablanca in 1956, staging both Western plays and his own original dramas. His work has a number of features in common with that of the Tunisian al-Madanī, both men being preoccupied with the question of how to use traditional Arabic literary forms (both 'elevated' and 'popular'), in a modern context. His *Dīwān Sīdī 'Abd al-Raḥmān al-Majdhūb* (1966), perhaps his best known work, is based on the life of the wandering poet after whom the play is named; it was followed in 1971 by *Maqāmat Badī' al-Zamān al-Hamadhānī*, an attempt to dramatise the medieval writer's *maqāmāt*. More recently, 'Abdelkrim Burchid has produced a number of modernistic plays, including *Imru' al-Qays fī Bārīz*, in which the author seeks to 'demythologise' a heroic figure, while implicitly commenting on the political and social situation in contemporary Morocco.

The course of theatrical development in Algeria has been even more precarious than in its Maghribi neighbours, not least because French colonialism there took a more oppressive form than in Tunisia and Morocco, threatening the existence of the critical mass of educated Arabic speakers required to sustain a thriving theatrical tradition in that language. Prior to the 1920s, theatrical performances appear to have been confined to 'colonial' productions in French, with a few local productions, often in the local dialect and usually of poor quality. As elsewhere, Algeria enjoyed tours by Egyptian companies, such as that by Jūrj Abyaḍ in 1921. Significantly, however, Abyaḍ's productions seem to have found less success there than in Tunisia, and though a few plays were written in the 1920s, such as Rashīd Qusanṭīnī's *Zawāj Bū Burmah* (1928), serious drama in Arabic does not appear to have played much part in the intellectual life of the country. Its potential, on the other hand, was clearly seen by the FLN during the struggle for independence during the 1950s and 1960s, when the organisation actively used the theatre as a propaganda tool, first in France (between 1955 and 1958) and later in Tunisia and elsewhere, and it was in this context that the well-known Algerian novelist al-Ṭāhir Waṭṭar (1936–)[36] actually started his writing career, with two dramas entitled *'Alā al-ḍaffa al-ukhrā* (1958) and *al-Hārib* (1960).

After independence in 1962, a national theatre (the Théâtre national algérien) was established and a number of troupes were formed in various towns. Political developments during the last years of the twentieth century, however, were not conducive to the development of a theatrical tradition in Arabic, and in general it would not be an exaggeration to say that serious Arabic drama in Algeria has yet to establish a solid basis for future development. The same judgement probably applies to Libya where, despite tours by Jūrj Abyaḍ and Italian companies in the 1920s, no local tradition of theatre in the Western sense appears to have been established as a result. Efforts were made at the beginning of the 1970s to stage a number of drama festivals and a number of theatrical companies were formed, but an attempt in 1973 to reorganise troupes on a professional basis failed, and local theatre stagnated; the present outlook for the theatre, as in much of the Arab world, therefore remains not merely precarious but even bleak.

Notes

1 See above, Chapter 4, pp. 115–17. For a fuller account of al-Ḥakīm's plays generally, see R. Long, *Tawfiq al-Hakim: Playwright of Egypt*, London, 1979; Paul Starkey, *From the Ivory Tower*, London, 1987.
2 For which, see above, pp. 115–16.
3 For whom, see above, p. 29.
4 For which, see above, p. 115.
5 See also above, Chapter 7, pp. 115–16.
6 *Ahl al-Kahf*, Cairo, n.d., pp. 32–3.
7 Though actually composed before *Ahl al-Kahf*. See Starkey, *From the Ivory Tower*, pp. 28–9.
8 *Pygmalion*, Cairo, n.d., p. 165.
9 On this, see Daly, M., *The Cambridge History of Egypt: Vol. 2*, Cambridge. For another use of historical analogy set in the Mamluk period, cf. Jamal al-Ghitani's *al-Zayni Barakat*, discussed above, p. 144.
10 *Masraḥ al-Mujtama'*, introduction, p. x.
11 For which, see above, Chapter 7.
12 For a fuller discussion, see Starkey, *From the Ivory Tower*, pp. 60–7.
13 Cachia, *Arabic Literature: an Overview*, pp. 148–9.
14 On which, see Starkey, *Ivory Tower*, pp. 72–4.
15 For which, see above, p. 165.
16 See also 'A god in spite of himself', P. Cachia (trans.), *JAL* 5 (1974), pp. 108–26.
17 On this play, see Mahmoud El Lozy, 'Censoring the Censor: The Politics of Satire in Nu'man 'Ashur's *Sima Awanta*', *Theater Three*, 6 (1989), pp. 31–46.
18 For this, see above, p. 116.
19 See above, Chapter 8.
20 English translation in M. Manzalaoui, *Arabic Writing Today: Drama*, Cairo, 1977, pp. 297–334.
21 English translation as ''Ali Janah al-Tabrizi and his servant Quffa', in S. K. Jayyusi and R. Allen (eds), *Modern Arabic Drama: An Anthology*, Bloomington, 1995, pp. 305–52.
22 English translation, as *The Comedy of Oedipus*, in S. K. Jayyusi and R. Allen (eds), *Modern Arabic Drama: An Anthology*, Bloomington, 1995, pp. 353–86.
23 In *Sahra ma'a Abū Khalīl al-Qabbānī* (1972) and *al-Malik huwa al-Malik* (1977). For Wannūs in general, see Roger Allen, 'Arabic drama in theory and practice: the writings of Sa'dallah Wannūs', *JAL* 15 (1984), pp. 94–113.
24 Damascus, 1996.
25 See Badawi, 'Drama Outside Egypt', *Theater Three* 6 (1989), pp. 53–63.
26 Translated into English as 'The Key', in S. K. Jayyusi and R. Allen (eds), *Modern Arabic Drama: An Anthology*, Bloomington, 1995.
27 Cf. the use of this theme by the Tunisian playwright 'Izz al-Dīn al-Madanī, discussed below, p. 195.
28 See 'El-Hakawati on Stage', *Saudi Aramco World* 39: 6 (1988), also Rachel Shteir, 'Al-Hakawati: chameleon with a voice', *Theater Three*, 6 (1989), pp. 47–52.
29 His name is given in other sources as al-Qurri.
30 Not published until 1955. For al-Mas'adī, see Ostle, R. C., 'Maḥmūd al-Mas 'adī and

Tunisia's "lost generation"', *JAL* 8 (1977), pp. 153–66.

31 Such as the Carthage Festival (for which, see the website at http://www.festival-carthage.com.tn).

32 For which, see Starkey, 'Quest for freedom: the case of 'Izz al-Dīn al-Madanī', *JAL*, 26 (1995), pp. 67–79.

33 On this, see al-Madanī's own preface to *Dīwān al-Zanj*.

34 See above, p. 194.

35 F. Abu-Haidar, s.v. 'Morocco, modern', *EAL*, II, p. 531

36 For whom, see above, p. 158.

11

Conclusion

'We have no theatre, no cinema, no research, no education. We have only festivals and conferences and a trunkful of lies.' (Ṣunʿ Allāh Ibrāhīm, on rejecting an Egyptian Higher Council for Culture award in 2003)

The preceding chapters have attempted to describe some of the main ways in which the literature of the Arab world has developed over the last two hundred years or so, since the time when the existing literary traditions of the Middle East outlined in the first chapter first became exposed on a large scale to the different literary forms of the West. The resulting 'revival', or *nahḍa*, centred initially in Egypt and Greater Syria, and greatly stimulated by the input of Arab émigrés to North and South America, has led to the emergence of a modern literature that has seen an Arab writer, Najīb Maḥfūẓ, win the Nobel Prize for Literature in 1988. As the preceding chapters have also shown, however, the path has been a far from smooth one. Literature in different areas of the Arab world has developed in different ways and at different rates, closely dependent on the political, social and cultural traditions of the individual regions. So great, indeed, have been these differences that some critics have questioned whether there is such a thing as 'Arabic literature' (as opposed to 'Egyptian literature', 'Tunisian literature' etc.) at all – and although, put in this form, the question may be no more than a debating point, it remains true that many Arab writers at times seem almost 'parochial', little concerned (the Arab-Israeli dispute excepted) with the wider Middle East outside their own individual countries.

What, then, of the future? By the nature of things, any survey of a contemporary literature must be an unfinished story. Of the three main genres which this book has discussed, the future outlook for poetry and imaginative prose seems in little doubt: the Arab world can boast an increasing number of imaginative and creative writers of novels and short stories, and although it is perhaps less easy to identify the leading figures in the next generation of poets, poetry in the Middle East continues to flourish and enjoy an esteem seldom paralleled in the West. The future for the drama seems perhaps less certain: despite the vigour of the theatre in certain periods and countries, despite the emergence of contemporary playwrights such as Lenin al-Ramlī in Egypt, and despite the efforts made to relate the theatre to political causes such as those of the Palestinians, many countries have failed to establish the sort of tradition of literary theatre envisaged by Tawfīq al-Ḥakīm and others. This is not only, perhaps, because the theatre has always the most vulnerable of the genres to political pressures (not least, because theatrical performances involve the gathering of crowds); but also because much theatrical talent is now being channelled into other forms of cultural expression such as cinema and television. Although the present work has discussed the theatre as a literary genre parallel to those of poetry, short story and novel, future surveys of Arab drama will probably more usefully be situated in the context of these newer forms of culture expression – the study of which, of course, requires a somewhat different approach. Also requiring a different approach is the study of 'popular' or 'folk literature', almost always in dialect, which although touched on at several points in the present work, has not been explored here in any systematic way.

A key factor in the reception of written literature in the Arab world continues to be the relatively small market, for although literacy rates in most parts of the Arab world have risen, often dramatically, during the twentieth century, the readership for most forms of literary expression remains a small one by Western standards. Some issues that have dogged the Arabic literary scene for decades, if not more, continue to remain unresolved, not least that of the colloquial vs classical (MSA) debate. But the greatest challenge to the contemporary Arab writer almost certainly remains, as it has through most of the period discussed, his or her relationship both to the state and to authority in other forms – a concern vividly expressed by Ṣunʻ Allāh Ibrāhīm in his words quoted above, as he rejected the award of an Egyptian state literature prize in 2003, on the grounds that that the Egyptian government lacked the necessary moral authority to make such an award. Official and unofficial censorship, political, moral and religious, together with the self-censorship that almost inevitably follows, continues to be a major factor in the development of literature in most parts of the Middle East. Violence against writers engendered by religious extremism has also been a feature of the area in recent years, as the murder of the Egyptian intellectual Farag Foda and the attack on Najīb Maḥfūẓ in the early 1990s demonstrate. In such circumstances, the outlook for the sort of literature discussed in this volume remains a somewhat precarious one, which is certain to present a formidable challenge to aspiring writers in the Arab world for many years to come.

Bibliography

This bibliography does not aim at completeness. Its aim is to suggest to the reader further sources of background information, and of more detailed information on the particular topics, authors and genres discussed. Most such works contain bibliographies of their own, which should be consulted for more detailed information. In accordance with the book's target readership, the main emphasis has been on sources in English, but I have included some books in other European languages, and a few in Arabic, where this has seemed necessary or helpful. After the introductory section, the bibliography is broadly arranged by genre (though there are inevitably a few overlaps between the different sections), with a list of selected English translations at the end. The Arabic literary publications referred to in the book have not been listed here, as in most cases this would merely mean duplicating publishing information already available in the book itself.

I. Reference and general background

ʿAbd al-Razzāq, Fawzī, 'Bāqāt min al-Maṭbūʿāt al ʿArabiyya al-ṣādira fī al-Amrīkatayn, *ʿĀlam al-Kutub*, 4 (4) (1991), pp. 546–76.

Abdel-Malek, Kamal and Wael Hallaq (eds), *Tradition, Modernity and Post-modernity in Arabic Literature: Essays in Honor of Professor Issa J. Boullata*, Leiden, 2000.

Al-Azmeh, A., *Ibn Khaldun: An Essay in Reinterpretation*, London, 1982; repr. 1990.

ʿAbduh, Ibrāhīm, *Ta'rīkh al-Waqā'iʿ al-Miṣriyya, 1828–1942*, Cairo, 1942.

Allen, Roger, *Modern Arabic Literature*, New York, 1987.

Allen, Roger, *The Arabic Literary Heritage*, Cambridge, 1998.

Allen, R., H. Kilpatrick and E. de Moor (eds), *Love and Sexuality in Modern Arabic Literature*, London, 1995.

Allen, R. and D. Richards, *Arabic Literature: The Post-Classical Period* (Cambridge History of Arabic Literature), Cambridge, 2006.

Altoma, Salih J., *Modern Arabic Literature: A Bibliography of Articles, Books, Dissertations and Translations in English*, Bloomington, 1975.

Altoma, Salih J., *Modern Arabic Literature in Translation: A Companion*, London, 2005.

'Antar and 'Abla: A Bedouin Romance, tr. Diana Richmond, London, 1978.

Ayalon, Ami, *The Press in the Arab Middle East: A History*, New York, 1995.

Badawi, El-Said and Martin Hinds, *A Dictionary of Egyptian Colloquial Arabic*, Cairo, 1986.

Badawi, M. M., *A Short History of Modern Arabic Literature*, Oxford, 1993.

Badawi, M. M., 'From primary to secondary *qaṣīdas*', *JAL* 11 (1980), pp. 1–31.

Badawi, M. M. (ed.), *Modern Arabic Literature* (The Cambridge History of Arabic Literature), Cambridge, 1992 [see also below, *Cambridge History of Arabic Literature*].

Badawi, M. M., *Modern Arabic Literature and the West*, London, 1985.

Badran, Margot and Miriam Cooke (eds), *Opening the Gates: A Century of Arab Feminist Writing*, Bloomington and Indianapolis, 1990.

Boullata, Issa J., *Critical Perspectives on Modern Arabic Literature, 1945–1980*, Washington, DC, 1980.

Brockelmann, C., *Geschichte der arabischen Literatur*, Leiden, 1943–9.

Brugman, J., *An Introduction to the History of Modern Arabic Literature in Egypt*, Leiden, 1984.

Cachia, Pierre, *An Overview of Modern Arabic Literature* (Islamic Surveys Series), Edinburgh, 1990.

Cachia, Pierre, *Arabic Literature: An Overview*, London, 2002.

Cambridge History of Arabic Literature, 6 vols, Cambridge, 1983–2006

'Abbasid belles-lettres (Cambridge History of Arabic Literature), ed. Julia Ashtiany et al., Cambridge/New York, 1990.

Arabic literature to the end of the Umayyad period (Cambridge History of Arabic Literature), ed. A. F. L. Beeston et al., Cambridge/New York, 1983.

Arabic Literature: The Post-Classical Period (Cambridge History of Arabic Literature), ed. R. Allen and D. Richards, Cambridge/New York, 2006.

The Literature of Al-Andalus (Cambridge History of Arabic Literature), ed. Maria Rosa Menocal, Raymond P. Scheindlin and Michael Sells, Cambridge/New York, 2000.

Modern Arabic literature (Cambridge History of Arabic Literature), ed. M. M. Badawi, Cambridge/New York, 1992.

Religion, literature and science in the 'Abbasid period (Cambridge History of Arabic Literature), ed. M. J. L. Young, J. D. Latham and R. B. Serjeant, Cambridge/ New York, 1990.

Camera d'Afflitto, Isabella, *Letteratura araba contemporanea: dalla* nahḍah *a oggi*, Roma, 1998.

Campbell, Robert, *A'lām al-adab al-'arabī al-mu'āṣir = Contemporary Arab Writers* (Beiruter Texte und Studien, 62), 2 vols, Beirut, 1996.

Classe, O. (ed.), *An Encyclopedia of Literary Translation into English*, 2 vols, London, 2000.

Commission des Monuments de l'Egypte, *Description de l'Egypte*, 1st edn, Paris, 1810–29.

Crabbs, J. A., *The Writing of History in Nineteenth-century Egypt*, Detroit, 1984.

Dāghir, Yūsuf As'ad, *Maṣādir al-dirāsāt al-adabiyya*, Beirut, 1956.

Daly, M. W. (ed.), *The Cambridge History of Egypt: Vol. 2: Modern Egypt from 1517 to the End of the Twentieth Century*, Cambridge, 1998.

Donohue, John J. and Leslie Tramontini, *Crosshatching in Global Culture: A Dictionary of Modern Arab Writers: An Updated Version of R. B. Campbell's 'Contemporary Arab Writers'* (Beiruter Texte und Studien, 101), 2 vols, Beirut, 2004.

Dunn, Ross, *The Adventures of Ibn Battuta*, London, 1986.

Encyclopaedia of Islam, new edn, Leiden, 1960– (in progress). [Electronic version also available.]

Findley, C. V., 'Knowledge and education in the modern Middle East', in G. Sabagh (ed.), *The Modern Economic and Social History of the Middle East in its World Context*, Cambridge, 1989.

Fliedner, S., *'Alī Mubārak und seine Ḫiṭaṭ* (Islamkundliche Untersuchungen, 140), Berlin, 1990.

Fontaine, J., *Histoire de la littérature tunisienne par les textes*, 2 vols, Bardo, 1988, 1994.

Fontaine, J., *La littérature tunisienne contemporaine*, Paris, 1991.

al-Ghazālī, 'Deliverance from Error ...', in *The Faith and Practice of al-Ghazali*, tr. W. M. Watt, London, 1953.

Gibb, H. A. R., *Arabic Literature: An Introduction*. 2nd edn, Oxford, 1963.

Haywood, John A., *Modern Arabic Literature: An Introduction with Extracts in Translation*, London, 1971.

Heyworth-Dunne, J., *An Introduction to the History of Education in Modern Egypt*, London, 1939, repr. 1968.

Hourani, A., *Arabic Thought in the Liberal Age, 1798–1939*, London, 1962.

Ḥusayn, Ṭāhā, *Mustaqbal al-Thaqāfa fī Miṣr*, Cairo, 1954.

Ibn Baṭṭūṭa, *The Travels of Ibn Battuta*, tr. H. A. R. Gibb, Cambridge, 1958–71.

Jones, Alan and Richard Hitchcock (eds), *Studies on the* Muwaššah *and the* Kharja*: Proceedings of the Exeter International Colloquium*, Reading, 1991.

Kaye, Jacqueline and Abdelhamid Zoubir, *The Ambiguous Compromise: Language, Literature and National Identity*, London and New York, 1990.

al-Kayyālī, Sāmī, *al-Adab al-'Arabī al-Mu'āṣir fī Sūriyya*, Damascus, 1959.

Lane, E. W., *Manners and Customs of the Modern Egyptians*, London, n.d. [1836].

Leder, Stefan and Hilary Kilpatrick, 'Classical Arabic prose literature: a researchers' sketch map', *JAL* 23 (1992), pp. 2–26.
Lewis, B. and P. M. Holt (eds), *Historians of the Middle East*, London, 1962.
Martínez Montávez, Pedro, *Introducción a la literatura árabe moderna*, Madrid, 1974.
Meisami, Julie Scott and Paul Starkey (eds), *Encyclopedia of Arabic Literature*, 2 vols, London and New York, 1998.
Mitchell, Timothy, *Colonising Egypt*, Berkeley, 1988.
Monroe, J. T., *The Art of Badī' al-Zamān al-Hamadhānī as Picaresque Narrative*, Beirut, 1983.
Nicholson, R. A., *A Literary History of the Arabs*, Cambridge, 1969 [1st edn, 1907].
Nicholson, R. A., *Translations of Eastern Poetry and Prose*, Cambridge, 1922.
Ostle, R. C., 'Modern Egyptian Renaissance Man', *Bulletin of the School of Oriental and African Studies*, 57 (1994), pp. 184ff.
Ostle, R. C. (ed.), *Modern Literature in the Near and Middle East 1850–1970*, London and New York, 1991.
Ostle, R. C. (ed.), *Studies in Modern Arabic Literature*, London, 1975.
Pantuček, S., *La littérature algérienne moderne*, Prague, 1969.
Pantuček, S., *Tunesische Literaturgeschichte*, Wiesbaden, 1974.
Pearson, J. D. et al., *Index Islamicus*, 1906–, London, 1958–.
Roper, G. 'Fāris al-Shidyāq and the Transition from Scribal to Print Culture in the Middle East', in G. N. Atiyeh (ed.), *The Book in the Islamic World*, Albany, c. 1995, pp. 209–32.
Sabagh, G. (ed.), *The Modern Economic and Social History of the Middle East in its World Context*, Cambridge, 1989.
Semah, David, *Four Egyptian Literary Critics*, Leiden, 1974.
Siddiq, Muhammad, 'Review of *Modern Arabic Literature*', in M. M. Badawi (ed.), *Journal of Arabic Literature*, 26 (1995), p. 270.
Snir, Reuven, *Modern Arabic Literature: A Functional Dynamic Model*, Toronto, 2001.
Stagh, Marina, *The Limits of Freedom: Prose Literature and Prose Writers in Egypt under Nasser and Sadat*, Stockholm, 1993.
Stetkevych, J., *Modern Arabic Literary Language: Lexical and Stylistic Development*, Chicago, 1970.
Straley, Dona S., *The Undergraduate's Companion to Arab Writers and Their Web Sites*, Westport, CT, 2004.
Tājir, Jāk, *Ḥarakat al-tarjama fī Miṣr khilāl al-qarn al-tāsi' 'ashar*, Cairo, c.1945.
Tibi, B., *Arab Nationalism*, London, 1981.
Tomiche, Nada, *La Littérature arabe contemporaine: roman-nouvelle-théâtre*, Paris, 1993.
al-Turk, Niqūlā (Nicolas Turc) *Chronique d'Egypte, 1798–1804*, ed. G. Wiet,

Cairo, 1950.
Vatikiotis, P. J., *The Modern History of Egypt*, London, 1969.
Wassef, Amin Sami, *L'Information et la presse officielle en Égypte jusqu'à la fin de l'occupation française*, Cairo, 1975, pp. 49–108.
Watt, W. M., *Muhammad at Mecca*, Oxford, 1953; *Muhammad at Medina*, Oxford, 1956.

II. Prose literature

Allen, Roger, *The Arabic Novel: an historical and critical introduction*, Syracuse, 1982 (2nd edn, 1995).
Allen, Roger, *Critical Perspectives on Yūsuf Idrīs*, Colorado Springs, 1994.
Allen, Roger, *A Period of Time*, Reading, 1992.
The Arab Novel since 1950: Critical Essays, Interviews and Bibliography, Cambridge, MA, 1992.
'Ayyād, Shukrī, *al-Qiṣṣa al-Qaṣīra fī Miṣr*, Cairo, 1968.
Boullata, I. J., 'Encounter between East and West: A theme in contemporary Arabic Novels', *MEJ* 30/1 (1976), pp. 44–62.
Cachia, Pierre, *Taha Husayn*, London, 1956.
Cohen-Mor, D., *Yūsuf Idrīs: Changing Visions*, Potomac, MD, 1992.
Cooke, Miriam, *The Anatomy of an Egyptian Intellectual*, Washington, DC, 1984.
Cooke, Miriam, *War's Other Voices: Women Writers on the Lebanese Civil War*, Cambridge, 1987.
Elad, Ami, *The Village Novel in Modern Egyptian Literature*, Berlin, 1994.
El-Enany, R., *Naguib Mahfouz: The Pursuit of Meaning*, London and New York, 1993.
Hafez, Sabry, 'The Egyptian Novel in the Sixties', *Journal of Arabic Literature* 7 (1976), pp. 68–84.
Hafez, Sabry, *The Genesis of Arabic Literary Discourse: A Study in the Sociology of Modern Arabic Literature*, London, 1993.
Hutchins, William M., *Tawfīq al-Ḥakīm: A Reader's Guide*, Boulder/London, 2003.
Jad, A. B., *Form and Technique in the Egyptian Novel 1912–1971*, London, 1973.
Kilpatrick, H., ''Abd al-Ḥakīm Qāsim and the Search for Liberation', *Journal of Arabic Literature* 26 (1995), pp. 50–65.
Kilpatrick, H., *The Modern Egyptian Novel*, London, 1974.
Kilpatrick, H., 'The Arabic Novel: a single tradition?', *Journal of Arabic Literature* 5 (1974), pp. 93–107.
Mahmoud, M., 'The Unchanging Hero in a Changing World: Najīb Maḥfūẓ's *al-Liṣṣ wa'l-kilāb*', *Journal of Arabic Literature* 15 (1984), pp. 58–75.

Malti-Douglas, Fadwa, *Men, Women and God(s): Nawāl El Saadāwī and Arab Feminist Poetics*, Berkeley, 1995.
Mehrez, S. 'Bricolage as hypertextuality: a study of narrative structure and narrative modes in the works of the Egyptian writer Gamāl al-Ghītāny'. Unpublished PhD dissertation, University of California, 1985.
Mehrez, Samia, *Egyptian Writers between History and Fiction (Essays on Naguib Mahfouz, Sonallah Ibrahim and Gamal Al-Ghitani)*, Cairo, 1994.
Meyer, Stefan G., *The Experimental Arabic Novel: postcolonial literary modernism in the Levant*, New York, 2001.
Michalak-Pikulska, Barbara, *The Contemporary Kuwaiti Short Story in Peace Time and War, 1920–1995*, Kraków, 1998.
Michalak-Pikulska, Barbara, *Modern Poetry and Prose of Oman, 1975–2000*, Kraków, 2002.
Moosa, Matti, *The Origins of Modern Arabic Fiction*, Washington, DC, 1983, 2nd edn, Boulder, CO, 1997.
Najm, Muḥammad Yūsuf, *al-Qiṣṣa fī al-Adab al-'Arabī al-Ḥadīth*, Beirut, 1961.
Nu'ayma, Mīkhā'īl, *Jubrān Khalīl Jubrān*, Beirut, 1932 (English version, *Kahlil Gibran*, New York, 1950).
Ostle, R.C., 'Mahmūd al-Mas'adī.and Tunisia's "Lost Generation"', *JAL* 8 (1977), pp. 155–66.
Ostle, Robin, Ed de Moor and Stefan Wild (eds), *Writing the Self: Autobiographical Writing in Modern Arabic Literature*, London, 1998.
Peled, M., '*al-Sāq 'alā al-Sāq*: a generic definition', *Arabica* 32 (1985), pp. 31–46.
Philipp, Thomas, *Gurgi Zaidan: His Life and Thought*, Beirut, 1979.
Ramsay, Gail, *The Novels of an Egyptian Romanticist: Yūsuf al-Sibā'ī*, Edsbruk, 1996.
Sakkut, Hamdi, *The Egyptian Novel and its Main Trends from 1913 to 1952*, Cairo, 1971.
Sakkut, Hamdi, *al-Riwāya al-'Arabiyya: bibliyūjrāfiyā wa-madkhal naqdī (1865–1995)/The Arabic Novel: Bibliography and Critical Introduction (1865–1995)*, Cairo, 2000.
Somekh, S., *The Changing Rhythm: A Study of Najīb Maḥfūẓ's Novels*, Leiden, 1973.
Starkey, Paul, 'Crisis and Memory in Rashid al-Da'if's *Dear Mr Kawabata*: an essay in narrative disorder', in Ken Seigneurie (ed.), *Crisis and Memory: The Representation of Space in Modern Levantine Narrative*, Wiesbaden, 2003, pp. 115–32.
Starkey, Paul, 'Egyptian History in the Modern Egyptian Novel', in *The Historiography of Islamic Egypt (c.950–1800)*, ed. Hugh Kennedy, Leiden, 2001, pp. 251–62.
Starkey, Paul, 'From the City of the Dead to Liberation Square: the novels of Yūsuf al-Qa'īd', *Journal of Arabic Literature* 24 (1993), pp. 39–61.

Starkey, Paul, *From the Ivory Tower: A Critical Study of Tawfīq al-Ḥakīm*, London, 1987.

Starkey, Paul, 'Quest for freedom: the case of 'Izz al-Din al-Madani', *JAL* 26 (1995), pp. 67–79.

Starkey, Paul, 'Some Aspects of the French Colonial Legacy in the Tunisian Novel of the 1960s and 1970s', *Oriente Moderno* XVI (LXXVII), n.s. (1997), pp. 151–61.

Tomiche, N., *Histoire de la littérature romanesque de l'Egypte moderne*, Paris, 1981.

Walther, Wiebke, 'Distant Echoes of Love in the Narrative Work of Fu'ād al-Tikirlī', in Allen, R., H. Kilpatrick and E. De Moor (eds), *Love and Sexuality in Modern Arabic Literature*, London, 1995, pp. 131–39.

III. Poetry

al-Abyārī, Ibrāhīm (ed.), *al-Mawsū'a al-Shawqiyya*, Beirut, 1994–5.

Adonis, *An Introduction to Arab Poetics*, tr. Catherine Cobham, London, 1990.

Allen, Roger, 'Poetry and Poetic Criticism at the Turn of the Century', in R. C. Ostle (ed.), *Studies in Modern Arabic Literature*, London, 1975.

Arberry, A. J., *Arabic Poetry: A Primer for Students*, Cambridge, 1965.

Arberry, A. J., *Modern Arabic Poetry: An Anthology of English Verse Translations*, Cambridge, 1980 (1st edn, 1950).

Badawi, M. M., *An Anthology of Modern Arabic Verse*, Beirut, 1969.

Badawi, M. M., *A Critical Introduction to Modern Arabic Poetry*, Cambridge, 1975.

Boullata, I. J., 'Mikhail Naimy: poet of meditative vision', *Journal of Arabic Literature* 24 (1993), pp. 173–84.

Bushrui, S. and J. Jenkins, *Kahlil Jibran: Man and Poet*, Oxford, 1998.

DeYoung, Terri, 'A New Reading of Badr Shākir al-Sayyāb's "Hymn of the Rain"', *Journal of Arabic Literature* 24 (1993), pp. 39–61.

Jayyusi, Salma Khadra, *Trends and Movements in Modern Arabic Poetry*, 2 vols, Leiden, 1977.

Khairallah, A. E., *Love, Madness and Poetry: An Interpretation of the Magnūn Legend*, Beirut, 1980.

Khouri, Mounah A., *Poetry and the Making of Modern Egypt*, Leiden, 1971.

Michalak-Pikulska, Barbara, *Modern Poetry and Prose of Oman, 1975–2000*, Kraków, 2002.

Moreh, S., *Modern Arabic Poetry 1800–1970*, Leiden, 1976.

Moreh, S., *Studies in Modern Arabic Prose and Poetry*, Leiden, 1988.

Nu'ayma, Mīkhā'īl, *Jubrān Khalīl Jubrān*, Beirut, 1932 (English version, *Kahlil Gibran*, New York, 1950).

Obank, M. and Shimon, S., *A Crack in the Wall: New Arab Poetry*, London, 2001.
O'Grady, Desmond, *Ten Modern Arab Poets*, Dublin, c.1992.
Ostle, R. C., 'Ilyā Abū Māḍī and Arabic Poetry in the Inter-War Period', in *idem* (ed.), *Studies in Modern Arabic Literature*, London, 1975.
Ostle, R. C., 'Khalīl Muṭrān: the precursor of lyrical poetry in modern Arabic', *Journal of Arabic Literature* 1971, pp. 116–26.
Sa'īd, Jamīl , *al-Zahāwī wa-thawratuhu fī al-jaḥīm*, Cairo, 1968.
Sells, Michael, *Desert Tracings: Six Classic Arabian Odes*, Middletown, 1989.

IV. Drama

Allen, Roger, 'Arabic Drama in Theory and Practice: the writings of Sa'd Allāh Wannūs', *Journal of Arabic Literature* 15 (1984), pp. 94–113.
Allen, Roger, 'Drama and Audience: the case of Arabic theater', *Theater Three* 6 (1989), pp. 7–20.
Allen, Roger, 'Egyptian Drama after the Revolution', *Edebiyat* 4/1 (1979), pp. 97–134.
Al-Khozai, M. A., *The Development of Early Arabic Drama (1847–1900)*, London, 1984.
Badawi, M. M., *Early Arabic Drama*, Cambridge, 1988.
Badawi, M. M., 'The Father of the Modern Egyptian Theatre: Ya'qūb Ṣannū'', *Journal of Arabic Literature* 16 (1985), pp. 132–45.
Badawi, M. M., *Modern Arabic Drama in Egypt*, Cambridge, 1987.
Ben Halima, H., *Les Principaux thèmes du théâtre arabe contemporain 1914–1960*, Tunis, 1969.
De Moor, E. C. M., *Un oiseau en cage*, Amsterdam, 1991.
El Lozy, Mahmoud, 'Censoring the Censor: The Politics of Satire in Nu'man 'Ashur's *Sima Awanta*', *Theater Three*, 6 (1989), 31–46.
'El-Hakawati on Stage', *Saudi Aramco World* 39 (6) (1988).
Fontaine, Jean, *Mort-resurrection: une lecture de Tawfiq al-Hakim*, Tunis, 1978.
Hutchins, William M., *Tawfiq al-Ḥakīm: A Reader's Guide*, Boulder/London, 2003.
Ismail, Abd El Monem, *Drama and Society in Contemporary Egypt*, Cairo, 1967.
Khouéiri, J., *Théâtre arabe: Liban, 1847–1860*, Louvain, 1984.
Landau, J. M., *Studies in the Arab Theater and Cinema*, Philadelphia, 1958.
Long, Richard, *Tawfīq al-Ḥakīm, Playwright of Egypt*, London, 1979.
Mandūr, Muḥammad, *al-Masraḥ al-Nathrī*, Cairo, 1959.
Moreh, Shmuel, 'Live Theatre and Dramatic Literature in the Arab World', Edinburgh, 1992.
Moreh, S., 'The Shadow Play' (*Khayāl al-Ẓill*) in the light of Arabic literature', *JAL* 28 (1987), pp. 46–61.

Moreh, S. and P. Sadgrove, *Jewish Contributions to Nineteenth-Century Arabic Theatre*, Oxford, 1996.
Al-Rāʿī, ʿAlī, 'Some Aspects of Modern Arabic Drama' in R. C. Ostle (ed.), *Studies in Modern Arabic Literature*, London, 1975.
Sadgrove, P. C., *The Egyptian Theatre in the Nineteenth Century*, Reading, 1996.
Shteir, Rachel, 'Al-Hakawati: chameleon with a voice', *Theater Three* 6 (1989), pp. 47–52.
Snir, Reuven, *Palestinian Theatre*, Leiden, 2005.
Starkey, Paul, *From the Ivory Tower: A Critical Study of Tawfīq al-Ḥakīm*, London, 1987.
Three Shadow Plays, Paul Kahle (ed.), prepared by Derek Hopwood and Mustafa Badawi, Cambridge, 1992.
Tomiche, Nada (ed.), *Le théâtre arabe*, Louvain, 1969.

V. English Translations

A comprehensive listing of English translations published between 1947 and 2003 is available in:

Altoma, Salih J., *Modern Arabic Literature in Translation: A Companion*, London, 2005.

Altoma's guide is particularly comprehensive for Arabic fiction. No attempt has been made here to duplicate the information provided by Altoma and the listings below are therefore restricted to: (a) translations mentioned in the body of the present book, either in the text or the footnotes, and (b) a small number of translations of individual works that have appeared since the cut-off date of 2003 for Altoma's listings.

ʿAbd Allāh, Yaḥyā Ṭāhir, *The Mountain of Green Tea*, tr. Denys Johnson-Davies, London, 1991.
ʿAbd al-Quddūs, Iḥsān, *I Am Free and Other Stories*, tr. Trevor LeGassick, Cairo, 1978.
ʿAbd al-Ṣabūr, Ṣalāḥ, *Murder in Baghdad*, tr. Khalil Semaan, Leiden, 1972.
Arberry, A. J. *The Koran Interpreted*, 2 vols, London and New York, 1955.
al-ʿAqqād, Maḥmūd ʿAbbās, *Sara*, tr. M. M. Badawi, Cairo, 1978.
ʿAwwād, Tawfīq Yūsuf, *Death in Beirut*, tr. Leslie McLoughlin, London, 1976.
Badran, Margot and Miriam Cooke (eds), *Opening the Gates: A Century of Arab Feminist Writing*, Bloomington and Indianapolis, 1990.
Baʿlabakkī, Laylā, 'Spaceship of tenderness to the moon', tr. Denys Johnson-Davies, in *Modern Arabic Short Stories*, London, 1976, pp. 126–34.
Barakāt, Ḥalīm, *Days of Dust*, tr. Trevor LeGassick, Wilmette, Illinois, 1974.
al-Ḍaʿīf, Rashīd, *Dear Mr Kawabata*, tr. Paul Starkey, London, 1999.

al-Ḍa'īf, Rashīd, *Passage to Dusk*, tr. Nirvana Tanoukhi, Austin, Texas, 2001.
al-Ḍa'īf, Rashīd, *This Side of Innocence*, tr. Paula Haydar, New York/Northampton, 2001.
Darwīsh, Maḥmūd, *Memory for Forgetfulness*, tr. I. Muhari, Berkeley, 1995.
Darwīsh, Maḥmūd, Samīḥ al-Qāsim, Adonis, *Victims of a Map*, poems tr. Abdullah al-Udhari, London, 1984.
Enani, M. (tr.), *Angry Voices: An Anthology of the Off-beat New Egyptian Poets*, compiled M. Metwalli, Fayetteville, 2003.
al-Faqīh, Aḥmad, *Gardens of the Night*, tr. Russell Harris, Amin al-'Ayouti and Suraya 'Allam, London, 1991.
Ghānim, Fatḥī, *The Man who Lost his Shadow*, tr. Desmond Stewart, London, 1980.
al-Ghīṭānī, Jamāl, *Incidents in Zafrani Alley*, tr. Peter O'Daniel, Cairo, 1986.
al-Ghīṭānī, Jamāl, *Zayni Barakat*, tr. Farouk Abdel Wahab, London, 1988.
Ḥabībī, Imīl, *The Secret Life of Saeed, the Ill-Fated Pessoptimist*, tr. Salma Khadra Jayyusi and Trevor LeGassick, London and New York, 1985.
al-Ḥakīm, Tawfīq, *The Maze of Justice*, tr. A. S. Eban, London, 1947; new edn, with foreword by P. H. Newby, London, 1989.
al-Ḥamad, Turkī, *Adama*, tr. Robin Bray, London, 2004.
al-Ḥamad, Turkī, *Shumaisi*, tr. Paul Starkey, London, 2005.
Ḥaqqī, Yaḥyā, *The Saint's Lamp and Other Stories*, tr. M. Badawi, Leiden, 1973.
Haykal, Muḥammad Ḥusayn, *Zainab*, tr. J.M. Grinsted, London, 1989.
Ibrāhīm, Ṣun' Allāh, *The Committee*, tr. May S. St Germain and Charlene Constable, Cairo, 2002.
Ibrāhīm, Ṣun' Allāh, *The Smell of It*, tr. Denys Johnson-Davies, London, 1971.
Ibrāhīm, Ṣun' Allāh, *Zaat*, tr. Anthony Calderbank, Cairo, 2001.
'al-Jabartī, 'Abd al-Raḥmān, *Napoleon in Egypt: al-Jabartī's Chronicle of the French Occupation, 1798*, tr. S. Moreh, Princeton, 1993.
Jabrā, Jabrā Ibrāhīm, *The Ship*, tr. A. Haydar and R. Allen, Washington, DC, 1983.
Jayyusi, S. K. and R. Allen (eds), *Modern Arabic Drama: An Anthology*, Bloomington (1995).
Kanafānī, Ghassān, *Men in the Sun*, tr. Hilary Kilpatrick, Washington, DC, 1985.
Kanafānī, Ghassān, *All That's Left to You*, tr. Mayy Jayyusi and Jeremy Reed, Austin, Texas, 1990.
Kanafānī, Ghassān, *Palestine's Children*, tr. Barbara Harlow, Washington, DC, 1985.
al-Kharrāṭ, Edwār, *City of Saffron*, tr. Frances Liardet, London, 1989.
al-Kharrāṭ, Edwār, *Girls of Alexandria*, tr. Frances Liardet, London, 1993.
al-Kharrāṭ, Edwār, *Rama and the Dragon*, tr. Ferial Ghazoul and John Verlenden, Cairo and New York, 2002.

al-Kharrāṭ, Edwār, *Stones of Bobello*, tr. Paul Starkey, London, 2005.
Maḥfūẓ, Najīb, *Children of Gebelawi*, tr. P. Stewart, London, 1981.
Manzalaoui, M., *Arabic Writing Today: Drama*, Cairo, 1977.
Mīnā, Ḥannā, *Fragments of Memory*, tr. L. Kenny and O. Kenny, Austin, 1993.
Naṣr Allāh, Emily, *Flight Against Time*, tr. Issa J. Boullata, Charlottetown, 1987.
al-Qa'īd, Yūsuf, *News from the Meneisi Farm*, tr. M.-T. F. Abdel-Messih, Cairo, 1987.
al-Qa'īd, Yūsuf, *War in the Land of Egypt*, tr. L. Kenny, O. Kenny and C. Tingley, London, 1986.
Qāsim, 'Abd al-Ḥakīm, *Rites of* Assent, tr. Peter Theroux, Philadelphia, 1995.
Qāsim, 'Abd al-Ḥakīm, *The Seven Days of Man*, tr. Joseph N. Bell, Cairo, 1990.
al-Sa'dāwī, Nawāl, *Memoirs from the Women's Prison*, tr. Marilyn Booth, Berkeley, 1986.
al-Sa'dāwī, Nawāl, *Two Women in One*, tr. Osman Nusairi and Jana Gough, London, 1986.
al-Sa'dāwī, Nawāl, *Woman at Point Zero*, tr. Sherif Hetata, London, 1990.
al-Sammān, Ghāda, *Beirut '75*, tr. Nancy N. Roberts, Fayetteville, 1995.
Shammās, Anṭūn, *Arabesques*, tr. (from the Hebrew) by Vivian Eden, New York, 1989.
al-Sharqāwī, 'Abd al-Raḥmān, *Egyptian Earth*, tr. Desmond Stewart, London, 1962 (new edn with foreword by Robin Ostle, London, 1990).
al-Shaykh, Ḥanān, *Beirut Blues*, tr. Catherine Cobham, London, 1995.
al-Shaykh, Ḥanān, *Only in London*, tr. Catherine Cobham, London, 2003.
al-Shaykh, Ḥanān, *The Story of Zahra*, tr. Peter Ford, London, 1986.
al-Ṭabarī, *The History of al-Tabarī: Ta'rīkh al-rusul wa'l-mulūk*, tr. F. Rosenthal et al. (Bibliotheca persica), Albany, c. 1985–98.
Ṭāhir, Bahā', *Aunt Safiyya and the Monastery*, tr. Barbara Romaine, Berkeley, 1996.
al-Ṭahṭāwī, Rifā'a Rāfi', *An Imam in Paris*, tr. Daniel Newman, London, 2004.
al-Takarlī, Fu'ād, *The Long Way Back*, tr. Catherine Cobham, Cairo, 2002.

Index

Dumas, Alexandre, 169
Dumū' Iblīs, 186
al-Durr al-manthūr fī ṭabaqāt rabbāt al-khudūr, 101
al-Duwayḥī, Isṭifānūs, 30

Egypt, 2, 12, 16, 23–9, 31, 35, 37–8, 43–7, 49, 51, 53–4, 57, 61, 64–5, 67–70, 73–5, 80–2, 84–5, 89, 91, 94, 97, 100–2, 105, 107, 109–10, 112, 117, 119–25, 130, 135, 141, 143, 145–6, 160, 165–7, 170–5, 178–80, 182, 186–7, 191, 194
  British occupation of (1882), 29, 97, 178–9, 186
  Free Officers' Revolt (1952), 80, 118, 123, 125–7, 139, 182, 184–5, 187, 190
  French occupation of (1798), 25, 26, 43
  General Foundation for Theater, Arts and Music, 188
  Zaghlūl rebellion/Egyptian Revolt (1919), 117. 178, 183, 185
Egyptian National Library *see* Dār al-Kutub
Egyptian National Theatre, 180
Egyptian State Prize for Literature, 123
Eliot, T. S., 80, 82–4, 88, 90, 118
  Four Quartets, 90
  The Wasteland, 80, 83
Eluard, Paul, 84
England, 66, 90, 98, 132, 163, 171

al-Fajr, 72, 110
fakhr, 50
al-Fallāḥ, 126–7
al-Faqīh, Aḥmad, 155
Farāfīr, 188
Faraj, Alfred, 187–9
Fāris, Bishr, 74
al-Fārisī, Muṣṭafā, 156, 195
Farmān, Ghā'ib Ṭu'ma, 130–1
al-Fāsī, 'Allāl, 57
al-Fatā al-rīfī, 101
al-Fatāh, 29
al-Fatāh al-rīfiyya, 101
Fatāt al-Fayyūm, 100
Fatāt Miṣr, 100
Fawwāz, Zaynab, 101
Fawzī, Ḥusayn, 109
al-Fayḥā', 62
al-Faytūrī, Muḥammad Miftāḥ, 85
Fayyāḍ, Niqūlā, 55–6
Fénelon, François, 27
Fī al-shi'r al-jāhilī, 104
Fī dawwāmat al-ḥubb wa-al-karāhiya, 149
al-Fikr, 156
Fikrī, 'Abd Allāh, 44
Fī Qāfilat al-Zamān, 122
France, 26–7, 46, 64, 102, 110, 149, 173, 196
France, Anatole, 169
Franco-Arab revue, 170
Frazer, Sir James, *The Golden Bough*, 83
French colonialism, 157, 186
French culture, 122, 156
French language, 115, 122, 134, 147, 151, 158–9, 164, 194
French literature, 47, 56, 70, 72, 74, 87, 90, 97, 99, 110
Fu'ād I Academy prize, 118
al-Funūn, 61, 63
Fuqahā' al-Ẓalām, 153
al-Furāt, 53
Fusḥa mustahdafa bayna al-Nu'ās wa-al-nawm, 151
al-Futūḥāt al-Makkiyya, 7, 145

Gallery 68, 139, 189
al-Garād, 95
Gebeyli, Claire, 147
Germany, 70
Ghābat al-ḥaqq, 35
Ghallāb, 'Abd al-Karīm, 135
Ghalwā', 73
Ghānim, Fatḥī, 125, 127–8
al-Ghazālī, 7–9
al-Ghirbāl, 64
al-Ghīṭānī, Jamāl, 7, 134, 144–5, 159
al-Ghufrān, 195
Ghuṣūb, Yūsuf, 73–4
Gorky, Maksim, 169
Greece, 1, 7, 11, 17, 68, 69, 87, 163–4, 180
Gulf states, 57, 148

al-Ḥabbūbī, Muḥammad Sa'īd, 49
Ḥabībatī, 76
Ḥabībī, Imīl, 151–2
al-Hadaf, 131
Ḥadā'iq al-Layl, 155
ḥadātha ('modernity'), 87, 91
Ḥaddād, 'Abd al-Masīḥ, 62
Ḥaddād, Najīb, 166
ḥadīth, 5–6
Ḥadīth al-Qarya, 145
Ḥadīth 'Īsā ibn Hishām, 28, 49, 97–9
Hadiyyat al-karawān, 66
Hadramaut, 186
Ḥaflat samar min ajl al-khāmis min Ḥazīrān, 191
al-Ḥājj, Unsī, 90
Hākadhā khuliqat, 103
ḥakawātī ('storyteller'), 187
Ḥakawātī Group/Theatre, 193
al-Ḥakīm, Tawfīq, 67, 104, 110–1, 115–17, 121, 123–4, 127, 135, 163, 165, 169–70, 173–4, 176, 178–88, 189, 200
Ḥalīma, 157
al-Ḥallāj, 7
al-Ḥallāj, Muṣṭafā, 192
al-Ḥamad, Turkī, 154–5
al-Hamadhānī, Badī' al-Zamān, 10, 98, 196
Ḥamlat taftīsh: Awrāq shashṣiyya, 127
al-Ḥamrāwī, 152
Hams al-Jufūn, 64
al-Hamsharī, 'Abd al-Mu'ṭī, 70, 73
Ḥaqqī, Maḥmūd Ṭāhir, 101
Ḥaqqī, Yaḥyā, 110–11, 121, 127, 141
al-Ḥaram, 127
al-Ḥarb fī barr Miṣr, 143
al-Hārib, 196
al-Ḥarīrī, 10
Hārūn al-Rashīd, 15, 17
Hārūn al-Rashīd wa-Hārūn al-Rāshid, 186
Harvard University, 90